To Be Young Was Very Heaven

To Be Young Was Very Heaven

Women in New York before the First World War

Sandra Adickes

St. Martin's Griffin
New York

TO BE YOUNG WAS VERY HEAVEN
Copyright © Sandra Adickes, 1997. All rights reserved. Printed in the
United States of America. No part of this book may be used or reproduced
in any manner whatsoever without written permission except in the case
of brief quotations embodied in critical articles or reviews. For information, address St. Martin's Press, 175 Fifth Avenue, New York, N.Y. 10010.

ISBN 0-312-22335-8

Library of Congress Cataloging-in-Publication Data
Adickes, Sandra, 1933-
    To be young was very heaven : women in New York before the First
World War / Sandra Adickes.
        p. cm.
    Includes bibliographical references and index.
    ISBN 0-312-16249-9 (cloth)   ISBN 0-312-22335-8 (pbk)
    1.Women—New York—History—20th century. I. Title.
    HQ1438.N57A35 1997 2000
    305.4'09747?dc21   97-9799
                                                                    CIP

Design by Acme Art, Inc.

First published in hardcover in the United States of America in 1997
First St. Martin's Griffin edition: February 2000
10 9 8 7 6 5 4 3 2 1

CONTENTS

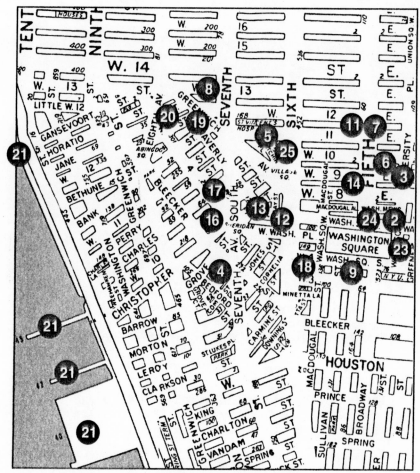

Greenwich Village

RESIDENCES

1. 210 East Thirteenth Street—Emma Goldman 1903-1913.
2. 3 Fifth Avenue?"A Club" Mary Heaton Vorse joined as an experiment in communal living in 1906.
3. 9 East Ninth Street—Inez Milholland 1909-1913.
4. 88 Grove Street—Mary Heaton Vorse 1910-1915.
5. Milligan Place—Susan Glaspell and George Cram Cook 1913-1922.
6. 23 Fifth Avenue—Mabel Dodge 1913-1917.
7. 15 East Eleventh Street—Inez Haynes Irwin 1915.
8. Thirteenth Street west of Seventh Avenue—Caroline Pratt and Helen Marot 1915-1940.
9. 42 Washington Square South—Louise Bryant and John Reed 1916-1919.
10. 118 Waverly Place—Crystal Eastman and Max Eastman 1909-1911; Ida Rauh and Max Eastman 1916.
11. 27 West Eleventh Street—Ida Rauh and Max Eastman 1912-1913.
12. 104 Waverly Place—Crystal Eastman and Walter Fuller 1916.
13. Waverly Place east of Sheridan Square— for $179.17 a month, Crystal Eastman rented a house that she and husband Walter Fuller shared with Max Eastman, Eugen Boissevain, and others in the winter of 1918-1919.

CENTERS OF VILLAGE LIFE

14. Eighth Street and Fifth Avenue—The Brevoort, where, "if the check had come," Villagers could dine.
15. 119 East Eleventh Street—Webster Hall, scene of the "Pagan Routs," *The Masses* "tumultuous" masked balls.
16. 1 Christopher Street—O'Connor's Saloon aka The Working Girls' Home, where Villagers never tired of singing "Frankie and Johnnie."
17. West Fourth Street and Seventh Avenue—The Golden Swan aka The Hell Hole, where Villagers made friends with members of the Hudson Dusters gang.

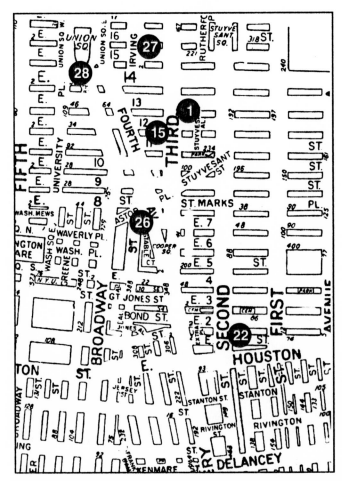

18. 137 MacDougal Street—The Liberal Club was established there in 1913 under the guiding force of Henrietta Rodman. Polly Holladay's restaurant was in the basement. Next door, the Provincetown Players scored a triumph in November, 1916, with Eugene O'Neill's "Bound East for Cardiff." In the summer of 1917, Dorothy Day shared an apartment above the theater with colleagues on *The Masses.*

19. 91 Greenwich Avenue—*The Masses,* a "revolutionary and not a reform magazine," had its office 1913-1917.

20. West Fourth and West Twelfth Streets—Caroline Pratt opened what would become City and Country School in the autumn of 1914.

21. The Hudson River Piers—Dorothy Day, Mike Gold, and Maurice Becker "sat on the ends of piers singing revolutionary songs into the starlit night" in 1917.

POLITICAL LANDMARKS

22. East First Street and Second Avenue—Women's Trade Union League headquarters opened in 1905.

23. Washington Place off Washington Square—The center of the shirtwaist-makers' strike 1909-1910; the Triangle Shirtwaist fire in the Asch Building on Washington Place in March, 1911 resulted in the loss of 146 lives.

24. Washington Square at Fifth Avenue—In May, 1911, suffrage parades began here. In May, 1913, Inez Milholland, mounted on a "splendid chestnut," led the parade up Fifth Avenue.

25. The Jefferson Market Court—1909-1910. Striking shirtwaist-makers and their supporters were tried here; Inez Milholland was twice thrown in jail.

26. Cooper Union on Astor Place—A feminist forum, "Breaking Into the Human Race," was held here in February, 1914. In November, 1917, suffragists gathered to celebrate winning the ballot in New York State.

27. Irving Place and East Sixteenth Street—A rally in support of mother-teachers was held at Washington Irving High School in November, 1914.

28. Union Square—With a touring car for a platform, Emma Goldman spoke to the crowd about birth control; Ida Rauh and Jessie Ashley were arrested for handing out "forbidden" birth control pamphlets in May, 1916.

This study of New York's first wave of women activists is dedicated to New York's second wave, but especially to Ruth Cowan, Janice Goodman, and Eleanor Jackson Piel.

Acknowledgements

My intention in writing this book was to demonstrate the personal connections—in terms of deep friendship, love, unity of purpose, rivalry, and opposition—among the women activists in New York during the early part of this century whose efforts to obtain the vote, decent wages and safe living conditions, access to birth control, and the enjoyment of personal development and free expression produced benefits to women in the entire nation. The creation of this overview would not have been possible without the work of many scholars listed in the bibliography. The following have been particularly useful: Mari Jo Buhle's *Woman and American Socialism 1870-1920*; Nancy Schrom Dye's *As Equals and As Sisters: Feminism, the Labor Movement, and the Women's Trade Union League of New York*; Nancy F. Cott's *The Grounding of Modern Feminism*; Judith Schwarz's *Radical Feminists of Heterodoxy: Greenwich Village, 1912-1940*; Dee Garrison's *Mary Heaton Vorse: The Life of an American Insurgent*; and Ellen Chesler's *Woman of Valor: Margaret Sanger and the Birth Control Movement in America*.

I am indebted for personal assistance to the following individuals: Dr. Michael Meeker, my colleague in the English Department at Winona State University, for time and again helping me manipulate the software that produced this work; Dena Hampton, assistant director of development at Elizabeth Irwin High School, for providing information about Elizabeth Irwin; Wendy Arozarena, director of development at City and Country School, for providing information about Caroline Pratt; Dr. Richard Reynertson of Gunderson Clinic, La Crosse, Wisconsin, for explaining Inez Milholland's final illness; Erika Gottfried, curator of Nonprint Collections, Tamiment Institute at New York University, for helping me obtain permission to use the photo of Elizabeth Gurley Flynn; Mike Smith, senior archivist of the Walter P. Reuther Library at Wayne State University, for searching the Mary

Heaton Vorse Collection and sending me requested materials; Lucille Swaim, director of negotiations, United Federation of Teachers of New York City, for information about women teachers' maternity rights; and Dr. Kathryn Sullivan, Helen Neavill, and Roy Smith of the Winona State University Library for assistance in obtaining materials from other libraries.

CHAPTER 1

Introduction

JOAN KELLY WROTE in "Did Women Have a Renaissance?": "To take the emancipation of women as a vantage point is to discover that events that further the historical development of men, liberating them from natural, social, or ideological constraints, have quite different, even opposite, effects on women."[1] Taking that vantage point, we probably would find that in our own country, no era could be described as a golden age for women. Young women in colonial Massachusetts often died in childbirth; wealthy widows in Salem were executed as witches. Frances Trollope found during her travels through this nation in 1828 that women were "guarded by a sevenfold shield of insignificance"; that daughters were "domestic slaves" until they took on the "still sadder burdens of a teeming wife," and that at thirty, women looked like grandmothers to their infants.[2] Willa Cather's novels describe the hardships and loneliness experienced by women who pioneered on the western frontier, and after industrialism had overtaken agrarianism, women fared no better as handmaidens to machines. The young women of New England recruited by Yankee capitalists to work in the textile mills of Lowell, Massachusetts, in the 1830s found themselves confined to the looms twelve hours a day, six days a week, twelve months a year.[3] Few women entered higher education and most were barred from entering the professions. For example, in 1875 the Supreme Court of Wisconsin refused to admit Lavinia Goodell to the bar on the grounds that it would be against nature for women to be "permitted to mix professionally in all the nastiness of the world which finds its way into the courts of justice."[4]

In the late nineteenth and early twentieth centuries immigrant women earned low wages working in unsafe factories, "sweated" in small shops by day, or did piecework day and night in crowded tenements. However, the pattern of this grim history was altered during the first wave of feminism when a period of forward movement seems, judging by the number and tenor of participants' memoirs, to have occurred in New York City—Greenwich Village in particular—during the years before the First World War.

The novelist Inez Haynes Irwin marked the years between 1900 and 1914 as a time when life was full of hope and freedom, when "great movements were stirring and the liberal's voice was the loudest in the land. Everyone was for something and everyone was sure of victory." According to Irwin, "a speaker with a microphone could go to the intersection of Forty-Second Street, Broadway, and Seventh Avenue and announce 'I am here to gather recruits for a movement to free . . .' and before he could announce the object of his crusade, he would be in the center of a milling crowd of volunteers."[5] Artistic movements kept apace with political movements. After establishing the modern dance movement in Europe, Californian-born Isadora Duncan, who saw herself as "the spiritual offspring of Walt Whitman," toured the country in 1912 to show Americans the way to a new freedom of the body and soul.[6]

Margaret Sanger, writing of the time before she began her crusade for birth control, cited the years just before World War I as "one of the most interesting phases of life the United States has ever seen." Sanger, a nurse, and her architect husband, William Sanger, lived in an apartment in uptown Manhattan that became a gathering place for liberals, anarchists, socialists—for "revolutionists of all shades." Almost without knowing it, according to Sanger, one quickly became "a comrade" among this group of "rebels and scoffers," who ranged from "'pink' parliamentarian socialists and theorists" to the Industrial Workers of the World. "The mental stirring," Sanger recalled, "was such as to make a near Renaissance." [7]

Sanger's friend, Mabel Dodge, whose apartment downtown at Ninth Street and Fifth Avenue was a celebrated gathering place where seemingly disparate groups came together, recalled 1913, the year she returned from living in Europe, as the time when "barriers went down" and "a new spirit" swept together people who had never been in touch before. According to Dodge, this "new spirit" was brought to life through the opening of the exhibition of Cubist art that she had helped to produce—the famous Armory show—whose hit attraction, Marcel Duchamp's "Nude Descending a Staircase," daily drew queues of titillated multitudes to the armory building on Twenty-fifth Street and Lexington Avenue.[8]

In the same period, Susan Glaspell found a less sensational, more homely way of life in the neighborhood slightly to the south and west of Dodge's apartment at 23 Fifth Avenue. Glaspell had never known "simpler, kinder or more real people" than she knew in Greenwich Village. None of them had much money; most were from families who thought one should be like everyone else. Drawn together by what they really were, Greenwich Villagers "were as a new family." They lent each other money, worried through each other's illnesses, ate together, and talked about their work. They were called radical, wild bohemians, but to Glaspell, it seemed "we were a particularly simple people who sought to arrange life for the thing we wanted to do, needing each other as protection against complexities," yet longing at the same time "to have a garden and neighbors, to keep up the fire and let the cat in at night."[9]

In her autobiography, Dorothy Day provides further evidence of the simple joyful pleasures of those years in New York. On the cusp of this nation's entry into the war, the editors of the radical magazine, *The Masses*, Max Eastman and Floyd Dell, left Day to "play with" the job of editor during the day; in the evenings she walked through the streets of New York with her *Masses* associates, Mike Gold and Maurice Becker, and sat "on the ends of piers singing revolutionary songs into the starlit night, dallied on park benches, never wanting to go home to sleep but only to continue to savor our youth and its struggles and joys." [10]

A Berkeley student during New York's radical heyday, Genevieve Taggard, the rebellious daughter of Disciples of Christ missionaries, resisted her mother's efforts to make her "a Christian gentlewoman," becoming instead a poet, "wine bibber," radical, and non-churchgoer who arrived in New York after graduation in 1919.[11] In her introduction to the poetry anthology *May Days,* Taggard invoked William

Wordsworth's description of the golden dawn of the French Revolution—"Bliss was it then in that dawn to be alive, but to be young was very heaven"—to express the mood of the city in those years. It was a "holiday time," when idealistic young people desiring to be more than happy, well bred, and lively were drawn to the abounding humanitarian crusades and amateur movements.[12]

The euphoria of that era was due in great measure to the energy generated by so many talented women—many of them known to one another—who were gathered in the city at the time. They were as diverse as Elizabeth Gurley Flynn, an organizer for the International Workers of the World (known as "the Wobblies," a name of unknown origin), the anarchist Emma Goldman, and Dorothy Day, who was to become a founder of the Catholic Worker movement. The amalgam of the women's many strengths was necessary to meet the three great struggles of the era: those for the rights to suffrage, birth control, and economic independence.

The women who came to New York from other parts of the country in these years were from middle-class or even affluent families. "Few of the Villagers came from New York City," Mary Heaton Vorse wrote in her novel *I've Come to Stay: A Love Comedy of Bohemia*. The Villagers came, according to Vorse, from "staid New England homes and from refined regions like Beloit"; most had fathers who were ministers, "or at the very least, deacons."[13] Vorse, whose ancestry on her mother's side went back to the seventeenth-century New England colonies, had grown up in a hilltop mansion in Amherst, Massachusetts, a community in which she never felt at home, and from which she fled as soon as she could.[14]

These women usually had some form of postsecondary education. Margaret Sanger was a trained nurse.[15] Vorse had attended art school in Paris.[16] Susan Glaspell had graduated from Drake University in Iowa and then worked for the *Des Moines Daily News*.[17] The percentage of college-educated women in this group of activists was much higher than that of the general population, for in 1910, women in college comprised only 3.8 percent of all women in the country between the ages of eighteen to twenty-one.[18] Some of the women activists also had professional training. Marie Jenney Howe, who founded the women's club Heterodoxy, had been trained as a Unitarian minister.[19] Crystal Eastman and Inez Milholland were lawyers as well as Vassar graduates; Eastman, who had graduated second in her class from New York University Law School in 1907, became the only female member of the New York State Employer's Liability Commission.[20] Elsie Clews Parsons received a Ph.D. in sociology from Columbia University and wrote a number of books on the condition of women in society before embarking on a career as an anthropologist.[21]

However, not all the women were college-educated. Some of the leading activists were schooled through political organizations or early trade union experience. A daughter in a Socialist family, Elizabeth Gurley Flynn began her political career at sixteen when she gave a speech, "What Socialism Will Do for Women," at the Harlem Socialist Club in January 1906.[22] Rose Pastor Stokes, a Russian-born former "stogy maker" who had captured the public's attention when she married J. G. Phelps Stokes, a wealthy socialite turned social worker, was a Socialist Party activist and labor organizer.[23] Emma Goldman—like Stokes, Russian born—had made her living as a factory worker before falling under the influence of Johann Most and becoming an anarchist and birth control political activist; her lectures and writings on politics, sexuality, and literature made her one of the era's most flamboyant women.[24] However, Goldman was not a supporter of suffrage. In 1906, she declared in "The Tragedy of Woman's Emancipation," an essay she wrote for the anarchist periodical she published, *Mother Earth*, that the struggle for equality was "but a slow process of dulling and stifling woman's nature, her love instinct and her mother's instinct."[25] Because she shared Margaret Sanger's belief in a woman's right to sexual pleasure, and because she also had been trained as a nurse and had witnessed the suffering and deaths brought on from too much childbearing, Goldman joined the campaign for birth control. In English and Yiddish, Goldman told women about contraceptives; her lectures led to her arrest, trial, and imprisonment.[26]

The struggle for legal birth control was in direct conflict with the puritanical legal code enacted through the fanatical efforts of the moral crusader Anthony Comstock. Moreover, the anti–birth control laws under which Goldman and Sanger were prosecuted were given added force because of the fear that immigrants from Southern and Eastern Europe and the "yellow wave" moving eastward over the

Pacific and "lapping at the shores of America" would outnumber Anglo-Saxon Americans.[27] "Race suicide" was a certainty if American women expressed the "abnormal" desire to limit their families or to pursue activities outside the home that would result in "unsexing" them.[28] Additionally, the unremitting opposition of the Catholic Church made the campaign for birth control long and bitter, and success did not come until the Supreme Court's 1965 decision in *Griswold v. Connecticut* guaranteeing Constitutional protection for the use of contraceptives.[29]

In contrast, the campaign for suffrage, already a half-century old, was gaining support. Optimistic New York suffragists injected drama into their campaign by staging a modest parade up Fifth Avenue in the spring of 1911. The following year, they provided the city with a celebratory pageant. On Sunday, May 5,1912, the *New York Times* reported that an "army" of woman's suffrage supporters, ten thousand strong, had marched up Fifth Avenue at sundown of the previous day "in a parade the like of which New York never knew before." The diversity among the marchers provided the spectacle: the march was made up of factory workers, affluent society leaders, nurses, teachers, cooks, writers, social workers, librarians, school girls, and laundry workers—women who worked with their heads and women who worked with their hands, and women who never worked at all, but all of them marching for suffrage.[30]

Promptly at five o'clock, over fifty horsewomen led their mounts out of Washington Square, followed by the Old Guard Band, "playing lustily," and after them came the parade's organizers, the leaders of the Women's Political Union, "a mass of gleaming white." As they proceeded northward, the various occupational groups flowed into the parade from the east and west sides of Fifth Avenue, most of these groups bearing a symbol of their occupation. The nurses bore a banner with the picture of a night lamp, honoring Florence Nightingale and Clara Barton. The banners of the writers honored the authors of *Little Women* and *Uncle Tom's Cabin*. The dressmakers' banner bore a sewing machine, the milliners' a hat, and the cooks' a kettle. Reverend Antoinette Brown Blackwell and other veterans of the struggle for suffrage rode in carriages. Despite these flourishes, the report stated that the "real excitement" of the parade, for which many of the spectators had waited since noon, "was the delegation of men." These marchers, as diverse a group as the women, had grown from the "scanty and much-derided eighty" of the previous year to close to a thousand.[31]

The weather was as perfect as had been anticipated, interest in the movement was high—for in the preceding months, the parade's organizers had distributed fliers and sponsored debates on suffrage—and New Yorkers were no doubt in a mood for celebration to banish the gloom that had descended on the city three weeks earlier following the sinking of the Titanic. The procession was much larger than it had been the previous year, and the crowd of spectators, including a greater number of "hoodlums," was at least five times greater; nevertheless, Police Commissioner Rhinelander Waldo had supplied even fewer policemen than he had for the previous year's much smaller parade. The result of this lack of preparation, Harriot Stanton Blatch (head of the Women's Political Union and daughter of suffrage pioneer Elizabeth Cady Stanton) complained in a letter to the *Times*, was that the lane of march repeatedly became so crowded that marchers had to rearrange themselves into twos, and on several occasions, sections of the parade were broken up by spectators. When the parade ended at Carnegie Hall, where a rally was to be held, the crush completely overwhelmed the police.[32]

The coverage of the parade was enthusiastic and expansive. Writing for *The World*, Winifred Harper Cooley, who marched with the suffragists, was thrilled by the cross-class alliance in the parade that was most strikingly represented when Mrs. Alva Belmont fell in at Forty-second Street at the head of a delegation of factory workers. Cooley invited her readers to marvel with her at the change wrought in the American ideal "when the manipulator of millions of dollars and the owner of thirteen automobiles walks the streets of New York past the great Vanderbilt palaces which she once planned and erected."[33] The *Times* devoted an entire special section to photos of the parade, but the editors were firmly opposed to women's suffrage. An editorial entitled "The Uprising of the Women" warned that men's complacency and women's persistence had led to a "dangerous" situation in which women certainly would get the vote "and play havoc with it for themselves and society, if the men are not firm and wise enough and, it may as well be said, masculine enough to prevent them."[34]

Correspondence from men and women on both sides of the issue poured in during the following weeks. The editions of three subsequent Sundays again devoted pages to the suffrage issue, including an article dealing sympathetically with the women who had made suffrage "a great river into which a vast number of small streams flow." Women identified with suffrage—Dr. Anna Shaw and Alva Belmont, for example—were acknowledged, but women less well known for their connection to suffrage also were cited; among these were Lillian Wald, head of the Henry Street Settlement House, and Ellen Glasgow, the author from Virginia.[35] But the *Times* editorials continued to prophesy disaster: women were swarming to the cities where they competed for jobs with men; thus, men had to wait longer to marry and rear families, and the result was "race suicide," a phrase that would be used repeatedly against women's quests for suffrage, birth control, and economic independence.

One response to these warnings came in the form of a taunting letter from Anna Cadogan Etz, the press secretary of the Women's Political Union, who reminded the *Times* editors that after the parade of 3,000 suffragists in May the year before, "You declared that woman suffrage had demonstrated its strength to such a degree that it was entitled to respectful consideration from all thoughtful people." Suffragists were glad, Etz stated, to be thus promoted out of the "funny column." But after the recent parade of 15,000, the *Times* had issued a "call to arms" to men to "save the world from the menace of woman suffrage." Suffragists were again glad, Etz concluded, for in one short year "to rise from a joke to the status of menace . . . seemed too good to be true."[36]

The élan Etz expressed in her letter would mark much of the activism of the struggle in the next years, for the long campaign for suffrage would successfully conclude with the passage of the Nineteenth Amendment to the Constitution in 1920. But Crystal Eastman saw the victory as the place for women to begin their struggle for freedom, not end it, and set forth the goals an organized feminist movement would have to achieve. The first, she stated, was freedom of choice in occupation and equal pay for equal work. Next, women must "institute a revolution" in the education of girls and boys; girls must be educated to earn their own living, boys to share in household work that could be simplified but not eliminated by "cooperative schemes and electrical devices." Birth control had to be an essential part of the feminist program; women must be able "to have children when they want them." And finally women who choose to bear and rear children must not be forced to "sink into" a dependent state from which it is difficult to rise. The occupation of raising children must be recognized as a service to the state for which women should receive "adequate economic reward from the government."[37]

The program Eastman outlined remains visionary, controversial, and, even these many years later, a long way from achievement. Much of the work she outlined was not really begun until the second wave of feminism occurred a half-century later. Moreover, political attitudes in the United States hardened during—but especially after—the First World War. Under the provisions of the 1918 Immigration Act, which made membership in anarchist organizations a transportable offense, Emma Goldman, though a United States citizen and a resident for over thirty years, was deported to Russia in December 1919.[38]

However, if the golden dawn of this century's hopeful activism was brief, it was glorious. During this era of youthful activism, women were larger-than-life figures. Films had not yet attained the iconographic power of later years, and women then were glamorized through the print media. The *New York Times* filled its society and drama section with photographic spreads of prominent socialites and actresses. But radical women were also glamorized. Rose Pastor Stokes, "the Jewish Cinderella," was an irresistible attraction for the reporters who thronged to record her words at labor rallies.[39] Similarly, Inez Milholland was the *Times*'s poster girl of radicalism. In cautionary articles about the Socialist Party's growing influence on college campuses and in photo collages of prominent suffragists, Inez Milholland's image smiled out at the reader as demurely as a debutante's.[40]

But the women activists were heroes as well to their contemporaries. While covering the 1912 strike of textile workers in Lawrence, Massachusetts for *Harper's*, Mary Heaton Vorse wrote of the power of the beautiful black-haired, blue-eyed Industrial Workers of the World organizer, Elizabeth Gurley Flynn, to stir the workers with her dazzling oratory.[41] Of Vorse, Inez Haynes Irwin would write in her autobiography that "any labor trouble found Mary immediately on the spot, and between strikes, she was always speeding on an important assignment to Europe."[42] When he was in college, Joseph Freeman, who was to become one of Max Eastman's assistants on *The Liberator*, attended a meeting for the defense of *The Masses* and found that Eastman's wife, Ida Rauh, and his sister, Crystal, seemed to "represent the romantic and revolutionary circle of writers and artists who were his [Freeman's] guiding stars" in the chaos of the times.[43] The untimely death of Inez Milholland, to whom Max Eastman briefly had been engaged, evoked this eulogy from him in *The Masses:* "I love to think of Inez Milholland as typifying in her flashing and heroic beauty of color and gesture the new ideal that is bringing to the world an enhancement of life more deep and sane than any that was ever written upon a page of history."[44]

Hardship, loss of love, even—as in the case of Emma Goldman—imprisonment and exile would be the fate of a number of these women in later years, but often the friendships formed in the years when they jubilantly strove to topple barriers sustained them in darker times. In the years before the war,the women activists brought joy to their struggles, together creating what Margaret Sanger termed "a near Renaissance."

CHAPTER 2

1912: New York Enters a New Era

THE YEARS BEFORE WORLD WAR I were marked by an exuberant optimism that participants in the movements and crusades of the era would remember fondly in later, gloomier times. Floyd Dell, novelist and associate editor of the radical magazine *The Masses,* found everywhere "evidence of a New Spirit come to birth in America"; he and his contemporaries "were in love with life, and willing to believe almost any modern theory which gave us a chance to live our lives more fully."[1] Dell's colleague Max Eastman agreed that, notwithstanding the violence and class conflict of labor struggles, "it was a protected little historic moment of peace and progress we grew up in," a "comparative paradise" that his generation mistook for the final reality that would come with the war.[2] A rising tide of political dissent, Margaret Sanger recalled, was spreading "like a religion without a name" over the country, and almost without knowing it, one became a "comrade."[3] Mary Heaton Vorse would recall the era as a time when radicalism was "in the air." "It was the time of Hull House. It was the time of social change. It was a natural thing. It was a time when great quantities of our people joined with the Socialist Party."[4] Mabel Dodge claimed that 1913, the year she returned from Europe, settled in New York, and helped to launch the Armory Show of Cubist art, was the year "when barriers went down and people reached each other who had never been in touch before."[5] However, Floyd Dell more accurately designated 1912 as the extraordinary year at the beginning of a special era, for it was marked by Woodrow Wilson's election and the proclamation by Democrats of a "New Freedom," the garnering of six percent of the presidential vote by the Socialists, intense women's suffrage activity, and a new spirit in the arts.[6] New York was the center of the new spirit in art, politics, and ideas. During these "May Days," declared the poet Genevieve Taggard, "the youth of the land was getting out of doors and all winter taboos were being broken," "humanitarian crusades abounded," and "amateur movements made a mushroom growth."[7]

The city also had experienced a mushroom growth. Between 1890 and 1900, New York City had grown at the rate of 3.20 percent, which was more than double the rate of gain in London and more than three times that in Paris, where the rate of gain had fallen from 1.04 to 0.48. In 1912 the population of the city had reached five million. In Manhattan, with two and one-third million residents, old buildings were being acquired and torn down to make way for new ones; apartment houses were rapidly replacing private residences, and residential neighborhoods were giving way to commercial districts. New York had a booming seaport, over 1,600 hotels, floor space in office buildings exceeding that in any other city in the world, and 20,000 factories employing more than 500,000 men and women.[8] The nation's economic situation was good, and, at least from the point of view of middle- and upper-class people, New York was flourishing.

Although Anglo-Americans dominated political, social, and economic life in New York, the Irish, Germans, Jews, and Italians had emigrated in large numbers since the late nineteenth century, along with smaller populations of other settlers, such as Syrians, Greeks, Poles, and African-Americans.[9] New housing rapidly was being built in Queens, the Bronx, and Long Island to accommodate newcomers, aspiring homeowners, and people moving out of less desirable neighborhoods. The expanding population also heightened the need for new lines to be added to the New York City transit system. The city's Board of Estimate and the Public Service Commission argued at length over plans for extending the subways, but eventually, the transit problems were settled, a plan was agreed upon, and the future for residential and industrial growth beyond Manhattan was assured. Two companies, the Brooklyn Rapid Transit System and the Interborough Metropolitan Company, would expand the connections between Manhattan and the other boroughs, connect Long Island with the Bronx, and extend service to outer areas of the boroughs. The new subways and elevated lines would supplement an already immense system; the New York subway system, begun in 1904, had, by 1912, developed a traffic of one million persons a day.[10]

The growing population in Manhattan and the spread of population to the outer boroughs brought crowding to the schools, requiring construction of a new high school in Bay Ridge, an annex to Bushwick High School in Brooklyn, and an annex to Commerce High School in Manhattan.[11] Teachers were needed for the expanding student population, and women benefited from the shortage of teachers. After years of struggling for salaries equal to those of men, women were granted equal pay under a change in the law. The increase in the salaries of women was balanced by a decrease in the salaries of men. Previously, female elementary school teachers were paid a starting salary of $600, male teachers $900. The maximum salary for men was $1,500, for women $1,250. After the equal-pay law was passed, the lowest salary for both was $720; the maximum was $1,280. Naturally, male teachers sought to regain their lost benefits, and there was support for their position. In a letter to the *New York Times,* John Martin, a member of the Board of Education, argued that the lowering of men's salaries would lead to the postponement of marriage, and that women, with greatly increased salaries, would go to Europe and have boxes at the opera, resulting in "the sacrifice of the race for the individual."[12] However, until later action by the Board of Education, the situation of female teachers did not change in one significant respect: married women, unless their husbands were mentally or physically incapacitated or had abandoned them for at least three years, could not apply for teaching positions.[13] One problem that teachers had not confronted previously was lack of discipline among the new student population. Elementary school teachers in Brooklyn complained that their male students smoked, drank, gambled, stole, shot spitballs, and pulled girls' hair.[14]

Meanwhile, the construction of Pennsylvania Station, with its marble columns, glass vaulted ceilings, and gracious waiting rooms designed for the comfort of the commercial and excursion passengers neared completion. Air travel was presaged by the flights in February of two pilots; George W. Beatty, who flew a Wright "airship" from

Nassau Boulevard into Manhattan, landing in Central Park; and Frank Coffyn, who flew a Wright "hydro-aeroplane" in a circle over the lower end of Manhattan, crossed to Brooklyn above the Navy Yard, and then passed under both the Manhattan and Brooklyn Bridges before landing in the water off the Fire Department Pier on the East River.[15] The challenge of flight had attracted many men and a few women to aviation, but the poor construction of early "airships" and the lack of understanding of the technology of flight had resulted in many fatalities—43 in this country in 1911—but ironically, the daring Coffyn, who made two more spectacular flights over Manhattan in February, met his death only one month later when he was thrown from his automobile after it skidded on a Central Park bridge.[16]

Coffyn's accident and other car fatalities did not halt the boom of what was to become Americans' most enduring passion. In January, record-breaking crowds poured into Madison Square Garden for the Twelfth Annual Automobile Show, deemed the "most brilliant automobile exhibit" ever seen there. Cars of all types, sizes, and colors were on display everywhere, along with over one hundred tons of accessories. Close to 100 vehicles from almost as many companies were on display—pleasure and commercial, open and closed—including some splendid vehicles long since vanished from the roads and highways: the Columbia Limousine, the Little Six Locomobile, the Lozier Riverside, the Simplex, the Speedwell, the Maxwell Big Six, the Pierce Arrow, and the Peerless.[17] Of course, the city already was burdened by the impact of automobile acquisition; because traffic was not regulated by a policeman at every intersection, speeding was common, and accidents, sometimes fatal, were frequent.

The ascendance of the automobile did not dim the charm of steamship travel for affluent American vacationers, who traveled first class on luxury liners. Servants to the wealthy and travelers of modest means traveled second class, and poor immigrants from Eastern and Southern Europe traveled by steerage. The tragic saga of this era of luxury began on the night of April 15, when the White Star Line's *Titanic*, on its maiden voyage, struck an iceberg in the North Atlantic and went down with a loss of nearly sixteen hundred lives.[18] Investigations in Washington and London revealed that the principal cause of the disaster was the failure of the *Titanic's* captain, Edward J. Smith, to heed messages that the ship was in the path of icebergs and ordered the ship to move too fast. Another possibly significant factor was the failure, in outfitting a $7,500,000 luxury liner to resemble a four-block-long, fifteen-story hotel, to provide the lookouts with good binoculars costing $50 each.[19] That so many lives were lost was due to the lack of enough lifeboats, the failure to hold lifeboat drills or assign responsibility for the lifeboats to specific crew members, and the dispatching of life boats only half full.[20] When the Cunard Line's *Carpathian* came into port on April 17 with 866 survivors, New York City opened "its hospitals and homes, and its people their hearts and purses."[21] Much attention was paid to the loss of prominent New Yorkers: department store owner Isador Straus and his fabled wife, Ida, who would not leave his side; realtor and corporate director John Jacob Astor; mining equipment industrialist Benjamin Guggenheim; and theater manager Henry B. Harris—but the steerage survivors were not forgotten. Mrs. Nelson H. Henry, wife of the surveyor of the port, immediately gathered prominent women—Mrs. Cornelius Vanderbilt, Miss Anne Morgan, Miss Sarah Cooper Hewitt, and Mrs. James Henry Aldrich among them—to form The Women's Relief Committee with the purpose of providing clothing, cash, homes, and work for "the unfortunates."[22] The committee moved into an office in the Metropolitan Life Building on Madison Square and soon informed the public—repeatedly—that they had raised more than enough money to complete their mission.[23] Perhaps the reason the committee had more resources than they needed was that so few steerage passengers survived to benefit from their charity. Of the 330 first-class passengers, 210 survived, but of the 750 steerage passengers only 200 survived, for these passengers were kept from climbing the five ladders to the lifeboat decks until the last boats were leaving.[24]

The steerage passengers' deaths symbolized the exclusion of many people from the prosperity the nation and the city were celebrating. In the year of the *Titanic,* more than 5,000 families in Manhattan were driven from their homes by order of the courts because they could not afford to pay their rents, which, along with the cost of food and clothing, had risen steeply, while their earning power had increased little. Some people, Jewish and Italian tenants on the Lower East Side in particular, dealt with the crisis by doubling in already cramped tenements or renting out rooms to boarders.[25] Without the social programs that have, since the 1930s, come to be seen as a safety net, people who no longer were able to make their way became desperate.

In January, a painter with failing eyesight who walked the city each day to sell paintings, often getting not even enough to buy supplies, ended his life by turning on gas.[26] That same month, a bricklayer, crippled because of a fall from a scaffold, ended his life by turning on gas because he feared being a burden to his sons.[27] In June, a once prosperous woman and her unemployed widower son, having sold all their possessions, were near starvation, yet refused to ask for charity, and also used gas to take their lives, along with the life of the man's two-year-old daughter.[28] In August, a young wife and mother, desperate because her husband's illness had cost him his job and the family was about to be evicted, strangled herself with a wet towel; the husband, meanwhile, had found someone willing to rent the family an apartment and another man, almost as needy as himself, willing to help the family move. He rushed home to tell his wife the good news and found his young son and daughter weeping by their mother's body.[29]

But even the employed could find the terms of their existence degrading and unbearable. In the wake of the 1911 Triangle Shirtwaist Factory fire that took 146 lives, a legislative investigation was made to determine what measures could be taken to prevent further such disasters. Sympathetic Vassar and Radcliffe students volunteered to take testimony from workers; asked what kind of fire protection she "enjoyed," one young woman replied she did not know and did not care, because the best thing that could happen to her was for a fire to come along and "end her miserable, work-a-day existence."[30]

Prostitutes, to be sure, labored under the most grim conditions. Approximately 600 women worked in twenty or more "disorderly resorts" operated by a vice "trust." Each woman was on duty from eight in the evening to four in the morning and paid three dollars for the room she occupied. The resort managers punched a card each time a client was serviced, each punch representing fifty cents. After a woman had her card punched six times, she was credited with payment for her room, and the remainder of her punches represented her small profit. In order to prevent a resort inmate from forging a punch, the card's shape was changed daily. Because the resort owners paid graft to corrupt policemen, these women at least had a measure of protection. Women who plied their trade in the streets were far more vulnerable, for they were frequently arrested—often through entrapment by young, attractive policemen—and taken to the Jefferson Market Night Court in Greenwich Village, there to join a "long procession of prodigals" who told their plights to a judge and received their sentences. Often, if a woman was over sixteen, she was sentenced to prison among hardened criminals.[31]

However, segments of the city's and the nation's work force were resisting the conditions imposed on them and demanding to be included in the general prosperity. At the beginning of 1912—during the coldest winter in forty-three years—New York laundry workers, most of them women and members of Local 126 of the Laundry Workers Union, went on strike.[32] The strikers were assisted by the Women's Trade Union League (WTUL), formed at the American Federation of Labor convention in 1903. The league had been active in the "women's strikes" in the garment industry, which had begun in 1909 with a strike by shirtwaist-makers at the Triangle factory in lower Manhattan. The harassment and arrest by police of the workers, some of them still in their teens, drew sympathetic coverage in the New York press and led to an expansion into "the uprising of 20,000" that ultimately reached 500 shops and brought production in the garment industry to a halt. The strikers did not win all their objectives; the Triangle workers who had started the strike returned to work without any gains for their action. However, the New York general strike inspired similar actions by workers in Chicago and Philadelphia and marked a new mood of militancy among women workers, long ignored by male leaders of the trade union movement.[33]

The most remarkable feature of the women's strikes was the alliance it produced among women of all classes through the WTUL. This alliance was evident in the laundry workers' strike: the WTUL leaders organized an auto parade, followed by a rally in the union headquarters at 211 East 124th Street, where the English suffragist Sylvia Pankhurst was the principal speaker.[34] The State Bureau of Mediation and Arbitration conducted an investigation of the strikers' working conditions during which a long line of witnesses complained of long hours, unsanitary conditions, and grinding labor. Many of the workers were underage; one fifteen-year-old, for example, testified that she worked fifty-six hours a week for four dollars. Although the State Labor Commissioner, John Williams, refused to prosecute owners for violations of the law, he did issue a report that would accelerate passage of a law limiting women's working hours to fifty-four hours a week.[35]

It was, in fact, a law limiting women's working hours without increasing their wages that led to another strike in January by textile workers in Lawrence, Massachusetts. This strike began with a walkout from the American Woolen Company by twelve women protesting a wage cut following passage of a law by the Massachusetts legislature reducing the work week for women and children from fifty-six to fifty-four hours. The International Workers of the World, under the leadership of "Big Bill" Haywood, were the principal organizers and leaders of the strike.

The WTUL, which included among its leadership a number of members of the Socialist Party, was ordered by the American Federation of Labor not to participate in the strike.[36] However, a number of New York activists were involved in the strike, among them Mary Heaton Vorse and Margaret Sanger, both Socialist Party members, and Elizabeth Gurley Flynn, a Socialist Party member before becoming an International Workers of the World organizer. Flynn led the organizing among the women, urging them to combat the old world attitude of man as the "lord and master" and take their rightful place as "valiant fighters on the picket line." Indeed, the women's participation produced an enduring moment in the Lawrence struggle when a group of young women strikers carried a banner with the words, "We want bread and roses, too."[37]

Meanwhile, Socialist Party women in New York provided support for Lawrence by arranging for the strikers' children to be sent to sympathetic people in other cities for the duration of the strike. On February 17, a trainload of 150 children left Lawrence escorted by a committee of New York activists headed by Margaret Sanger, a trained nurse and chair of the Women's Committee of the Socialist Party.[38] Five thousand people were waiting in Grand Central Station to meet them. In a letter to her friend Arthur Bullard, Mary Heaton Vorse described their arrival. The idea was fine, Vorse wrote, but "Haywood was managing it, and now look what happens: Isn't this like Radicals all over?" No one knew when the children were arriving; the temperature was below zero. But finally, Vorse wrote, "I found out more about it than anyone knew from headquarters by getting in with a wide-faced Irish cop who was . . . keeping tabs on the babies as they came down." Lots of social service "hens," Vorse complained, were in attendance, and the Anarchists wouldn't do anything they were asked to do. Finally, the children arrived and were taken on the Third Avenue El to the Labor Temple on East Eighty-fifth Street, where they were distributed to their host families. "The whole thing," Vorse concluded, was "a curious little summary of the weakness and strength of the whole extreme wing of the Radical proletariat."[39]

One week later another group of forty children and their parents were attacked by the Lawrence police as the children were boarding a train for Philadelphia; the assault provoked outrage and won sympathy for the workers, whose strike ended in an agreement that brought them pay increases.[40]

Following Lawrence, Haywood was involved in a strike in New York in late May by waiters in hotel dining rooms and restaurants, members of the International Hotel Workers' Union. At a mass meeting in the Amsterdam Opera House on West Forty-fourth Street, Haywood exhorted the waiters, who were striving to gain recognition from the hotel owners for their union and hoping to affiliate with the American Federation of Labor, to get other workers to support their strike and in turn to support strikes by other workers, resonating the IWW's theme that every man and woman in the United States should belong to one big union.

In response to the hotel owners' claim that they would replace striking workers with college students, Negroes, and women, Haywood claimed that college boys would not be waiters; that since the Civil War, Negroes had better conditions in the South than in New York; and that there were not enough women in New York capable of being waiters.[41] The next night, waiters from Delmonico's restaurant and the Hotel Savoy crowded into the Netherland Hotel at Fifty-ninth Street and Fifth Avenue, determined to drag out the waiters who were still working; their attack resulted in a call by management to the "strong arm squad" from the Sixty-seventh Street precinct to stop the assault. Six of the waiters were sentenced to terms in the workhouse.[42]

Efforts to recruit hotel chambermaids, scrubwomen, and laundresses into the strike were made with some success by Socialist Party activists Theresa Malkiel, who had been active in the shirtwaist-makers' strike and the Lawrence strike; Anita Bloch, editor of the women's department of the Socialist Party newspaper, the *Call*; and another activist in the shirtwaist-makers' strike, Rose Pastor Stokes—a Russian-born former cigar maker married to the socially prominent J. G. Phelps Stokes.[43] The strikers had some success; some hotel and restaurant managers and owners, at least for a time, agreed to recognize the union and made some concessions. But the concessions later were withdrawn, and the strike was not successful. Bill Haywood's prophesy was inaccurate; the hotel workers were easily replaced, and when they voted at the end of June to return to work, many were not reemployed. Of the men he refused to rehire, the restaurant manager known as Oscar of the Waldorf said, "a job at the Waldorf is not an apple hanging from a tree."[44]

Concurrent with the waiters' strike, a protest of another kind took place in Brooklyn, where housewives, angry at the rise in meat prices, broke butcher-shop windows, invaded shops, poured kerosene on meat bought by nonprotesters, threatened butchers' meat stock, and told them to close their shops.[45] The meat protest spread to Manhattan and the Bronx, where it was expressed, for the most part, in picketing and boycotting. Housewives on the Lower East Side organized a house-to-house canvass in their efforts to stop the purchase of meat and held community meetings at which local butchers pleaded for their businesses, blaming wholesalers for the high price of meat. However, there were exceptions to nonviolent protest, as one butcher found when he tried to leave his shop with four chickens under his coat and had to be rescued by four policemen from the wrath of pursuing housewives.[46]

Of course, some of the population pursued their interests outside the law, with the result that New York in 1912 had a significant criminal element, whose influence, in some cases, extended to the upper reaches of political circles. At a distance, the violence of the gangsters is muted by their colorful names: "Roughhouse" Hogan, "Yakey Yake" Brady, "Eat-em-Up" Jack McManus—but their activities on behalf of themselves or the interests they represented were nevertheless lethal. They fought each other on the Lower East Side, usually waging war, like medieval mercenaries, on behalf of gambling-establishment owners. A historic battle was fought under the Rivington Street elevated railway, with fifty men, including policemen, blazing away at one another, while tenement residents and storekeepers cringed in panic. A gang leader, Monk Eastman, a man with twenty previous arrests but excellent connections to Tammany politicians, was arrested again and ultimately acquitted.[47] Eventually, however, even he exceeded the limits of his power and was sent away to prison. Some of his confederates renounced gang life and claimed, at least, to enter legitimate enterprises, but they quickly were succeeded by other gangsters who fought just as viciously for control of the Lower East Side, where their open warfare in the streets often resulted in the deaths of innocent bystanders.[48]

Rival Chinatown gangs—known as tongs—also engaged in open warfare, but the police, who were tolerant of second-generation, American-born criminals, were extremely vigilant—"thick as flies"—to bring the foreign-born perpetrators to justice.[49] In June, the police department's Lieutenant Charles Becker, leader of the "strong-arm squad," very aggressively led his men in arresting young novices in the Lower East Side and Chinatown and bringing them to justice.[50] Just weeks later, Becker himself became the central figure in a murder that exposed the "system," a partnership for profit among politicians, police, and criminals.

Early on the morning of July 16, Herman Rosenthal, owner of a Lower East Side gambling establishment, was shot to death as he left the restaurant of the Metropole Hotel on West Forty-third Street. Rosenthal, a police informer, had been on the verge of revealing in a court case that Lieutenant Becker was "a silent partner" in his gambling establishment.[51] The murder was carried out by a group of men who escaped after the slaying in an auto and fled the city.[52] With no due diligence, the police began a search for the slayers; the *New York Times*, meanwhile, located a witness to the murder who revealed that the police had cleared the area around the Metropole prior to Rosenthal's exit and execution. The anonymous witness also revealed that, while the actual shooter was bending over the body of his victim, his cap had fallen off, revealing his bald head.[53] This man, "Billiard Ball

Jack" Rose, fearing vengeance from the police, gave himself up to District Attorney Charles Whitman and revealed that Becker was the principal figure in the case; Rose also named Becker's confederates: "Lefty Louie" Rosenzweig; "Whitey" Lewis; Harry Horowitz, known as "Gyp the Blood"; and "Dago Frank" Cirofici. Becker was arrested, indicted, and confined to the Tombs to await trial.[54] He was found guilty of murder in the first degree in October, and successfully appealed for a new trial, but was again found guilty. Becker died in the electric chair at Sing Sing Prison in July 1915.[55] His four accomplices, after their capture, trial, and conviction, had previously been executed in Sing Sing in April 1914.[56]

The accounts of the Rosenthal murder revealed how pervasive was the system of graft extorted from saloon keepers, brothel keepers, and gambling-establishment owners by the police and politicians, with the result that factions of the city administration hurried to name each other as wrongdoers. District Attorney Whitman accused the police of trying to prevent key witnesses from testifying and failing to act promptly to capture Becker's accomplices.[57] Mayor William Gaynor took control of the police away from Commissioner Rhinelander Waldo, and some police officials were suspended from duty or demoted.[58] The city's legislative body, the Council of Aldermen, meanwhile, resisted the efforts of Mayor Gaynor to control their own investigation of police misconduct, for fear of a "whitewash"; the mayor retaliated by accusing the aldermen of collecting graft through the issuance of licenses to newsstand vendors and found a witness to back him up.[59]

The public was sufficiently aroused by the widespread police and political corruption to gather in unprecedented numbers at Cooper Union to protest politically protected crime, in the process forming a committee to "solicit funds, engage counsel, and do whatever is, in its judgment, necessary to vindicate law and order in this city."[60] The agitation for reform led to palliative actions by the state legislature, but the changes were superficial. Rhinelander Waldo remained in his post as police commissioner. William Gaynor's plans to run for reelection the following year ended when he died of a heart attack while sailing to Europe.[61] When Charles Becker was on Death Row in Sing Sing, the only man who could have pardoned him was Charles Whitman, whose political career, launched by his prosecution of Becker, had culminated in his election as governor of New York State in November 1914.[62]

Meanwhile, the efforts of reformers in 1912 had not deterred less flamboyant entrepreneurial criminals from spending the summer of that year busily burglarizing the homes of vacationing executives. One insurance broker complained that 1912 was "the toughest year we've ever known," adding that New York was the only city in the country where insurance companies were losing money.[63] However, so long as violent crime was confined to the city's underworld and burglary was confined to wealthy people who could afford the losses, the passions of the average New Yorker were not stirred for long. The death rate was low; the health of the populace was good, and the nation was at peace.

Nevertheless, much was going on in the world beyond the U.S. borders: In China, the Qing dynasty had been overthrown, and after a period of conflict between the rebels and the supporters of the empire, a republic had been established under Sun-yat Sen.[64] Insurgents were rebelling against the governments of Cuba and Mexico; these events brought stern warnings that the United States might intervene if the heads of state were incapable of quelling unrest.[65] Indeed, at the request of the president of Nicaragua, American marines did land in that country to protect American property against rebellious insurgents.[66] At the time, most New Yorkers, like most Americans, did not question their government's right to intervene in the affairs of other nations. Just before the November presidential election, the outbreak of conflict between the Balkan states—Greece, Serbia, and Bulgaria—and Turkey signaled the beginning of the conflict that later engulfed all of Europe, eventually drawing in America and ultimately changing the national destiny of all the combatants.[67]

The still inward-looking American nation was not too concerned by foreign conflicts, but much interest was aroused by the presidential election of 1912. The former president of Princeton University and governor of New Jersey, Woodrow Wilson, was nominated as the Democratic Party's presidential candidate. When Theodore Roosevelt was denied the nomination of the Republican Party and President William Howard Taft was again the party's candidate, Roosevelt formed the Progressive, or Bull Moose, Party and ran for the office. Lukewarm to suffrage until then, he threw the convention open to women, and some notable suffragists—Margaret Dreier of the WTUL and Jane Addams, founder of Chicago's Hull House, among them— became delegates. More typically, however, Roosevelt's belated welcome to women drew a skeptical response from most suffragists. What did Addams gain, Ida Husted Harper queried in a letter to the *New York Times,* that she could not have gained from neutrality? Addams had been unsuccessful in her contest for the rights of Negroes within the Progressive Party, Harper pointed out, as Roosevelt, to appease Southern whites, had refused to recognize Southern blacks as delegates. Roosevelt's assessment that he would lose votes among blacks in the South but gain votes in the North was, in Harper's view, a concise expression of his character.[68] In a later letter to the *Times,* Harper pointed out that, in a revised version of his convention speech published as a Senate document, Roosevelt had amended his support for suffrage by proposing that in conservative states, the question of suffrage be submitted to a vote by women.[69]

Gertrude Atherton, another suffrage activist, claimed in her letter to the *New York Times* that Roosevelt had decided "he must have the women" because women "can vote in six states, they love a real man, and many of them are fools." "These Roosevelt women," Atherton acknowledged, were putting their heads in the sand; such women might be attracted to Roosevelt only because they were not clever and led narrow, dull lives and they should be judged with charity. On the other hand, she stated, women of intelligence "have grown to distrust the influence exerted upon them by the 100 percent male."[70] In rare agreement with the suffragists, the *New York Times* pointed out in an editorial that Roosevelt, while not enthusiastic about women's suffrage, was in a "white heat" for his candidacy and had flattered women into working for him.[71] Recognizing that Roosevelt was on to a good thing, Republicans and Democrats followed his lead, enlisting women as aides in their campaign.[72]

Women's energy was an important factor in preserving the stability of civic life in New York. During the Gilded Age, great concern had been aroused by the stream of young American women of newly minted fortunes making marriages with titled, impecunious foreigners. The *New York Times* periodically railed against the "transfer of numerous large fortunes to Europe." In March, 1877, for example, the

Times editor had protested against the "barter between American women of beauty and fortune and broken-down Marquises, worthless Counts, and other titled vagabonds" in which the only return to "ambitious mammas is a worthless son-in-law with a worthless name."[73] At that time, the events of American women's lives were not noted significantly in the *Times*.

Marriages of New York women were reported under "Local News In Brief" in the back pages, but space on the front page was reserved for marriages between members of European royalty and those made by daughters of famous American men. The marriage in the White House of President Ulysses S. Grant's daughter, Ellen, to Algernon Charles Frederick Sartoris was, of course, reported on the front page of the May 22, 1874 edition.[74]

Marriages between Americans of great wealth or even infamy on either side were also noted, as in the case of the marriage of William H. ("Boss") Tweed's daughter, Mary, to Arthur Ambrose Maginnis, reported in the June 1, 1871 edition. Under the heading "A Costly Wedding," the *Times* reported in detail the gifts to the bridal couple from Tweed's cronies (all of whom were accompanied "by their wives and daughters in magnificent apparel"), which filled an entire room, and included forty silver sets—one containing 240 pieces—and forty pieces of jewelry, one containing "diamonds as big as filberts."[75] Because the *Times* reports of weddings and other social events usually contained details of the splendor and the costs of decorations and gifts, it is difficult to determine if the account of the wedding presents to Mary Tweed was a tongue-in-cheek reminder to readers that the public, through graft, was in part contributing to the largess; in any event, the wedding marked William Tweed's last hurrah, preceding by only a few months the downfall and imprisonment of the political leader, who for years had been the target of *Times* editorials.

The lack of attention to women ended when Adolph Ochs became publisher in 1896. Ochs introduced a Sunday supplement, and by 1912, the Sunday *Times* had expanded to eight sections, well on its way to its present size. The first section, a pictorial section, featured photographs of current events: the Equitable Life Insurance Building after it was destroyed by fire in January; the striking Lowell textile workers confronting the Massachusetts National Guard; American forces protecting American property in China. Important works of art recently acquired or on exhibition also were shown. But the most lavish attention was paid to displays of prominent women recently engaged or married, at dances—often in costume—and at charity balls. So, too, the children of prominent families frequently were pictured. These glamorous images were important factors in gender construction; not every woman, of course, could see her name in the *New York Times,* but the roles of prominent women as wives, mothers, and benefactors were roles to which all women might aspire. Edith Wharton demonstrated the influence of the women's pages of the daily press in her 1913 novel, *The Custom of the Country,* in which the social-climbing central character, Undine Spragg, consults a newspaper advice column before responding to a dinner invitation and throughout the novel documents her ascendance through a collection of clippings about her triumphs.[76]

To reinforce the process of gender construction, these images of glamour always were followed by advertisements for aids to and enhancers of beauty: dresses, dressmakers, shoes, hats, beauticians, and corsetiers. The most prominently advertised garments were corsets, each brand advertising the superiority of its construction. The firmness of steel stays was weighed against the suppleness of bone; the garments were guaranteed not to stretch or give, to retain their shape until worn out, and to "serve as a preventative of those ailments of weakness from which millions of women suffer, and as a cure for them." The display of corset ads in the pictorial section seemed to imply that in exchange for physical bondage, a woman might achieve the ideal of perfection represented by the most prominent women in the city.

As if to underscore this message, the *Times* included less prominent women in its pages. The seventh section of the Sunday edition, while concentrating on the activities of the most socially prominent women, also included announcements of the engagements and marriages of middle- class women, along with the births of their children, the parties they gave and attended, and the charity events they sponsored. The *Times,* as a family newspaper, included along with announcements of the retreat of the wealthy and well-known to Europe and Newport in the summer and Southern spas in the winter announcements of the vacations of middle class families at less famous and affluent resorts: Rockaway Beach, Long Island; Lakewood, New Jersey; or the White Mountains of New Hampshire.

Ochs clearly had aspirations for his audience as well as his newspaper. By the journalistic standards of the day, the *Times* was restrained, although it did not meet the editorial credo in the initial issue expressing Ochs's "earnest aim" to give the news concisely, clearly, promptly, and impartial, without fear or favor. Ochs was shaping his newspaper by including not just all the news "fit to print" but only such as "does not soil the breakfast cloth." Therefore, the staples of William Randolph Hearst's *Journal* and Joseph Pulitzer's *World*—lurid crime, sex, and rival versions of "The Yellow Kid," a cartoon that came to be synonymous with "yellow" journalism, were absent from the *Times*.[77] By 1912, the *Times*'s advertising revenues outstripped those of its rivals, and its identity as a family newspaper had been secured. The *Journal* and the *World* included news of society and cultural events, but never to the extent that the *Times* did, for their readers were less well educated and less affluent. Nevertheless, corset ads also were prominently displayed in those newspapers.

Gender construction was also a significant part of public education. Some high schools were for girls, others for boys, and within schools, some courses were also designated for one sex or the other. Mayor Gaynor made his contribution to girls' education during his visit in February 1912 to Public School 4, when he advised the girl graduates that they have been taught useful things for homemaking, not for work in a cigar factory because the right kind of woman "knows how to sing a little, dance a little . . . and at the same time knows how to cook to make her husband good natured." Miss Rector, the principal, thanked the mayor for reinstituting sewing in the schools instead of replacing it with science.[78]

With respect to young women of fortune, those who traveled to Europe to find suitors continued to incur the disdain of the *Times* editors, who described these young women as "dollar princesses."[79] On the other hand, splendid unions between upper-class Americans continued to be reported in lavish detail. When Edward T. Shaftesbury gave a gift of pearls to his intended bride, the widow of Oliver Cromwell, a late partner of J. P. Morgan, the *Times* account noted that the future Mrs. Shaftesbury could wrap the necklace around her neck seven times and the lower strand could still reach her waist. J. P. Morgan also was munificent to the future Mrs. Shaftesbury, giving her one diamond necklace with a pendant of a pear-shaped diamond the size of a robin's egg and another diamond necklace with a pendant whose center stone was a sapphire the size of a thumbnail said to be worth $100,000.[80] In another breathless account, the *Times* reported that at a dinner honoring the Russian ambassador and his wife—for which lilies were imported from England at a cost of $8,000 and at which the forty guests dined on gold service—Mrs. Edward B. McLean wore the Hope Diamond on her head and the ninety-eight-carat Star of the East Diamond on a platinum chain around her neck.[81]

However, much of the glitter of the Gilded Age had, as if by a corset, been trimmed and tamed. In the post–Civil War era of robber barons and great fortunes, wives of newly wealthy men were expected to display their husbands' conquests through splendid clothes, jewels, and grand entertainments in oversized, overfurnished houses. But in the dawn of the Progressive era, the wives of wealthy men were expected to atone by their good works for the entrepreneurial depredations that might provoke social unrest. Upper-class women were expected to be models of propriety, inspirations in character as well as dress for women further down the social scale, and many socially prominent women stepped forward to assume these roles. Mrs. William K. Vanderbilt set up sunny, airy apartment homes for people with tuberculosis. She was spurred by the involvement of Jewish and Catholic charities on behalf of children of those faiths to act on behalf of Protestant children. Her involvement led to the establishment of "Big Sisters," patterned after the "Big Brothers" organization founded in 1904. She interested her two sisters, Mrs. F. C. Havemeyer and Mrs. Stephen H. Olin, along with many other prominent women to visit the homes of girls in need, assisting them, and encouraging them to stay in school.[82]

A paragon among altruistic society women was Mrs. Nelson Henry, who had organized, among other philanthropies, the Titanic Relief Committee to assist steerage survivors. Still another form of guardianship was exercised by Mrs. Charles Henry Isaacs, who formed the Committee on Amusement and Vacation Resources whose function was to watch the dance halls of New York and suppress such close-contact dances of San Francisco origin as the "Turkey Trot," the "Grizzly Bear," and the "Bunny Hug." When the committee was reminded sarcastically by skeptics to consider the morals of the upper-class as well as those of the working-class, its members asked patronesses of debutante cotillions not to depart from the traditional dance forms.

In January, at the height of New York's debutante season, a committee member was delegated to attend a cotillion at Sherry's to see whether the two-step and the waltz had been replaced by "a series of indecent antics to the accompaniment of music." The undercover dance policeman was able to report to the committee that he had seen nothing out of the way.[83] In June, Mrs. Isaacs assembled 600 society people, settlement workers, city officials, writers, artists, actors, and License Bureau Inspectors for a conference in Delmonico's restaurant that included a demonstration of the "indecent" dances by Al Jolson and Alice Cable, then appearing at the Winter Garden, that brought gasps from the committee. Young women of privilege must not engage in such dances, Mrs. Isaacs firmly declared, for "the girl who dances at Sherry's has just as much responsibility for the welfare of the girl who dances at the Murray Hill Lyceum as has the recreation supervisor in that district."[84]

In November, however, Mrs. Isaacs changed her mind, apparently coming to agree with Oscar Wilde that the purpose of the working class was to set a good example for the upper class. If the working girl-patron of the dance hall could be persuaded to dance the Tangle Two-Step, the Aviation Glide, the Fourstep, and the Danube Waltz instead of the "vulgar" dances, Mrs. Isaac believed, perhaps the society girls would dance them also. The indefatigable dance reformer was determined to purge the dance halls of gang influence; each evening, a volunteer force of dancers went to the dance halls, where the men danced with girls while the women danced with gang members, from whom they picked up much evidence to persuade dance hall operators that they could banish gangs and still make a profit.[85]

The Committee's zealous efforts to reform society girls and working girls did not satisfy all critics, however. A Miss Trenholm, head worker of the settlement house she established at East Seventy-second Street, declared to a *New York Times* reporter that New York's biggest problem was "not the police . . . it's its girls." The women of New York, she declared, "are frequently without a God, and just now very frequently without a petticoat." The responsibility for the decline of the morals of working women, according to Miss Trenholm, lay with society women, whose immodest dress—a "paralyzing" problem—and "reckless" and "indecent" dancing, originating in the "vicious dives" of San Francisco's Barbary Coast, influenced women farther down the social scale; thus, through the decline of the morals of future mothers, the entire nation was imperiled.[86] To Miss Trenholm's indictment, Mrs. Nelson Henry, so much identified with altruistic movements, responded that, on the contrary, far from being the idle rich, young women of privilege as never before were setting their less fortunate sisters an example of self-denial and altruism through such good works as the Big Sisters, the Titanic Relief Committee, the Playgrounds Association, and other philanthropic works, such as serving as waitresses to "shop girls" at the Grace Church Deaconesses' House, that did not always attract attention from the general public.[87]

Women might achieve prominence in New York through wealth and good works, but one area of the city's life endowed women with unqualified glory: the theater. New York had at least thirty theaters in operation during the theatrical season, not taking into account the vaudeville theaters and theaters operating in the Bronx and Brooklyn, and ten more were to be added to the Times Square district before winter of 1913.[88] New Yorkers in 1912 demanded theatrical entertainment and theater managers obliged. The plays, usually comedies, musical comedies, or farces, were slight and transient; their success depended on the female stars, some of whose names still can be remembered today, for their careers continued long after their ingenue years. Among these were Ethel Barrymore, who had a long and distinguished stage and film career; Laurette Taylor, who, long after performing as Luana, the Hawaiian princess in *The Bird of Paradise,* came out of retirement to triumph as Amanda Wingfield in *The Glass Managerie;* Peggy Wood, who played the central character in the television series *I Remember Mama;* and Billie Burke, the star in 1912 of *The Mind-the-Paint Girl,* who can be seen as Glinda the good witch every time *The Wizard of Oz* is shown on television or video.

The feature "Plays and Players of the Week" in the Sunday *Times's* seventh section always focused on the women who were appearing in the new entertainments; the male performers received much less attention, and the reviews also focused on the female stars. An era of "woman plays" was declared, with "mere men in reality [playing] second fiddle." If a woman did not figure prominently in the title, she still was the important part of the show, as evidenced by such productions as *The Woman Bought and Paid For, The Bird of Paradise, The Quaker Girl, The Trail of the Lonesome Pine, The Talker,* and *The Butterfly in the Wheel.*[89] Aware of the appeal of actresses and the popularity of theatrical entertainment, suffragists planned their strategy accordingly. The 1912 May suffrage parade was held on a Saturday rather than on Sunday, as had been the case the previous year, thus ensuring coverage in the more widely read Sunday newspapers. For months before, suffragists appeared on street corners making speeches and handing out leaflets. In March they flaunted "Votes for Women" sashes at the Women's Industrial Exhibition, infuriating its anti-suffragist managers.[90] That same month suffragists sponsored a debate during which prominent suffragists, including Charlotte Perkins Gilman and Inez Haynes Irwin, "knocked into a cocked hat" objections from anti-suffragists; only one half of those who wanted to hear the debate were able to get into the hall, and the speakers agreed to repeat themselves for the overflow crowd, while the lone policeman assigned to the debate was forced to call for help.[91]

The suffragists recruited intensely among working women, not omitting in their campaign performers in the Barnum and Bailey circus.[92] In April, the Women's Political Union had a benefit matinee at the Republic theater, with skits about the campaign by English suffragists.[93] The flourishes of the suffrage parade—a troop of women on horseback in the lead, one of them dressed in armor to represent Joan of Arc; the sashes, the white dresses, the banners; the flow of occupational groups into the line of march—all bore the imprint of dramatic imagination. Nor did the theatricality end with the suffrage parade. In September, through the efforts of the actress Fola La Follette, daughter of Wisconsin Senator Robert La Follette, a group of

suffragists appeared for a week in the Hammerstein's Victoria vaudeville theater on West Forty-second Street.[94]

Clearly, activist women in New York—those already in residence
and those streaming in to free themselves from the narrow provincial-
ism of the nation's small towns—were gripped by the spirit of that age
and place. These women were not willing to accept the limits imposed
on their political status, nor the confinements of traditional roles.
They were not willing, either, to adopt the conservatism of earlier
generations of suffragists. "I wanted two things as a girl," Mary Heaton
Vorse reflected in 1923; "I wanted to be loved. I wanted expression. I
have had both things. I have run head on into middle life and have
never had time to fear for the future."[95] Activist women in New York
wanted the ballot, but they also wanted love, and this dual demand of
a younger generation of suffragists resulted in tandem campaigns for
birth control as well as for suffrage.

Greenwich Village, physically isolated from the rest of Manhattan
until the opening of the West Side subway in 1917,[96] was the
intellectual and spiritual center of these movements—a tiny island
within the island of Manhattan where people were young and free, but
serious, with high ethical standards. There, in a community where, for
a brief time, art and politics, earnestness and good companionship
mingled, one could rent for thirty dollars a month "whole floors in old
houses, each with two enormous rooms—high-ceilinged rooms, with
deep-embrasured windows, and fireplaces—and a hall bedroom, a
kitchen with a gas range, and a bathroom."[97]

The women of Greenwich Village defied the *Times's* decorous
homemaking advice column by decorating these inexpensive apartments in shades of orange and black. They bobbed their hair, and,
eschewing corsets, wore loose, comfortable clothing, often with sandals. They gathered to sing "Frankie and Johnnie" at The Working
Girls' Home and The Hell Hole, two of the Village's favorite saloons, or
ate at the restaurant on MacDougal Street, where its owner, Polly
Holladay from Evanston, Illinois, "looking very madonna-like presided with benignant serenity over a wild and noisy horde of young
people," assisted in her enterprise by her lover, cook, waiter, and
dishwasher, Hippolite Havel, an anarchist with a penchant for
denouncing the diners as "bourgeois pigs." For serious discussion,

debate, poetry reading, drama production, and socializing, they went to the Liberal Club, or a branch of it that Henrietta Rodman brought to the Village and established upstairs from Polly Holladay's restaurant when the branch in Gramercy Park refused to accept African Americans as members. The latest works of modern art were hung on the walls, and an old electric piano allowed for dancing closely in the style that so outraged uptown society, but that permitted the partners to feel they were doing something for humanity as well as themselves.[98]

They read and wrote for the radical journal *The Masses*, presided over by the triumvirate of Max Eastman, Floyd Dell, and John Reed, who were committed—if self-serving—feminists, and they turkey-trotted in costumes (some of which were rumored to be largely painted and not of cloth) at *The Masses's* annual masked ball, the gala social event of the year.[99] *The Masses* was organized as a collective in which contributors and close friends gathered for "large and tumultuous" meetings, often at Mary Heaton Vorse's home, to accept or reject contributions by writers and artists. "Nothing more horrible can be imagined than having one's pieces torn to bits by the artists at a Masses meeting," Vorse recalled. Nevertheless, "there was no greater reward than having them stop their groans and catcalls and give close attention; then laughter if the piece was funny, finally applause."[100] The magazine's political cartoons were its most distinctive feature: John Sloan, Art Young, Maurice Becker, and Charles Winter mocked capitalists, the mainstream press, and organized religion with irreverent fervor, while Alice Beach Winter and Cornelia Barns made feminist statements in cartoons such as Winter's "Discrimination,"[101] which showed a girl looking wistfully into a butcher's window that bore a sign reading, "Boy Wanted," and Barns's "Patriotism for Women," which featured a woman holding a baby and a note under the drawing that informed the reader of the encouragement by European governments of soldiers to marry before enlisting in order to maintain posterity, a policy that led England to reduce the cost of a marriage license, but not "the cost of raising a baby."[102]

The most far-reaching and long-lasting Village institution nurturing women's activism was the Heterodoxy Club, a women's luncheon club that met more or less regularly for almost thirty years and included as members in the pre–World War I years most of the major activists in the important political, social, and artistic movements of the era. Among the members were actresses, such as Fola La Follette, Margaret Wycherly, and Beatrice Forbes-Robinson; writers, such as Mary Heaton Vorse, Rheta Childe Dorr, Alice Duer Miller, Zona Gale, Inez Haynes Irwin, Mary Austin, Susan Glaspell, and Katherine Anthony; social scientists, such as Elsie Clews Parsons and Leta Hollingsworth; lawyers, such as Crystal Eastman and Inez Milholland; educators, such as Henrietta Rodman and Elizabeth Irwin; feminist activist and political organizer Marie Jenney Howe; labor organizers Rose Pastor Stokes and Elizabeth Gurley Flynn; member of the National Association for the Advancement of Colored People Grace Nail Johnson; physician and child health care administrator Jo Baker; and economic theorist and writer Charlotte Perkins Gilman.[103]

Heterodoxy members, suffragists to a woman, were interested in more than the vote, envisioning the women's movement as revolutionary. Many of the Heterodoxy members were Socialists, but, as feminists, they were skeptical that a socialist state would bring all the benefits the party promised unless women struggled for them. So exasperated was Mary Heaton Vorse with Socialist Party leadership that she wrote a friend in 1913, urging her to pay her party dues in order to vote in the party election to thwart "the attempts of all those old, hide-bound, sausage-eating, fat-witted Dutchmen who call themselves Socialists to try and get control of the party and squash any truly revolutionary movement in it."[104] Vorse cheered the violence of the British suffragists, writing to a friend, "I cannot imagine anything that would affect better the moral health of any country than something which would blast the greatest number of that indecent, immoral institution—the perfect lady—out of doors and set them smashing and rioting."[105] Vorse later recalled that another Heterodoxy member, Rose Strunsky, "had a lot of dynamite in her room that she'd cached for someone. The owner of the house would come in and say, 'I smell something stuffy in here!' Being social minded—you didn't have to search at all . . . because it was in the air."[106]

For a few years, until the tide of reaction, racism, xenophobia, and class warfare brought an end to the euphoric golden dawn of their activism, women in New York lay the foundations for social, political, intellectual, and artistic movements that have remained influential.

Having a mission, in the years before this nation entered the Great War, did not mean one did not have a good time, and Greenwich Village was the place where good times were to be had. There, living in inexpensive apartments, enjoying the "flavor of those days," Susan Glaspell recalled, "one could turn down Greenwich Avenue to the office of The Masses, argue with Max, or Floyd, or Jack Reed; then after an encounter with some fanatic at the Liberal Club, or (better luck) tea with Harriet Rodman, on to the Working Girls' Home . . . or if the check had come, to the Brevoort." Art and politics, Marx and Freud coexisted good-naturedly among people bursting with joyful and frantic self expression. In those early years of psychoanalysis in the Village, Glaspell recalled, "one could not go out for a bun without hearing of someone's complex." [107]

Beyond the Village, however, women's claims and desires met with opposition on every level; they even were blamed for the streamlined clothing they wore. The narrower skirts, and the reduction in the number of petticoats that became the fashion in 1912, produced denunciation from a fashion critic who accused the women of being responsible for the loss of jobs in the garment industry.[108] Women's desire for political and economic autonomy brought the charge of ruinous self-indulgence; self-supporting, independent women were held responsible for taking jobs from men, with the result that men could not start families. White Anglo-American ruling class males feared that if white Anglo-American women limited their child-bearing, the population would shift from Northern-European descended Americans to large families from Eastern and Southern Europe, with "race suicide" the result.[109] But women would not be deterred from their goals; they continued to struggle, and their efforts laid the groundwork for benefits women enjoy today.

Chapter 3

Movers and Shakers: The Forerunners

IF ONE WOMAN CAN BE DESIGNATED as principal foremother of the "first wave" of twentieth-century feminism, Charlotte Perkins Gilman deserves that designation. Born in 1860, Gilman grew up in a household in which her father, Frederick Beecher Perkins (Harriet Beecher Stowe was his aunt) frequently was absent, and, in any case, was so poor a provider that her mother, Mary Fitch Westcott Perkins, was forced to move nineteen times in eighteen years; her mother's life, in Gilman's view, was "one of the most painfully thwarted" she had ever known. When she was fifteen, her family settled in Providence, and Charlotte, who had received most of her education at home, attended the Rhode Island School of Design, supporting herself by working as a commercial artist, art teacher, and governess. In 1884 she married Charles Walter Stetson, a promising Providence artist, and gave birth to a daughter, Katherine Beecher Stetson, the following year.

Charlotte, who had been happy and full of vitality before marriage, was overcome by spells of weeping and depression brought on by her effort to fulfill the roles of wife and mother. When she went unaccompanied to visit family friends in Pasadena, California, the illness abated, but returned in full force when she returned to her husband. Eventually, convinced that despite her love for her husband, her marriage threatened her sanity, she separated from him, and, after attempts at reconciliation failed, the couple were divorced in 1894.

Charlotte moved with her daughter to the San Francisco Bay area and struggled for a living by taking in boarders, publishing poetry and fiction—including the short story "The Yellow Wallpaper," a fictionalized account of her breakdown—and lecturing to women's clubs, labor unions, and suffrage groups. However, her work was interrupted by frequent periods of collapse from the "permanent mental injury" she attributed to her marriage. After her former husband married her close friend Grace Channing, Charlotte sent Katherine to live with the couple in order to secure for her daughter the advantages she could not provide. Believing herself at thirty-five to be a "repeated, cumulative failure," Charlotte lived a nomadic existence for the next five years, traveling across the country to work for suffrage and socialism.[1]

In 1898, Gilman published the work for which she is best known, *Women and Economics*. Her thesis was that women's subordinate position was due to their dependence on men, for while men produce wealth, women "receive it at their hands," and all that a woman may wish to have or do "must come to her through a small gold ring." She argued that equality would transform women from "mere creatures of sex into fully developed human beings"; they would enter industry, join clubs, and bring about social improvements. She issued a warning against the injurious social and economic effects of limiting woman to the role of "priestess of the temple of consumption":

> the consuming female, debarred from any free production, unable to estimate the labor involved in the making of what she so lightly destroys, and her consumption limited mainly to those things which minister to physical pleasure, creates a market for sensuous decoration and personal adornment . . . which operates as a most deadly check to true industry.

Gilman advocated that cooking and cleaning be performed by specialists who could perform those tasks more efficiently, and in less time, than individual women in their individual homes could perform them, and she argued further that children also be turned over to experts because the private home was no longer sufficient for their rearing. Gilman believed a child socialized outside the home "learns that he is one among many" and that a mother who is out in the world doing work she enjoys will love her baby more when she is with it. Women's economic independence, according to Gilman, would produce happier homes, for if husbands were freed from the burden of domination and wives were freed from the degradation of dependence, they would be each other's friends, sharing common interests in the world around them, and serving equally as true companions to their children.[2]

After reading *Women and Economics*, Marie Jenney, a twenty-nine-year-old Unitarian minister in Iowa, wrote Gilman that her book was one "I have been waiting all my life to read." Marie Jenney asked Gilman to write her with instructions on what to read, for "you have found a disciple, whether you will or no." If Gilman would help her now, Jenney promised, "perhaps in the end I shall be able to help you also."[3]

In 1912, Marie Jenney, no longer preaching in Iowa but living in New York as the wife of Frederic Howe, a lawyer and Commissioner of Immigration, became chair of the Twenty-fifth Assembly District division of the New York City Woman Suffrage Party and formed the New York State Suffrage League. In 1912 she organized Heterodoxy, a club for "luncheon and debate" that probably began its meetings in one of the popular Greenwich Village gathering places, Polly Holladay's restaurant on MacDougal Street,[4] but later moved to the Town Hall club.[5]

According to another activist of the era, Mabel Dodge, Heterodoxy "was composed of women whose names were known," "women who did things and did them openly."[6] And one of the foremost of these, for a time, was Marie Jenney Howe's hero, Charlotte Perkins Gilman, who in 1900 had married her first cousin, George Houghton Gilman, a New York lawyer seven years her junior with whom she lived "happy ever after."[7] If Marie Jenney Howe had lapsed from the discipleship she had pledged in her 1899 letter to Gilman, and if, after her marriage, everything came to her through a small gold ring, she perhaps had compensated for what Dodge termed "the sterility of her domestic life"[8] by gathering together some of the most remarkable women of the era.

Charlotte Perkins Gilman influenced the activists who came of age in the twentieth century, but she also had a strong influence on her near contemporary, Rheta Childe Dorr. Born in Nebraska in 1866, Dorr, at the age of twelve, defied her father to hear Elizabeth Cady Stanton lecture on women's rights and immediately joined the National Woman Suffrage Association. Her formal education ended in

1885, when, while a student at the University of Nebraska, she
followed a professor's recommendation to read Henrik Ibsen's *A Doll's
House* and was inspired to leave the university and become economi-
cally independent. She worked in a post office, then as an insurance
underwriter before going in 1890 to New York, where she studied art
for a while, but soon turned to writing fiction and verse. In 1892, she
married John Pixley Dorr, a conservative Seattle businessman fourteen
years her senior. Influenced by the writings of Gilman and other
feminists, she continued in her quest for wider experience, seeking out
Alaska miners and prospectors in Seattle and writing accounts of these
adventures for New York newspapers. Because her husband remained
unsympathetic to her need for self-expression, she left him in 1898,
taking her two-year-old son, Julian, and returning to New York,
determined to make her way as a journalist.

Her most interesting newspaper work was a series of articles about
the condition of working women on the Lower East Side. These
accounts led to an appointment in 1904 as chair of the Federation of
Women's Clubs' committee on the industrial conditions of women and
children. Assisted by two important advocacy organizations for working women, the Association of Social Settlements and the Women's
Trade Union League, Rheta Dorr's committee persuaded Congress in
1905 to authorize the Bureau of Labor to conduct the first official
investigation of the condition of working women in the United States.
In 1906, Dorr went to Europe as a freelance correspondent; while there
she attended a meeting of the International Woman Suffrage Alliance
and met Christabel Pankhurst and other English suffrage leaders. On
her return to New York in 1907, she worked as a laundress, seamstress,
and factory hand in New York sweatshops in order to write authentic
articles on the conditions of working women. For a time, she wrote for
Hampton's, an aggressive, short-lived reform magazine. Her articles
formed the basis of her 1910 book, *What Eight Million Women Want,*
one of the notable works of the muckraking era.

In 1912, on a second trip to Europe, she interviewed suffragists
and feminists, and on her return she reported on Mrs. Emmeline G.
Pankhurst for *Good Housekeeping* magazine. After her return to the
United States, Dorr, who briefly had been a Socialist, joined Mrs.
Pankhurst's American disciples, Alice Paul and Lucy Burns, in urging

militant action to achieve a women's suffrage amendment. In 1914, she became the first editor of the *Suffragist,* official organ of the Congressional Union for Woman Suffrage, forerunner of the National Woman's Party.

The outbreak of World War I produced a change in Dorr's political views; her support for the war drew her away from reformist causes and estranged her from her friends.[9] Her pro-Allies position, though a minority view among women activists of the era, was shared by Charlotte Perkins Gilman, whose earlier opposition to this nation's entry into the war had been overcome by her vehemently anti-German feelings. The two women had been Heterodoxy members, but resigned from the club because of its members' opposition to the war.[10]

Inez Haynes Irwin's unpublished autobiography contains one of the fuller descriptions of Heterodoxy, which began with twenty-five members and ultimately included seventy-five members; its meetings were almost invariably addressed by members, and everything that was said was off the record.

> What did Heterodoxy talk about? It talked about everything. Hetero-
> doxy members were . . . Democrats, Republicans, Prohibitionists,
> socialists, anarchists, liberals and radicals of all opinions. . . . The
> rosta included many publicists, newspaper-women, war correspon-
> dents, radio commentators. There were dramatists, novelists and
> poets; painters and musicians. Our occupations and preoccupations
> ranged the world. Many of our members were working for various
> reforms. A sizable proportion were always somewhere else. During
> the First World War, when no Americans were supposed to enter
> Russia, always, at least two members of Heterodoxy were there
> writing articles.[11]

Irwin recalled as especially memorable the "background talks," in which a member would speak about her girlhood and young woman-hood. These talks ranged

> from the midwestern farm on which Leta Hollingsworth's childhood
> was spent, where all her dresses were made from flour bags which
> had the manufacturer's name printed on them, through a life of

inherited rebelliousness, like that of Charlotte Perkins Gilman . . . to
the fiery shadow of Emma Goldman, in which Stella Comen
Ballantine, who was her niece and adoring partisan lived . . . to the
quiet of Helen Hull's early life in the Middle West which was so like
that of her own rich novels.[12]

In other meetings, members and nonmembers addressed the club on
such subjects as pacifism, birth control, the Russian revolution, health
issues, infant mortality, anarchism, women's education, black civil
rights, disabled women, free love and changing sexual mores.[13]
Reflecting on the years from 1912 to 1917, Rheta Childe Dorr
observed, "We thought we discussed the whole field, but we really
discussed ourselves."[14]

One of the early activists, the writer, Socialist, and suffragist Inez
Haynes Irwin (known in these years as Inez Haynes Gillmore through
her first marriage to Rufus Gillmore), was born in 1873 in Brazil,
where her father had taken his family while on a brief and unsuccessful business venture, and had grown up and been educated in Boston,
her family's original home. She graduated from the Boston Normal
School in 1893, taught grammar school for three and one half years,
and then, from 1897 to 1900, attended Radcliffe College, a center of
feminist activity. In 1900, Gillmore and her friend Maud Wood
founded the Massachusetts College Equal Suffrage Association, which
later evolved into the National College Equal Suffrage League and
became an active force in the suffrage movement. Irwin and her then
husband, Rufus Hamilton Gillmore, whom she had married in 1897,
moved to New York where both hoped to become writers.

In 1907, the couple went to Paris, where Irwin first learned of
Socialism through meeting William English Walling and his wife, Rose
Strunsky, who had been witnesses to the 1905 Russian revolution, and
the circle of refugees from that revolution who had settled in Paris. She
also met Leo and Gertrude Stein and the Impressionist painters: Henri
Matisse (who, according to Irwin, had been discovered and supported
by the Steins early in his career and thus, after he was recognized and
wished to enlarge his clientele, was pressured by the Steins to sell them
everything he painted at their price), Georges Braque, Pablo Picasso,
André Derain, and other members of the group.[15]

Irwin wrote her first novel in Paris and, after returning to New York, began to sell her short stories to magazines. She had already published *June Jeopardy* (1908), a novel of mystery and romance among the Harvard-Radcliffe set, two works of children's fiction: *Ernest and Pheobe* (1911) and *Maida's Little Shop* (1911), when Piet Vlag, manager of the basement restaurant of the Rand School on East Seventeenth Street, "a gathering place of all the utopians, muckrakers, young intellectuals, and elderly malcontents south of Forty-Second Street,"[16] asked her to be fiction editor of *The Masses*, the journal that, between 1911 and 1917, became the rallying center for "everything that was then alive and irreverent in American culture."[17]

Under a series of editors in the first months of the magazine's existence, most of the fiction selections were translations of European authors; when Vlag became editor as well as publisher in January 1912 and invited Irwin to be fiction editor, she provided publishing opportunities for new writers. Irwin herself was a frequent contributor, relying upon the subjects of her popular fiction: the plight of poor children and life among the Harvard-Radcliffe set. Under Irwin's leadership as fiction editor of *The Masses*, a significant number of women authors were introduced to its readers. In most of the stories, the characters and settings are American; the protagonists are poor or working-class people, viewed sympathetically but from a sentimental, middle-class point of view.

The spirit of cooperation reflected in the fiction owed more to Christian perfectionism than to the Marxist concept of class conflict. For example, in Ethel Lloyd Patterson's story in the January 1912 issue, "Things for Dolls: Mamie Tuttle's Story and Its Unusual Climax," a part-time sales clerk in a toy store becomes enraged and smashes a doll because the wealthy matron she is serving is spending on dolls and "things for dolls" an amount of money that could pay to cure her own sick sister and end her mother's poverty. Her outburst arouses the sympathies of her co-workers who have been unfriendly to her, and the department manager pleads her case with the store owner, an unseen but apparently benevolent capitalist, who rules that if the sales clerk will pay for the damage she has caused, she will be promoted to full-time employment with a raise that will enable her to send her sick sister to Colorado.[18]

In addition to providing publishing opportunities for new writers, Irwin actively recruited a writer she admired to contribute fiction to *The Masses*. In January 1912 she wrote to Mary Heaton Vorse explaining that although she had never met Vorse (both Irwin and Vorse later would become members of Heterodoxy), she had heard "so much that is charming" about her "from those of my friends who happen to be your friends—that I have a feeling that you will not resent my request." Irwin prefaced her request with an explanation that the magazine called *The Masses* was the result of a decision by a few artists, illustrators and authors to turn out "a magazine that should stand for socialism and yet be artistic," that although these people had contributed illustrations, fiction, and editorials, "one giant of a Dutchman," Piet Vlag, was entirely responsible for getting it out. She followed the explanation with praise for Vorse's stories, despite hating to "throw bouquets in a letter in which I ask a favor," and added a postscript: "Please don't think I'm sending these letters out wholesale. You are the only unknown I have ventured to address. But I feel the socialist—whether conscious or unconscious I don't know—in all your work."[19]

Vorse did not resent the request, which was for anything in her "literary barrel" that had "been the rounds and can never go again," and shortly contributed a story, "The Day of a Man," about an unemployed construction worker cadging a living on the Bowery who regains his dignity during his final day of life by giving his last quarter to a poor young widow and then, while saving a child from drowning in the East River, is drowned himself.[20]

Like Inez Irwin, Vorse came from an old New England family. Born in 1874 and reared in Amherst, Massachusetts, a community she described as "seemingly free of the knowledge that there was such a thing as pain or death," Vorse traveled in Europe with her parents during her childhood and later studied art in Paris.[21] As a young woman, Vorse demanded that her family send her to art school in New York. Her insistence on having an independent life and career rather than following her mother's plan that she should marry, have children, and confine herself to domestic life caused an estrangement between them, and her wealthy mother disinherited her.[22] "I never took it into account," Vorse wrote in her journal years afterward, "that the poor old goose who laid the golden eggs might go on a goose strike and stop laying."[23]

In 1898, Vorse married the editor and writer Albert White Vorse and settled with him in Greenwich Village, which already was becoming a bohemian haven. Their son, Heaton, was born in 1901. In 1903, the Vorses moved to France, where they could live more cheaply while Bert Vorse devoted himself fully to his writing. During a difficult time in their marriage, Vorse traveled with her son and his nurse to Italy, where, freed from her husband's criticisms and demands, she began her writing career in earnest and had more success than her dilletantish, philandering husband. Bert Vorse joined Mary in Venice in 1904, and Mary continued to try to reconcile her mother's ideal of a woman's true destiny with her own ambition.

The Vorses were in Venice during the Italian general strike, and Mary witnessed the power of labor solidarity for the first time. The Vorses returned to America in 1905, residing in Amherst and Provincetown. In 1906, they joined sixteen other people in a communal housing venture, A Club, at 3 Fifth Avenue, a few blocks from Washington Square and across the street from the Brevoort Hotel. The other communards were people of intellect, most of them writers, reformers, or social workers associated with University Settlement; they included Rose Strunsky and her husband, William English Walling, who had been witnesses to the 1905 Russian revolution; Rose's sister, Anna; Charlotte Teller Hirsch; Howard Brubaker; and Arthur Bullard. Mark Twain, Frances Perkins, Dolly and John Sloan, and William Glackens were frequent visitors; other visitors included Theodore Dreiser, Maxim Gorky, and Mother Jones.

In 1907 Mary gave birth to her daughter, Ellen. That same year she purchased a home in Provincetown, Massachusetts that was to become, in the peripatetic years that followed, her home and refuge. In this period, Vorse was bringing up two small children and establishing herself as a writer of short stories, articles for magazines, and novels based on her family life: *The Breaking In of a Yachtsman's Wife* (1908), *The Very Little Person* (1911), and *The Autobiography of an Elderly Woman* (1911). Finally, her success and her husband's frequent infidelities put more strain on the marriage than it could bear, and Vorse and her husband separated in 1909. He died suddenly in 1910; when Vorse's mother learned of his death the next day, she died of heart failure. Now totally dependent on her ability as a writer to support her young daughter and son, as well as a father who was lapsing into madness, Vorse nevertheless continued her involvement in Greenwich Village community life. She was a member of the Socialist Party and had been active in the pure milk campaign, launched to ensure that poor and working-class mothers could obtain pasteurized milk free or at low cost, for, before 1912, milk was often produced in unsanitary conditions.[24]

Inez Haynes Irwin's invitation to become a *Masses* contributor coincided with Vorse's desire to turn her writing in a different direction as a result of her experience in the 1912 textile workers' strike in Lowell, Massachusetts. Initially curious and mildly concerned about the strike, Vorse had "wangled" an assignment from *Harper's* to report on the strike; once in Lawrence, however, Vorse became aware for the first time of the cost of the human cost of industrial strife. In her native New England, armed troops—"uniformed boys"—were being called out against workers while the "comfortable people" like those she had known in Amherst—clergymen, business men, civic leaders—were bitterly unsympathetic to the workers. On the other side, she saw the redemptive power of a common struggle. For a moment in Lawrence, "people were swept up outside of their small personal existence and into the august flow of the strike."

Vorse was moved by the commanding presence of "Big" Bill Haywood, leader of the International Workers of the World, the strike organizers, and by the beauty and stirring speeches of Elizabeth Gurley Flynn, with whom she formed an enduring friendship. Witnessing for the first time the victory won by collective action over great odds was a conversion experience for Vorse. She could not be an organizer or a labor leader, but she could write. She could try to make other people, who were ignorant but not indifferent, see what she had seen, feel what she had felt, and become as angry as she was. Vorse wanted "to see wages go up and babies' deaths rates go down," and she went away from Lawrence "with a resolve to write of these things always."[25]

Vorse's story "The Day of a Man" marked not only the beginning of a long association with *The Masses,* but the start of a new life as well, for after she returned to New York, she married Joe O'Brien, a fellow journalist who had shared the Lawrence experience with her. The couple were quickly absorbed into the corps of talented people who had been drawn together through their association with the magazine. The group included the writers Inez Haynes Irwin, William English Walling, Eugene Wood, Louis Untermeyer, and Ellis O. Jones, and the artists John Sloan, Boardman Robinson, Charles and Alice Winter, Maurice Becker, and Art Young.[26] Young later described Vorse as "pallid and unassuming," taking her time in conversation, pausing to lift her cigarette with "a slow, sinuous curve of her arm, taking an indifferent puff, then lazily saying something neither brilliant nor very interesting." However, according to Young, when many of those who came to the meetings became better acquainted with Vorse and her work, they grew to admire her. Young recorded that when Vorse was not at *Masses* meetings, she was "out on some errand of the heart among striking workers in the textile, steel, or mining sections of the country."[27]

Like Vorse, the most notorious activist of the era found her life transformed by a labor struggle, but not one that she had witnessed. Emma Goldman, born in Russia in 1869, settled with her family in Rochester, New York after her arrival in the United States when she was seventeen. She went to work in a factory, and to relieve the oppression and tedium of her job, she began attending meetings held by German socialists. One Sunday, a speaker from New York, Johanna Greie, related the events surrounding the Haymarket tragedy. In 1886, Labor strikes had broken out in America over the demand for an eight-hour day. A meeting of striking employees of the McCormick Harvester Company in Chicago, the center of the eight-hour movement, was attacked by police; many strikers were beaten and several were killed. A mass protest meeting was held in Haymarket Square on May 4 at which Albert Parsons, August Spies, Adolf Fischer, and others spoke. Satisfied that the meeting was orderly, the mayor of Chicago, Carter Harrison, left, but a Chicago police officer then came to the square and ordered the meeting to disperse. When the organizers protested, police attacked the gathering. A bomb was thrown, killing a number of police officers and wounding others. Not much effort was made to determine who was responsible for the bombing, but the speakers at the Haymarket meeting and other prominent anarchists were arrested and charged with the crime.

A number of factors combined to doom the accused: the bitter opposition of employers to the eight-hour movement; the inflammatory campaign of police and press to arouse the public against them; the intimidation of witnesses; and prejudicial denunciations of the men by the judge. Five men—Albert Parsons, August Spies, Louis Lling, Adolph Fischer, and George Engel—were sentenced to be hanged. Two men were sentenced to life imprisonment, and one man was sentenced to fifteen years in prison. The five condemned men were hanged on November 11, 1887; the anniversary of their martyrdom was observed in following years by anarchists and socialists, and Goldman would often return to the event in her imagination and refer to it in her writing.[28]

However, the defining event in Goldman's life was her involvement in a plot with Alexander Berkman to assassinate Henry Clay Frick, general manager of the Carnegie Company. Goldman and Berkman had been born in the same Russian city, Kovno;[29] Goldman met him on the day of her arrival in New York City in August, 1889, after she had left the dreariness of factory life in Rochester and a brief, failed marriage to Jacob Kershner. Goldman had been quickly enfolded into the anarchist movement. But the drudgery of making a living as a seamstress or as a factory worker dragged down Goldman's energy and spirit, so she welcomed the opportunity, in 1892, to join another comrade, "Fedya"—Modest Stein—and Berkman first in Springfield, then later in Worcester, Massachusetts. At the suggestion of their Worcester landlord, the trio opened an ice cream parlor and were doing a profitable business when actions of Frick against the striking steelworkers at Homestead, where the largest of the Carnegie mills were located, determined the trio to return to New York. Without knowing much beyond the newspaper accounts, without consulting the Homestead strikers about whether they viewed such an action as in their interest, Berkman determined to kill Frick.[30]

Using a text by the anarchist Johann Most, Berkman bought materials with the money made from the ice cream parlor venture and tried to build a bomb—at night, in the flat of a comrade who had agreed to put them up—while Goldman, terrified that something might go wrong and bring harm to others, persuaded herself that the ends justified the means and that she could do no less than "share to the uttermost with the beloved." When Berkman tested the bomb on Staten Island, it failed, so he decided he would use a gun. Goldman confided their plan to Joseph Peukert, the leader of one of the anarchist factions, who flatly turned down her request for a gun or funds to buy one. Inspired by Sonia, the character in Fyodor Dostoyevsky's *Crime and Punishment* who supported her family through prostitution, Goldman thought she would raise the money by marketing sex on East Fourteenth Street. With money borrowed from her host's servant, Goldman bought material and made appropriate garments. However, when potential customers approached her, she fled. Finally, "a tall, distinguished looking person" approached her and invited her to have a drink. The "affable stranger" told her she did not have the knack for prostitution and gave her ten dollars to cover her expenses to "rig" herself out. Goldman eventually borrowed the money Berkman needed from her sister.[31]

Berkman, with almost no experience with guns, traveled to Pittsburgh and shot Frick three times; however, Frick lived and Berkman was tried, convicted of attempted murder, and sentenced to twenty-two years in prison. Emma's connection to Berkman became known; she was arrested in Philadelphia after a fiery address on class warfare at a mass meeting in Union Square. This speech inspired the press to label her "Red Emma," a name that followed her for the rest of her life. She was brought back to New York, tried and convicted of inciting to riot, and sentenced to one year in Blackwell's Island.[32]

In prison, Goldman assisted a visiting physician and learned enough of nursing, by the standards of the times, to take up that work once she left prison. Through the support of Ed Brady, who had become her lover in 1893, she studied nursing in Vienna, earning a degree for midwifery and a degree for nursing. But political activism claimed Goldman's spirit, and she continually was involved in protesting injustice, traveling around the country lecturing on anarchism, and maintaining an ongoing effort to win a commutation of Berkman's sentence.[33]

Her reputation as the most dangerous woman in America followed her—she was even accused of involvement in the assassination of President William McKinley.[34] But in 1912, Goldman was living in relative stability at 210 East Thirteenth Street. Alexander Berkman—

Sasha—whose sentence had been reduced to fourteen years—had been freed in 1906, the same year in which Goldman began publishing *Mother Earth*, a journal designed to offer a place of expression for "young idealists in art and letters."[35] Her interests never had been confined narrowly to political ideology; she lectured across the country as often on drama as on anarchy, and her circle of friends had widened to include the young activists who were settling in Greenwich Village. She and Berkman were no longer lovers, but were strongly bound to each other as friends, colleagues, and comrades. When Ed Brady proved too jealous and demanding, Goldman, determined never to be controlled by a lover, parted from him, but she was on good terms with him when he died in 1903.[36]

She had affairs during and after her relationship with Brady, but in 1912, Goldman was passionately in love with Ben Reitman, a doctor who left medicine to aid homeless men and then became her assistant. She was, in sum, a lovesick woman in her forties "carried away by a mad attraction for a young man" who did not share her ideals and who was repeatedly unfaithful to her with women he claimed he did not love.[37] The incredibly energetic Goldman lectured on literature and politics around the country, served numerous causes, and issued *Mother Earth* almost single-handedly—yet this middle-aged woman, whom Mabel Dodge described as "a severe schoolteacher in a scolding mood,"[38] still had the strength to pour out her soul in long anguished letters to Reitman.

At the other end of the broad spectrum of activists was Alva Erskine Smith Vanderbilt Belmont, who was born in Mobile in 1853 and, after being educated in France, where her family had moved after the Civil War, came with her mother and sisters to New York in the early 1870s as part of the influx of outsiders whose social climbing was depicted in Edith Wharton's novels. In April, 1875, Alva Smith married William Vanderbilt, and, though the marriage was the great social event of the season, she was not accepted by Mrs. William Astor, who presided over the inner circle of New York society. The social acceptance Alva Vanderbilt strove for was accomplished through a fabulous costume ball held in March 1883 at the three-million-dollar chateau she had had constructed at Fifth Avenue and Fifty-second Street. In order that her daughter might be invited to the ball, Mrs. Astor finally made a call upon Mrs. Vanderbilt.

In 1895, Alva Vanderbilt divorced her husband on the grounds of adultery, receiving as a settlement an income of $100,000 a year and retaining sole custody of her two sons and her daughter. Later that year, she introduced her daughter, Consuelo, to society and, in the manner of socially ambitious Gilded Age mothers, forced Consuelo to abandon the man to whom she had been secretly engaged and marry the Duke of Marlborough, an unhappy union that was annulled two decades later.

In 1896, Mrs. Vanderbilt married Oliver Hazard Perry Belmont, a Vanderbilt family friend five years her junior. After his death in 1909, Alva Belmont came under the influence of Anna Howard Shaw and was transformed into a militant feminist, devoting the rest of her life and much of her fortune to suffrage and other reform causes. She supported the Women's Trade Union League during the garment workers' strikes of 1909 and 1916 and was an activist and financial supporter of the National Woman Suffrage Association; the Political Equality League, a New York suffrage organization she had founded; and the National Woman's Party, which elected her its president in 1921. In her later years, Alva Belmont lived most of the time in France, dying in Paris shortly after her eightieth birthday.[39]

Another of the great suffrage leaders of the era, Harriot Stanton Blatch, was born in 1856 to Henry Brewster Stanton and Elizabeth Cady Stanton, whose leadership in the early suffrage movement inspired Harriot to take on a leadership role in the twentieth-century women's movement. Harriot Stanton graduated with honors from Vassar in 1878, spent a year at the Boston School of Oratory, and then traveled abroad serving as tutor to several young girls. She returned home to assist her mother and Lucy Stone in writing the *History of Woman Suffrage*. In 1882, Stanton married an English businessman, William Henry Blatch, and lived with him for twenty years in the small town of Basingstoke, forty miles west of London. She had two children—Nora Stanton, born in 1883, and Helen Stanton, who was born in 1892 but died in childhood.

Harriot Stanton Blatch became active in the era's reform movements and was, of course, drawn to the cause of woman suffrage. She was inspired by the leadership of Emmeline Pankhurst, one of the founders of the short-lived Woman's Franchise League, which had successfully organized a movement for suffrage among mill hands and factory workers in the north and midlands of England.

In 1902, the Blatch family settled in the United States, and Harriot became active in the women's suffrage movement in New York. Drawing on her experience in England, she launched the Equality League of Self-Supporting Women, an organization that drew nearly 20,000 women workers in factories, laundries, and shops. Under Mrs. Blatch's leadership, the suffrage movement was enlivened by outdoor meetings, suffrage parades, testimonials at legislative hearings, and campaigns in election districts. In 1910, the league became the Women's Political Union, and a vigorous but ultimately unsuccessful drive for a state constitutional suffrage amendment was launched.

In 1915, William Blatch was accidentally killed through contact with a fallen power line on a neighbor's Long Island home, and Mrs. Blatch went to England to settle his affairs. When she returned to the United States and resumed her suffrage activism in 1917, she helped to fuse the Congressional Union—which had previously merged with the Women's Political Union—with the Woman's Party, organized in 1916 to secure the votes of enfranchised women in the western states against Democrat incumbents who opposed women's suffrage. Blatch campaigned against Wilson, and in order to be able to vote herself, established residence in Kansas, where her mother had campaigned for suffrage about fifty years earlier.[40]

Women like Alva Belmont aroused the suspicion of women like Theresa Serber, who was born in Russia in 1874, emigrated to America in 1891, found work in the garment trade, and soon dedicated herself, as did many of her generation of Jewish female immigrants, to the labor movement and to socialism—and later to suffrage. In 1900, she married Leon A. Malkiel, also a socialist and a lawyer who also dealt in real estate. In 1903, Theresa gave birth to a daughter, Henrietta. Theresa's marriage enabled her to leave work in the sweatshop, and though her family moved from the Lower East Side to the Upper West Side of Manhattan—and later to Westchester—she remained committed throughout her life to socialist politics and to helping immigrant women.

In 1907, a large influx of native-born and immigrant radical women, Malkiel among them, reacted to the male-centered culture of the Socialist Party. The demands for women's suffrage created a dilemma for these women, for although the Second International Meeting of the Socialist Party had encouraged socialists to work for women's suffrage, it prohibited them from allying themselves with "bourgeois" women and organizations. Malkiel was torn on this issue; on the one hand, she held the class struggle and profound social change as her priorities, but on the other, she viewed the vote as essential to women's emancipation. During the "women's strikes" of 1909-1911, Malkiel worked for the strikers in her capacity as a member of the Women's Trade Union League executive board and as a journalist writing articles for the *New York Call,* which printed excerpts of what became her best known work, *The Diary of a Shirtwaist Maker,* published in 1910.[41]

In this fictionalized diary, Mary, a shirtwaist-maker from an "American" working-class family, gains awareness of class struggle and an understanding of the difficult lives of immigrant working women through participation in the "Uprising of 20,000." When Jim, her fiancé, objects to her involvement in the strike because he feels threatened by her new independence, Mary tells him that until she left her workbench, she "was no better than a cow in a stall."[42] A scene in which Mary attends a mass meeting at a hall hired by Alva Belmont expresses Malkiel's ambivalence about wealthy sympathizers of working women. She is curious to see Mrs. Belmont and thinks that "she must be better than the rest of her kind if she is willing to help us girls rather than give a monkey dinner or buy a couple of new pet dogs." However, after she has been caught up in the meeting and has found the feeling of being surrounded by thousands of people all assembled for the same purpose "like an immense giant born for the purpose of doing justice to all," Mary decides she "ain't got much use for the rich," for if they were human, "they couldn't stand for all this misery."[43]

Despite her hostility to rich suffragists like Belmont, Malkiel continued to work for suffrage within the Socialist Party, reaching out to groups not embraced by the mainstream movement. Along with other New York women socialists, she participated in a large "anti-preparedness" campaign protesting America's imminent entry into World War I in January 1916, and went on a nationwide speaking tour in opposition to the war. After 1919, like other Socialist Party women,

Malkiel drifted away from political involvement and became active in adult education. She died in 1948.[44]

Pioneer in child health care Sara Josephine Baker was born in 1873 to an affluent Poughkeepsie, New York lawyer, Orlando Daniel Mosher Baker, and a Vassar College graduate, Jenny Brown Baker. Her pleasant, privileged childhood ended with her father's death when she was sixteen.[45] With scholarship aid and some support from her family, Baker—who was always known as "Jo"—studied medicine at the women's medical college attached to the New York Infirmary for Women and Children established by Dr. Elizabeth Blackwell. After graduating second in a class of eighteen in 1898, Baker interned at the New England Hospital for Women and Children, returning to New York the following year to set up a practice on New York's Upper West Side with another doctor, Florence Laighton, who worked and lived with Baker for many years.[46]

After earning only $185 in her first year of practice, Baker secured an appointment in 1901 as a medical inspector for the New York City Health Department at a salary of $30 a month. In the summer of 1902 she was assigned to seek out sick babies by climbing up and down flights of tenement stairs on the West Side's "Hell's Kitchen" neighborhood. In 1907, Baker was appointed assistant to the health commissioner and in the summer of 1908 she undertook a mission of teaching the principles of child care to poor mothers in order to reduce the mortality rate among children under five, who comprised a third of all deaths in New York City each year. The efforts of Baker and a team of nurses resulted in a drop of 1,200 infant deaths in an East Side district, while the rates in other districts showed no significant change[47]

Baker cited this achievement as marking the "actual beginning" of her life's work, for in August 1908, the Health Department established the Division (later Bureau) of Child Hygiene with her as its chief.[48] Baker developed what became known as public health education. Under her leadership pamphlets on hygiene were distributed; a free training school and licensing procedures for midwives were established; and "baby health stations" for distributing pure milk and infant care advice were set up. Tests for diphtheria, influenza, and other infectious diseases were given to children in the schools, where "Little Mother's Leagues" were organized to provide information on proper child care.[49]

Baker's attention to details led her to design a sanitary container for eye medications administered at birth to prevent infant blindness. She also designed a pattern for baby clothes the opened down the front "like a fireman's clothes" that the ... Call Pattern Company adapted for commercial use.[50]

Baker's achievements brought her recognition as a public health authority. For fifteen years, beginning in 1916, she lectured annually at New York University–Bellevue Hospital Medical School. Her arrangement with the school enabled her to pursue a doctorate in its new public health course; her thesis was a study of the relationship between classroom ventilation and respiratory diseases among children. In 1917, she received a Doctorate of Public Health, the first awarded to a woman.

By the time she retired from the Child Hygiene Bureau in 1923, a Children's Bureau had been created within the United States Department of Labor, and similar agencies had been established in every state and several foreign countries. Retirement did not mark an end to her career. She remained active in local, state, and national medical societies and she was a consultant to the federal Children's Bureau and Public Health Service and to the New York State Department of Health. She represented the United States on the Health Committee of the League of Nations from 1922 to 1924, and in 1935 and 1936 she served as president of the American Women's Health Association. She published three books in 1920—*Healthy Babies, Healthy Mothers*, and *Healthy Children*. To these she added *The Growing Child* in 1923 and *Child Hygiene* in 1925. She contributed over 200 articles to the popular press and over 50 articles to the *American Journal of Public Health*. Her autobiography, *Fighting for Life*, was published in 1939. She spent her final years at her home in Belleville, New Jersey. Baker died of cancer in 1975.[51]

Before coming to New York, Helen Marot, who was born in 1865 and Quaker-educated, worked in Philadelphia, where she was employed by the University Extension Society from 1893 to 1895, and then in Delaware, where she was a librarian at the Wilmington Public Library in 1896. In 1897, she returned to Philadelphia and organized the Library of Economics and Political Science, which became a center for radical thought. With the educational reformer Caroline Pratt, she investigated the custom tailoring trades in Philadelphia for the United States Industrial Commission in 1899. As Mary Heaton Vorse was afterward transformed by her experience in Lowell, Marot's Philadelphia investigation awakened her to the condition of the working classes. Marot, a slender, plain woman of medium height who wore glasses, parted her auburn hair in the middle and pulled it back into a bun, and habitually wore mannish clothing, was transformed from a Quakerish librarian into an aggressive, partisan activist. In 1902, she was invited by the Association of Neighborhood Workers in New York City to investigate the child labor situation there; her work resulted in the formation of the New York Child Labor Committee in 1902. The committee's report supported the campaign that led to the enactment by the New York State legislature of the Compulsory Education Act of 1903. From 1904 to 1905, Marot served as secretary of the Pennsylvania Child Labor Commission, and in 1906, she joined the Women's Trade Union League in New York, serving as its executive secretary from 1906 to 1913.

Marot was deeply involved in organizing the women garment workers' strikes in 1910 and 1911. The strikes, while not entirely successful, brought women workers into the labor movement and laid the foundations for the International Ladies Garment Workers Union. Marot remained involved in the conditions of women workers, organizing protests following the Triangle Shirtwaist fire in 1911 and organizing women during the laundry workers' strike in 1912. In 1913, she began writing regularly for *The Masses* on labor unions and served on the magazine's editorial board. In October 1918 Marot joined the staff of *Dial* magazine, helping to transform it from a staid literary magazine into a journal of liberal opinion, and as part of this effort she recruited John Dewey and Thorstein Veblen to the staff. In 1920, worn out by decades of activism, Marot, then fifty-five, retired and lived pleasantly in Greenwich Village, spending summers with Pratt in West Becket, Massachusetts until her death, after a short illness, in New York City in 1965.[52]

In her principal work, *American Labor Unions,* published in 1914, Marot reflected on the discrimination against women within labor unions, commenting that labor union men were no different from other men, for they were not eager to trust office-holding to women.

However, Marot continued, labor union women were no different from other women, for they lacked the courage and determination to overcome the prevailing attitude that women are unfit to assume responsibility. Women's domestic relations, their lack of support from their partners, created the real stumbling block to their advancement in unions; thus, Marot concluded, the lack of executive representation of women in executive positions endowed the labor movement with a masculine point of view and limited it to masculine ability.[53]

Marot, like the rest of the early women activists, had devoted her career to improving the condition of working women and also aided the younger women who came to New York after these older women had spent years blazing trails for suffrage and women's economic advancement. The foremothers befriended, mentored, and, in some cases, protected the younger women, who, with daring and panache, continued the work of previous generations of feminists.

CHAPTER 4

Movers and Shakers: The New Women

THE FOUNDER OF THAT WONDERFUL WOMEN'S CLUB, Heterodoxy, Marie Jenney Howe, was born in 1870 in Syracuse, New York to Edwin Sherwin Jenney and Marie Saul Jenney, both of whom were members of prosperous old New York families. In 1893, in pursuit of her desire to be a minister, she went to the Unitarian Theological Seminary in Meadville, Pennsylvania, where, because of her striking good looks, the townspeople could not take her ambition seriously. The skeptics included the man who would become her husband, Frederic C. Howe, a young law student who met Jenney when he returned to his hometown for a visit.

In his first meeting with her, Howe "quoted a remark of Heine's that every woman who did anything in the world had one eye on her work and the other eye on a man. The only exception was the Countess Somebody or Other, but then she only had one eye."[1] The joke did not amuse Marie Jenney, who seemed quite willing to see Howe go. Nevertheless, Howe—who was attracted to her beauty even though he found her ideas about woman's independence in conflict with his ideas about woman's "place"—pursued Jenney. He continued the courtship through letters after Jenney graduated in 1897 and departed from Meadville for Sioux City and later Des Moines, Iowa to be an assistant to another woman minister, Mary A. Sanford. Howe, in the meantime, had become an idealistic lawyer, working as an active

Cleveland municipal reformer. His letters must have been persuasive, for in 1904, Marie Jenney gave up the ministry and married him.[2]

The Howes moved to New York in 1910, when Frederic became Commissioner of Immigration. Marie became active in the suffrage movement and the National Consumers' League, an organization of middle-class women who sought to improve conditions for working women. In 1910, she became chair of the Twenty-fifth Assembly District division of the New York City Woman Suffrage Party, which, under her leadership, became known as the "Fighting Twenty-fifth." Here she met women like Mary Heaton Vorse, Crystal Eastman, and Henrietta Rodman and, in 1912, began assembling what Vorse's biographer, Dee Garrison, has justly called "the largest group of intellectually exciting American women ever gathered in one room."[3] The rule that Heterodoxy meetings were off the record was broken on several occasions; one revealing account that seems in conflict with the image of Heterodites' image of intellectuality was recorded in Dr. Sara Josephine Baker's autobiography, where she described the address to the club by Amy Lowell:

> She dealt very pleasantly with her theories of poetry and such general subjects and then asked if anyone would like her to read some of her poems. That produced a landslide of requests. Member after member demanded a special favorite, and each selection was more sentimental than the last. . . . It was all so sad that Rose Pastor Stokes turned around and laid her head on her neighbor's shoulder and cried down her neck, sobbing an obbligato to Miss Lowell's sonorous voice. The poetess stood it as long as she could and then:
>
> "I'm through," she said. "They told me I was to speak to a group of intellectual, realistic, tough-minded leaders in the women's world. Instead I find a group that wants nothing but my most sentimental things. Good afternoon!" And she poked her cigar into her mouth and walked out glowering.[4]

The Heterodoxy meetings resembled the "consciousness-raising" groups of the 1960s feminist movement, in which women broke through their isolation to discover that, despite the differences in their backgrounds, their socialization had imposed limitations on all of them that they were determined to remove. Feminism was incubated in Heterodoxy, and when the concept was more fully developed, Marie Jenney Howe led dynamic meetings at which her colleagues defined its aspects.

In 1927, Howe published *George Sand: The Search for Love*, a work that surprised her by its good reception from critics and readers. Hutchins Hapgood offered a dissenting opinion by claiming that Howe had written the biography because she, like Sand, was "unhappy in a harsh world," and, like other sensitive women of her time, incorrectly thought "men were the cause of all their inward woe."[5] However, in a letter to Fola La Follette, Howe confided that her motivation for writing Sand's biography was to prove that she could accomplish something beyond being simply "poor domestic Marie." And when letters came from strangers who had drawn strength from her portrait of Sand, she again wrote to La Follette, stating that such letters should come when writers are working and need confidence, and that La Follette had given her "encouragement at the right time."[6]

Howe died in 1934, greatly mourned for "her genius for friendship" and for her ability to overcome her moments of regret for involving herself in "this hydra-headed Heterodoxy, with its everlasting eating and smoking, its imperviousness to discipline and its strange incapacity for boredom," for the real Heterodoxy "is a warm and friendly and staunch spirit, in which our conglomerate personalities all have a share."[7]

Like Emma Goldman and Theresa Serber Malkiel, Rose Pastor Stokes was another radical Russian-Jewish immigrant, but the attention she drew from the press of the day was due to the rags-to-riches direction of her life. Born in 1879, she emigrated in early childhood to London with her mother, after her father had left the family and emigrated to the United States. Her mother, who worked as a seamstress, later married Israel Pastor, whom Stokes described as a kind but improvident man. The family moved to America in 1890 and settled in Cleveland, where, after her stepfather deserted the family, Rose went to work in a series of cigar factories rolling "stogies." When a fellow worker brought in a copy of the *Jewish Daily News* that included an invitation to readers to write letters about their work, Rose responded. Her correspondence evoked so favorable a response from readers that the editors offered her a full-time position, and she went to live in New York.[8]

As a journalist, she interviewed J. G. Phelps Stokes, a socialite turned social worker at the University Settlement—a "seething center for the exchange of ideas"—who reminded her of a "young Abe Lincoln." Their romance and subsequent engagement brought constant attention from the press. She refused to have the word "obey" included in the ceremony during her marriage to Stokes on her birthday, July 18, 1904.[9] However, she wore a silver cross about her neck, an act that outraged Jews.[10] Overwhelmed by the luxury of her husband's family's home and furnishings and rebelling against assuming the role of an alms-bestowing Lady Bountiful, Stokes joined the Socialist Party—afterward persuading her husband to become a member—and threw herself into labor organizing. She participated in the shirtwaist-makers' strike of 1909-1910, marching on the picket line and speaking at rallies.[11] When the International Hotel Workers' Union called a strike in 1912, she urged the waiters to organize against the "master class" that despised them.[12] The Socialist Jewish Cinderella was an irresistible attraction for the reporters who thronged to hear her speak and record her appearance: the New York Times reporter wrote that there is "little of the Jewess about Rose Pastor Stokes, except the melancholy associated with her race."[13] As figures in "our greatest social romance," she and her husband were popular speakers, invited even by patriotic and conservative groups like the Daughters of the American Revolution to "come and tell us about Socialism."[14]

The sociologist Elsie Clews Parsons began life far from the working class, having been born into a prominent New York family in 1875. In 1896 she graduated from Barnard College and continued her studies at Columbia, where she received her doctorate in 1899. She taught sociology at Barnard from 1899 to 1905. In 1900 she married Herbert Parsons, a lawyer who served as a Republican congressman from 1905 to 1911 and thereafter was a leader in the New York County Republican Party. Parsons, who had four surviving children, held political and social views that strongly differed from her husband's. And while Herbert Parsons did not oppose his wife's career, he did not encourage it or take an active interest in it. Of course, there were strains in such a marriage, but eventually the couple achieved an acceptance of each other that endured until Herbert Parsons' death in 1925.[15]

Elsie Clews Parsons's career was divided into two stages. In the first stage, she produced sociological studies: *The Family* (1906); *Religious Chastity* (1913), published anonymously to protect her husband's political career; *The Old Fashioned Woman* (1913); *Fear and Conventionality* (1914); *Social Freedom* (1915; and *Social Rule* (1916).[16] The central purpose of these works was to examine controls in the form of barriers, taboos, assigned roles and classifications used by all societies against groups or individuals. Parsons urged change and movement toward a society "where age will not bully youth, nor youth misprize age; and where the impulses of sex will not be restricted in their expression to conjugality, nor will conjugality be considered as necessarily a habit for a lifetime."[17]

Parsons's essays for *The Masses* reflected her thinking in this stage of her career. In "Facing Race Suicide" in the June 1915 issue of that magazine, she addresses the concern of conservatives about the falling "native birth-rate" by asking if the "race suicide croakers" were prepared to eliminate the distinction between legitimacy and illegitimacy, or to reform other conditions that make child-bearing impossible or possible only at great sacrifice by women they consider desirable mothers. If these conservatives did not see that such women had been educated for lives they were not allowed to live and that the roles imposed upon women were likely to make them "the colorless, untemperamental, unsexed women Europeans consider the American type," then they should be satisfied by having the population maintained by those immigrants "whose peasant education is consistent with the conditions for mating and childbearing obtaining in America—or in that part of America, shall we say, represented by the Board of Education that excludes the teacher-mother or by the State Legislature that makes the control of conception illegal."[18]

The psychological and philosophical concepts Parsons expressed in her books and *Masses* essays did not bring her recognition from either a scholarly or a general audience. While remaining concerned with the interrelation between personality and cultural forms, she turned from sociology to anthropology, undertaking a meticulous and rigorous study of other cultures as a means of illuminating her own, in the conviction that scientific work, rather than propaganda, would promote her ideas more effectively. In this second stage of her career, she explored the cultures of the Pueblo Indians of the American Southwest and American and West Indian blacks and achieved as an anthropologist the recognition that had eluded her as a sociologist.[19]

Mabel Dodge Luhan, born in 1879 to a Buffalo family whose money came from banking, became during this period a major mover and shaker of the arts scene.[20] Her first husband, Karl Evans, by whom she had a son, John,[21] was killed in a shooting accident. She married her second husband, Edwin Dodge, an architect, in Paris; the couple then purchased a villa in Florence, which Edwin reconstructed while Mabel furnished it.[22] The villa absorbed their income for years; "it drank money."[23] But during her years in Europe, Mabel Dodge came to know and appreciate the work of Picasso and Matisse, and to know as well the art patrons Leo and Gertrude Stein.[24] However, the stimulating European life failed to mask Dodge's realization that after ten years of marriage, she found Edwin a "wet blanket."[25]

In the autumn of 1912, Dodge made arrangements for her son to be educated in the United States and sailed back from Europe, unhappily convinced that there was "no place" in her own country for a person like her. The Dodges settled into an apartment at 23 Fifth Avenue; Edwin worked as an architect, but Mabel was unhappily convinced she had "nothing to do" in New York and the couple drifted apart. Through the writer Hutchins Hapgood—the confidant of all her years in New York—she met Emma Goldman and Margaret Sanger, and before long she had gathered a large collection of new acquaintances. She became involved in organizing her "own little Revolution," the Armory show of Cubist painters, which she considered "the most important thing that ever happened in America."[26]

At the suggestion of her friend Lincoln Steffens, Mabel Dodge had "Evenings" at her lower Fifth Avenue apartment. Her home became a center

> where Socialists, Trade-Unionists, Anarchists, Suffragists, Poets, Relations, Lawyers, Murderers, "old friends," Psychoanalysts, I.W.W.s, Single Taxers, Birth Controlists, Newspapermen, Artists, Modern Artists, Clubwomen, Place-is-in-the-home Women, Clergy-

men, and just plain men all met there and, stammering in an
unaccustomed freedom a kind of Speech called Free, exchanged . . .
Opinions.[27]

Through these evenings, Dodge met more and more people, first
because she wanted to know everybody, and second because everybody wanted to know her. She wanted, in particular,

> to know the Heads of things. Heads of Movements, Heads of
> Newspapers, Heads of all kinds of groups of people. I became a
> Species of Head Hunter, in fact. It was not dogs or glass I collected
> now, it was people, Important People. I vaguely believed that anyone
> who reached eminence in the community, raised themselves above
> others, must have attained excellence, and excellence I have always
> revered. . . . Each of these "leaders" brought his or her group along,
> for they had heard about the Evenings (by this time called a Salon)
> and they all wanted to come.[28]

One night Mabel Dodge, with her friends Hutchins Hapgood and his
wife, Neith Boyce, attended a party at the barely furnished Greenwich
Village apartment of Bea Shostak, a schoolteacher and Bill Haywood's
sometime lover. Haywood, "a great battered hulk of a man," spoke
there of his inability to publicize the strike of silk-loom workers in
Paterson, New Jersey that he was leading with the other members of
the International Workers of the World triumvirate, Carlo Tresca and
Elizabeth Gurley Flynn. Dodge suggested that Haywood bring the
workers to Madison Square Garden and reenact the strike. The
attractive young journalist John Reed immediately volunteered to
organize the pageant, and Mabel Dodge, who had lost interest in her
Evenings, "gave up everything to work on the Paterson pageant."
    The recreation of the scenes of the strike, including the graveside
speeches of the leaders at a funeral of a nonstriking worker whom the
police had killed, was an artistic success and won much sympathy for
the silk workers. But the pageant had lost money and the effort to
launch it resulted, according to Elizabeth Gurley Flynn, in a diversion
of 1,000 of the best workers from actual strike activity and jealousies
among the strikers as to who would perform in the pageant. The strike

ended with little real change in the speedup system—requiring workers to produce at a faster and faster rate—that had produced it. The day after the strike, Mabel Dodge and John Reed sailed for Paris, where they consummated the love that had developed as they had worked together.[29]

Dodge had attended Heterodoxy meetings, admiring the "fine, daring, rather joyous and independent women" who were its members.[30] Through her Evenings, she had helped to popularize the ideas of Sigmund Freud. She had become interested in *The Masses* because it was "fearless and young and laughing at everything solemn and conservative."[31] But after she began her affair with John Reed, "Nothing else in the world had, any longer, any significance" for her.[32] Then, when the affair ended in late 1914, she said "good-bye forever to Reed" in her heart, and good-bye as well to "the Labor Movement, to Revolution, and to anarchy."[33] But Mabel Dodge did not end her career as an activist; she turned her energies to the arts, and her principal accomplishment in that endeavor was to create an arts community, not in New York, but in Taos, New Mexico.

Margaret Sanger, one of the radicals Dodge came to know in her early days in New York, was born in 1879 in Corning, New York, the sixth of eleven children born to Michael and Anne Purcell Higgins. Her father was a nonconforming first-generation, Irish-American, a stonemason whose love of drink and talk led to periods of unemployment that forced his children to support the large family.[34] Margaret's mother died from chronic tuberculosis aggravated by weakness caused by her frequent pregnancies. Stricken by the loss of her mother and the realization that she could have done nothing to save her, Margaret became a nurse.

During the course of her training in New York City, she met and married Bill Sanger, an architect, and moved with him to an apartment on Manhattan's Upper West Side, where the Sanger living room, on a smaller and less opulent scale than Mabel Dodge's downtown salon, became a "gathering place where liberals, anarchists, Socialists, and I. W. W.'s could meet." In those days, Sanger recalled, their guests "really came to see Bill"; she made the cocoa. The Sangers' guests also included people who flocked to Mabel Dodge's Evenings: Emma Goldman, Alexander Berkman, Bill Haywood, and John Reed.[35] Sanger and Dodge became friends in this period, Dodge recalling Sanger as "the Madonna type of woman, with soft brown hair parted over a quiet brow, and crystal-clear light brown eyes," the first person Dodge had ever known "who was openly an ardent propagandist for the joys of the flesh."[36] Sanger remembered Dodge at her "famous soirees" as a listener more than a talker, who sat "near the hearth, brown bangs outlining a white face, simply gowned in velvet, beautifully arched foot beating the air."[37] Sanger's memory of Emma Goldman was as vivid as Dodge's; she remembered Red Emma as a "true Russian peasant type" whose way with people "was to berate and lash with scorn."[38] And like Mary Heaton Vorse, she recalled Elizabeth Gurley Flynn's dramatic beauty, "with her black hair and deep blue eyes, her cream-white complexion set off by the flaming scarf she always wore at her throat."[39]

Sanger joined the Socialist Party and wrote articles for the party newspaper, the *New York Call*. One of these was about the 1912 strike by laundry workers, whom she found to be the hardest worked and poorest paid of any union members. She was especially sensitive to the needs of the women, who, though concerned as the men were with wages and working conditions, were more distressed by having too many children.[40] During the strike by textile workers in Lawrence, Massachusetts, Sanger was designated, in her capacity as a nurse, to accompany the children on the train that brought them to New York, where they were turned over to foster parents who cared for them for the duration of the strike.[41] Sanger also was involved in the Paterson silk workers' strike, and the failure of the pageant, which left her despondent, brought a "fitting conclusion to one period" of her life. Sanger's involvement with strikes had left her believing that the struggle for pennies was futile "when fast-coming babies required dollars to feed them."[42]

Sanger's true career was determined by her experiences as a nurse. Working among the poor on the Lower East Side, she witnessed the agony and early deaths of women with too many children who died in childbirth or through "butchery" by "five dollar abortionists." What Sanger was afterward to cite repeatedly as an "awakening" was her work with a young Jewish immigrant, Sadie Sachs, whom she nursed in a Hester Street tenement through the complications of a self-induced abortion. Mrs. Sachs pleaded for contraceptive information, which Sanger lacked; the attending physician turned aside his patient's pleas with the advice to tell her husband, Jake, "to sleep on the roof." Inevitably, Sanger was called back to the Hester Street tenement three months later to find Mrs. Sachs dying of septicemia. From that night on, Sanger declared, she resolved to "abandon the palliative career of nursing in pursuit of fundamental social change."[43]

The Socialist, feminist, and lawyer Crystal Eastman was born in upstate New York in 1881. Her father was a minister, but when he became disabled from his Civil War injuries and unable to work, her mother, Annis Ford Eastman, took up the ministry, becoming the first ordained minister in the Congregational Church of New York. The household, according to her brother, Max, "was run on feminist principles."[44] Eastman graduated from Vassar College in 1903 and earned a master's degree in sociology from Columbia University and a law degree—graduating second in her class—from New York University in 1907. In 1909, she was appointed by New York's governor, Charles Evans Hughes, to the Employer's Liability Commission and became the only woman to serve on that commission. As secretary of that commission, she drafted New York State's first worker's compensation law, which thereafter was used by many states as a model. Her 1910 book, *Work Accidents and the Law,* resulted in significant movement toward worker safety.

Eastman married an insurance salesman, Wallace Benedict, in 1911 and went to live in Milwaukee, where she worked on the suffrage referendum. After the referendum was defeated by the German brewery interests, who feared that women's suffrage would lead to prohibition, she returned to New York—her marriage later ended—and in 1914 formed the Woman's Peace Party of New York, serving as its president until 1919. She also helped to create two other anti-war organizations: the national Woman's Peace Party (WPP)—known today as the Women's International League for Peace and Freedom—and the American Union Against Militarism (AUAM). Eastman recruited Heterodoxy members Katherine Anthony, Marie Jenney Howe, Freda Kirchwey, and Margaret Lane for leadership positions in the WPP, which was far more militant and confrontational than other women's anti-militarism organizations, and whose debates between pro-military businessmen and anti-militarists were broken up by violent patriots, frequently in uniform. Ironically, on these occasions the WPP, rather than the attackers, received unfavorable press criticism.

In 1915, with the support of the AUAM and the Woman's Peace Party of New York, Eastman launched the "Truth About Preparedness Campaign," which, through mass meetings in many cities, "won hundreds of columns from an unwilling press." As a result, the AUAM grew into an organization of 6,000 members with committees in twenty-two cities. But Eastman's flamboyant and confrontational tactics alienated other reformers in the anti-militarism campaign. The WPP-sponsored "War Against War" exhibit, which drew crowds of New Yorkers for several months to hear its militant speakers and view its display of vivid cartoons and colorful posters, offended a number of women involved in the anti-militarism campaign. So, too, did the irreverent and radical tone of the New York WPP meetings, and Eastman was the target of their criticism.[45]

However, Eastman maintained that both private lobbying and more confrontational public activism were necessary to change government policy. This strategy proved effective in averting war with Mexico, when, after clashes between American and Mexican soldiers, private mediation efforts by Mexican and American labor officials were accompanied by the AUAM's publicity campaign demonstrating that most of Mexico's wealth was controlled largely by North American interests. In response to the union's efforts, President Woodrow Wilson appointed a commission to mediate differences with Mexico, and war was averted. The success of the AUAM in this instance encouraged Eastman to believe that such a policy could end war in Europe.[46]

Eastman did not support Charles Evans Hughes in the 1916 presidential election, even though he was progressive and pro-suffrage, because he, unlike the anti-suffrage Wilson, proclaimed himself in favor of the war. Her position caused a breach with suffragists who opposed Wilson, but after Wilson betrayed the anti-militarists, the suffragists again closed ranks. As the United States moved inexorably toward war, Eastman worked tirelessly for peace, taking time off to have her first baby, Jeffrey, her son by her second husband, the British pacifist Walter Fuller, whom she had married in 1916.

Eastman's support for *Four Lights*, the newsletter launched by New York's WPP, caused tension between Eastman and AUAM leaders Jane Addams and Lillian Wald. Modeled in format and style on *The Masses*, which Eastman's brother edited, *Four Lights*, first issued in January 1917 criticized within the AUAM leadership anti-militarist women who had abandoned their position to assist the war relief work of conservative groups. Three months after the United States entered the war, *Four Lights* editorialized against President Wilson's lack of action following the race riot in East St. Louis in which scores of black people were beaten or killed. In March 1917 *Four Lights* announced in a banner headline that it hailed "the Russian Revolution with mad glad joy." Although each issue was independently edited, the newsletter reflected Eastman's style and tone and, as she presided over the organization that produced it, the newsletter became one more reason many conservative reformers were alienated from her.

Further alienation occurred when Eastman, together with Roger Baldwin and Norman Thomas, established an AUAM committee, the Civil Liberties Bureau—forerunner of the American Civil Liberties Union—to establish conscientious objection to the war as a legal option to conscription. By November 1917 the Socialist Party activism of Eastman and her associates in the Woman's Peace Party of New York, as well as in the activities of the Civil Liberties Bureau, caused a breach with reformers such as Jane Addams and Lillian Wald, and the powerful alliance the AUAM had represented disintegrated.

The Espionage Act and the Sedition Act of May 1918 rendered all Eastman's wartime activity illegal and resulted in a ban on sending through the mails all radical publications, including *Four Lights* and *The Masses*. The laws suspended civil liberties, and freedom as America's citizens had known it was changed beyond recognition. Eastman continued to act on her socialist beliefs and to struggle for the restoration of democracy in the United States.[47]

Eastman's closest friend until political differences divided them, Inez Milholland, was born in Brooklyn, New York in 1888, the elder daughter and first of three children of Jean (Torrey) and John Elmer Milholland, a reporter and editorial writer for the *New York Tribune*. In 1905 Inez entered Vassar, where she was an outstanding athlete and campus leader. Inspired by Charlotte Perkins Gilman's *Women* and Economics, then "the Bible of the student body," she enrolled two-thirds of the students into a suffrage organization and organized a branch of the Socialist Party. When Mrs. Gilman and Vassar alumna and suffragist Harriot Stanton Blatch visited the campus, Milholland defied a college ban and organized a meeting in a nearby cemetery.[48] Her activities were noted in Socialist Woman, where Milholland was described as "one of the most brilliant and popular girls in the college" and "a tireless organizer of her fellow students."[49] In 1912, the New York Times included a photo of Milholland in an article expressing alarm about the growth of Socialism's grip on American college campuses, but in acknowledgment of the effective opposition to Socialism by faculty and administrators at women's colleges, the paper noted that the local Milholland organized "did not survive her college days."[50]

After graduating from Vassar in 1909, Milholland went to England with the intention of entering Oxford or Cambridge to study law, but those universities refused to admit her. Returning to America, she applied to the Harvard University Law School, but was again refused admission on the basis of her sex. New York University Law School granted her admission, and she received an L. L. B. degree in 1912, thereafter joining the firm of Osborne, Lamb, and Garvan.[51] While in law school, Milholland continued her political activity, supporting the shirtwaist strikers in 1910—on one occasion getting herself arrested— and periodically addressing crowds on suffrage. During a visit to New York by President William Taft, she rented a room facing the Fifth Avenue parade route, from which she shouted, "votes for women!" through a megaphone and made a speech to the crowd.[52]

Her involvement in the crusades of the era brought her into contact with the Greenwich Village artists and radicals. She became a close friend, and for a time the fiancée, of Max Eastman, the editor of The Masses. In December 1912 she introduced Eastman to Alva Belmont, who contributed several thousand dollars to aid the strug-gling magazine.[53] Milholland's beauty and social position made her politics newsworthy and glamorous; articles about her activities were published in the city's newspapers, usually accompanied by a photo-graph. She was on the cover of the September 1914 issue of Every-woman magazine, and she was assumed to be involved in every protest

Figure 1: Inez Milholland at suffrage march in Washington, D.C., 1913.
Reproduced by permission of the Schlesinger Library, Radcliffe College.

or demonstration. When 120 children of striking Lawrence mill
workers were sent to New York in February 1912, reporters rushing to
the office of the Italian Socialist Federation were informed by an
exasperated Theresa Malkiel that only working people were serving as
hosts to the children and neither Inez Milholland nor Alva Belmont
had anything to do with helping them.[54]

Milholland's frequently projected image was useful in contrasting
the "gentle charms" of the American suffragist with the frightening
window-smashing assault tactics of the British suffragists. An accomplished horsewoman, she was a member of the group of riders that led
the suffrage parade in New York in 1912 and was a white-robed
mounted herald in the suffrage march to the United States Treasury
Building in Washington, D.C. in 1913.[55] "Almost the best reason I
know for being a Suffragist," Milholland declared in one of her
speeches, "is that there is so much fun and gladness in it—so much
good will—so much healthy activity."[56] Although she was serious

about suffrage, economic justice, and political reform, Milholland pursued those commitments with style and panache. When John Mitchel defeated the Tammany candidate for mayor in November 1913, Inez Milholland and he "turkey trotted all evening to the great delight of the onlookers, who thought their mayor-elect would not dare do so in a public place."[57]

Milholland, a feminist and advocate of women's "sex rights" in public, conducted a number of love affairs in private (her personal papers include a birth control pamphlet) before her marriage in London in July 1913 to Eugen Boissevain, a Dutch-born importer. Discovering on her return to the United States that she had lost her American citizenship, she persuaded her husband to become an American citizen.[58] Milholland then resumed her professional and political activity. As a lawyer, she specialized in criminal and divorce cases; she was an opponent of capital punishment and an advocate of prison reform. She was a member of the Women's Trade Union League and the National Association for the Advancement of Colored People.

During 1915 Milholland served as a war correspondent for a Canadian newspaper in Italy, sailing to that country with Guglielmo Marconi, the inventor of the wireless. She entered the war zone and wrote a series of pacifist articles that caused the Italian government to request that she leave the country. She returned to the United States, only to set off for Europe again in December on Henry Ford's "Peace Ship," but she left the group in Sweden because of lack of confidence in the leaders and her belief that the group was undemocratically run.[59]

Claiming that suffragists must put women first, Milholland campaigned for Charles Evans Hughes in the presidential campaign of 1916. While on a national tour, during which "she spoke day and night, took a train at two in the morning to arrive at eight, and then a train at midnight to arrive at five in the morning,"[60] Milholland collapsed during an appearance in Los Angeles, stricken by a disease, aplastic anemia, that was diagnosed too late and from which she never recovered. The tributes that followed her death showed the depth of affection Milholland had inspired among her associates. Tributes to Milholland from around the nation culminated in a memorial service on Christmas Day in Statuary Hall of the Capitol in Washington,

D.C.[61] Representatives of all the major reform movements, including suffragists and pacifists, paid tribute to Milholland. Crystal Eastman, whose support for Wilson had estranged her from Milholland, her closest friend, declared that the outpouring of grief demonstrated that all the great movements claimed Inez Milholland, whose "whole aspiration was for fuller liberty."[62]

For a number of years Harriet Rodman was at the center of almost every movement in New York. Born in Astoria, New York to Washington and Henrietta Rodman in 1877, she graduated from Teachers College and taught in the city's public schools for twenty-five years. She was active in building the Teachers' Union and recruited colleagues to the cause of teacher unionism, as well as to the cause of other labor struggles.[63] Taking her inspiration from Charlotte Perkins Gilman, Rodman organized the Feminist Alliance, an organization that aimed, as one of its goals, to design a twelve-story apartment house, "with all the mechanical fixtures needed to relieve women of work that machines can do" and to operate it on the plan for professionalized household care developed by Gilman in *Women and Economics*.[64] (There is no evidence that the building was ever constructed.)

When Rodman later was suspended from her teaching position because of her opposition to the New York City School Board's policy against allowing mothers to teach, Gilman, her mentor, was one of her strong supporters.[65] During the heyday of the prewar years, Rodman was active in Heterodoxy and the "moving spirit" of the Liberal Club. Floyd Dell later described her as naive and reckless, "believing in beauty and goodness, a Candide in petticoats and sandals," who was "laughed at a good deal and loved very much indeed, and followed loyally by her friends into new schemes for the betterment of the world." Dell credited Rodman with attracting academics and social workers to the Liberal Club, where, mixing with the literary and artistic crowds, they gave the Village an entirely new character, one that was soon exploited by real estate interests. As a result of the interaction of these disparate groups Rodman brought together in the Village, Dell reported that "ideas now began to explode there, and soon were heard all the way across the continent."[66]

The daughter of a "shanty Irish" father who was a quarry laborer and a "lace curtain Irish" mother who was a skilled tailor, Elizabeth

Gurley Flynn was born in Concord, New Hampshire in 1890 and settled with her parents and three siblings in the South Bronx when she was ten years old. In their poor household, reading was the only amusement, and Flynn was significantly influenced by such books as Edward Bellamy's *Looking Backward* and Upton Sinclair's *The Jungle*. Socialist politics absorbed the Flynn family, and at a meeting of the Harlem Socialist Club in January 1906 Elizabeth's skill in oratory, developed through participation in a grammar school debating society, together. with information drawn from wide reading, led to a triumph at sixteen in her first public speech, "What Socialism Will Do for Women." Her career as a public speaker was launched; her youth, beauty, and passion drew much attention. The theatrical producer David Belasco invited her to appear in a labor play, an offer to which she replied heatedly, "I'm in the labor movement and I speak my own piece."[67]

Although a good student, Flynn left Morris High School without graduating and joined the International Workers of the World (IWW) as an organizer.[68] With her parents' reluctant consent, she attended the IWW convention in Chicago in 1907, stopping to speak in midwestern cities on her return to New York, where, after travel and the charm of meeting new people, she found herself bored. She eagerly accepted an invitation from an IWW organizer, Jack Jones, to travel to Minnesota's Mesabi Range to speak on behalf of miners. Stirred by the adventure in "a rough, wild country," Flynn fell in love and married Jones.[69] After her marriage, Flynn traveled in the west, speaking in IWW halls, learning about the lives of migratory workers, and occasionally being arrested.

Their work as organizers kept Flynn and her husband apart; eventually Jones wanted her to give up her work and live with him. Flynn, who had lost one child after its birth, was again pregnant, but she was no longer in love with her husband, and, wanting "to speak and write, to travel and meet people, to see places, to organize for the IWW," she refused to give up her work for her husband. She returned to New York and the warm embrace of her family, who cared for her son, Fred, after he was born, while she continued to organize workers.[70]

Early in her career, Flynn had met other women activists in New York. While still in high school, she had met Emma Goldman, heard her speak, and was surprised by the "force, eloquence and fire that poured from this mild-mannered motherly sort of woman."[71] In 1910,

Figure 2: Elizabeth Gurley Flynn addressing Paterson, NJ silk strikers, 1913. Reproduced by permission of the Taminent Institute Library. Elizabeth Gurley Flynn Collection.

Rose Pastor Stokes, concerned for Flynn's health after the birth of her child, invited her and her son to spend the summer at the Stokes home on Caritas Island off the Connecticut shore.[72] During the shirtwaist-makers' strike that year, she met Henrietta Rodman, who led 500 teachers in a meeting to pledge aid to the strikers.[73]

Flynn's work with in the Lawrence textile workers' strike brought her into contact with Margaret Sanger, who accompanied the strikers' children when they were evacuated to New York.[74] And she formed an enduring friendship with Mary Heaton Vorse, who had come to Lawrence as a reporter and was thereafter converted to the workers' cause for the rest of her life. One activist of whom Flynn disapproved was Mabel Dodge, who had conceived the idea of the Paterson Pageant at Madison Square Garden. In 1914, Flynn made a speech, "The Truth About The Paterson Strike," in which she gave credit for the pageant not to "the dilettante element who figured so prominently, but who would have abandoned it at the last moment," but to the New York silk workers who advanced $600 to keep it going.[75]

A fateful meeting for Flynn was with Carlo Tresca, an Italian-born IWW organizer and a married man; his "roving eye had roved" in Flynn's direction during the Lawrence strike and then, after they had worked and lived together for thirteen years, began "roving elsewhere."[76] Although a committed revolutionary, Tresca resented Flynn's total involvement in politics, and as much as she was in love with Tresca, she refused—as she had refused her husband—to give up her work for him and remain in her family's South Bronx apartment Not even her son's claims on her could keep her there; when the IWW summoned her, Flynn traveled to the Mesabi Range, to San Francisco, to Seattle—to wherever she might assist workers in labor struggles.[77]

By 1914, after eight years of witnessing the exploitation of workers, "more and more the iron" had been driven into her soul.[78] The repression of civil liberties and mob violence that accompanied the Espionage Act of 1917 and the Deportation Act of 1918 confirmed Flynn then and ever afterward as "a mortal enemy of capitalism."[79] Flynn gave up her activities as an IWW strike leader and organizer in 1918 and subsequently worked to protect civil liberties and the rights of labor during the hysterical xenophobia and hostility to dissent that seized the United States during World War I and the years immediately following it. From 1920 to 1927 Flynn, then working in New York for the Workers Defense Union, was intensely involved in the struggle to free the Italian anarchists Bartolomeo Vanzetti and Nicola Sacco, who were accused, tried, and convicted of robbery and two murders in Massachusetts and ultimately were executed despite worldwide protest that they were innocent of these crimes.[80]

In 1926, worn out by twenty years of hard work, concerned that she was not spending time with her son, and depressed by Carlo Tresca's infidelities, Flynn suffered a mental and physical collapse. She spent most of the next ten years in Portland, Oregon, living and recuperating at the home of Dr. Marie Equi. In 1937, she returned to her family in New York, joined the Communist Party, and resumed political life.[81]

One of the later arrivals to New York's radical activism, Dorothy Day, was born in Brooklyn in 1897, but moved with her mother, her newspaperman father, and her siblings to Berkeley and then Oakland, California, and later, because of her father's work, to Chicago. The failure of newspapers that employed her father brought spells of poverty to the Day family, but Dorothy remembered her childhood as a happy one—due, she believed, to her mother's optimism and skill in homemaking.[82]

When she was sixteen Day won a scholarship to the University of Illinois at Urbana, where, "happy as a lark to be leaving home," she took courses without planning to pursue a degree, for, having been stirred by reading Upton Sinclair and Jack London, among others, during her adolescence, she was more concerned with class conflict than with her studies. She was often in need of money, but found her freedom "worth going hungry for." She formed a deep friendship with another student, Rayna Prohme, and lived with her during her sophomore year. With Rayna and her friends, Dorothy went to hear the lectures by political activists Rose Pastor Stokes and Scott Nearing and poets Edgar Lee Masters and John Masefield.[83]

In the summer of 1916, her father took a job in New York with the *Morning Telegraph,* and Dorothy, realizing she needed her family, moved with them. At first, finding no work and having no friends, she felt a "long loneliness" descend on her, yet she was drawn to the districts inhabited by the poor of the city and wanted to go live among them. When Day was hired, at a salary of five dollars a week, by the Socialist newspaper the *Call,* she left her family's apartment and took a furnished room in the tenement apartment of the Gottliebs, a family she came to love.

Day's work on the *Call* took her to strike meetings, peace meetings, and picket lines. She covered these meetings and marches to City Hall, as well as appeals for playgrounds, babies' clinics, and better schools. In the course of covering strikes, Day came to know labor leaders and she found those of the IWW "outstanding." When Day heard Elizabeth Gurley Flynn speak at meetings for the Mesabi Iron Range strikers, she was "thrilled by her fire and vision," as Flynn herself had been thrilled years before by the fire and vision of Emma Goldman.[84]

Day's work, though it provided a vast education to a woman just twenty years old, involved moving at a pace too fast for reflection on the events she was witnessing. Moreover, she found the Socialists too "doctrinaire and foreign," too much rooted in past struggles. Her work with a group of students opposed to the war led to an offer to work on *The Masses*, an association that lasted for the final six months of that magazine's existence.[85]

In early summer, 1917, the magazine's principal editors were occupied with projects closer to their hearts. Max Eastman was writing poems, lecturing, and working on a "scientific explanation of humor."[86] John Reed was preparing to join his wife, Louise Bryant, in Europe, before going on with her to Russia to witness and report on the Russian Revolution.[87] Floyd Dell was out of the city on a month's vacation. The only member of the magazine's staff left in the office was Day, the recently hired assistant editor, who had just had what she considered a marvelous piece of good luck, for she had moved into an apartment on MacDougal Street that the vacationing owners had loaned for the summer to members and friends of the *Masses* collective. Her friend Rayna Prohme came to visit her and after Day completed her work at the magazine, they walked the streets of New York with two *Masses* contributors, Mike Gold and Maurice Becker, singing revolutionary songs and savoring their youth.[88] In that innocent-seeming summer, Day's selection of some of the articles and cartoons for the August issue of *The Masses* led to the indictment of the editors on a charge of treason.[89] The idyllic summer and the "comparative paradise" of the era was at an end. The "real thing" in the form of war was before them.[90]

CHAPTER 5

The Great Movements: Suffrage

THE MOVEMENT FOR WOMEN'S SUFFRAGE in the United States may be dated from the 1840 World's Anti-Slavery Convention in London, when Elizabeth Cady, then the twenty-five-year-old bride of the abolitionist leader Henry Stanton, met the forty-seven-year-old veteran Quaker abolitionist Lucretia Coffin Mott. After the male delegates, despite strong dissent, voted to exclude female delegates from the convention, the women were obliged to watch the ten-days proceedings from behind a curtained gallery or in their quarters and to meet together in a room in a Quaker meeting house reserved for "rejected delegates." Stanton and Mott, who were staying at the same hotel, found common cause in their exclusion and talked together at length about holding a women's rights convention when they returned to the United States.[1]

The meeting, which was the first of many such conventions that were ridiculed in the press and denounced in the pulpits, did not take place until July 19 and 20, 1848, at the Wesleyan Chapel in Seneca Falls, New York.[2] Stanton, though trembling with fear, nevertheless made a maiden speech that was full of the eloquence that would distinguish her speeches for the next fifty years. Others spoke and discussion followed the resolutions presented to implement the Convention's Declarations of Principles, modeled on the Declaration of Independence. The most controversial of these was read by Mrs. Stanton: "Resolved, that it is the duty of women of this nation to secure to themselves the sacred right to the elective franchise." At the conclusion of the meeting, sixty-eight women and thirty-two men—a third of those who had traveled to the convention from as far as fifty miles on foot, in carriages, or in horse-drawn farm carts—signed the Declaration of Principles. Among the signers was nineteen-year-old Charlotte Woodward, a farmer's daughter who aspired to be a typesetter and who was the only woman present at the Seneca Falls meeting who lived to vote for the president of the United States in 1920.[3]

In the years following the Seneca Falls meeting, Lucy Stone, Susan B. Anthony, and many other women joined the struggle for women's rights. When the Civil War broke out, the women, still as much abolitionists as they were suffragists, suspended their conventions and devoted themselves to the war effort. After the war, they resumed their demands for suffrage, expecting the Republican Party to reward them for their many contributions during the war, but the party leaders, while thanking the women for their "noble devotion to the cause of freedom," informed them that it was "the Negro's hour," and women's rights must wait.[4]

The Fourteenth Amendment, which inserted the word "male" into the United States Constitution for the first time, divided the suffragists. One faction, including Susan B. Anthony and Elizabeth Cady Stanton, wanted the amendment defeated. Others, including Lucy Stone, argued that if women could not achieve political equality, Negro men should not be prevented from achieving theirs. This and other issues on which suffragists divided led to the establishment of two organizations in 1869: the National Woman Suffrage Association, led by Stanton and Anthony, which believed enfranchisement would come through federal actions, and the American Woman Suffrage Association, led by Henry Ward Beecher and Lucy Stone, which concentrated on enfranchisement through state action. The division lasted until 1890, when the two factions merged into the National American Woman Suffrage Association (NAWSA).[5]

In the years following the Civil War, American society was undergoing great changes, and suffrage was only one of the reform movements as the home became less and less the center of women's lives.[6] Higher education was opening to women, especially in the midwest, where Antioch had joined Oberlin in 1852 as a coeducational college; where, in 1858, Iowa had been the first state university to accept women; and where, in 1863, Wisconsin admitted women to "normal" schools for teacher training. In the east, a few institutions adopted coeducation. Vassar was chartered as a college for women by New York State in 1861, followed by Wellesley and Mount Holyoke. By 1890 more than 2,500 women had bachelor of arts degrees; 250,000 women were teachers; and 4,500 women were physicians, surgeons, and other medical service workers.[7] Women's clubs grew in such numbers and accommodated such a breadth of interests that in 1890 the General Federation of Women's Clubs was formed, followed in 1894 by the formation of state federations.[8]

Women also were becoming wage earners in urban industries and services, as office workers, retail workers, and telephone operators. College graduates were founding settlement houses and developing the social work profession. At the beginning of the twentieth century, women were becoming doctors and lawyers, public health officers and social investigators, architects and planners, journalists and novelists, and teachers in universities as well as elementary schools.[9]

This growth of women's employment outside the home and the increased diversity of the patterns of women's lives set the stage for a new readiness for the women's suffrage movement. However, the linkage between the abolitionist and suffrage movements broke down in these years. The middle-class, Anglo-Saxon, Protestant suffragists were no longer committed to the democratic principles of the abolitionist generation of leaders. A principal factor in this shift was resentment that Negro men and illiterate males who had emigrated to the United States in the last decades of the nineteenth century could vote while women could not. Classism and racism formed the basis for the argument offered by suffragists in this period that national stability depended upon the governance by "intelligent" people of "unfit" groups.[10] This position was strengthened by the growth of the women' suffrage movement in the South in the 1890s, and the argument originally offered by the abolitionist suffragists that the franchise was their right as citizens, created equal to men, with the same inalienable right to vote for the class that governed them, was replaced by the expedient argument that women's suffrage would preserve white supremacy.[11]

In these years a new generation of women leaders was developing to replace veterans such as Anthony, Stanton, and Stone. These younger women were not, for the most part, marked by the visionary views of their predecessors.[12] The gulf between women of privilege and working women widened. NAWSA's organization was declining, and the routes to suffrage were markedly unsuccessful. The strategy of achieving the franchise through federal action favored by Susan B. Anthony had been fostered by annual NAWSA conventions in Washington that once had secured respectful hearings before Congressional committees, but no favorable committee reports were issued after 1893. The alternate route to suffrage through amendment of state constitutions declined apace in influence. From 1870 to 1910, 480 campaigns to get the issue submitted to voters were held in thirty-three states, of which only seventeen resulted in actual referenda, and of these, only two—in Colorado and in Idaho—were successful. Only the admission of new states, Wyoming in 1890 and Utah in 1896, resulted in suffrage for women.[13]

The old NAWSA had lost influence, but suffrage activity revived in the states, beginning in New York. When Harriot Stanton Blatch returned to the United States after a twenty-years residence in England, she found that the suffrage movement of which her mother had been one of the founders was completely in a rut in New York State. It bored its adherents and repelled its opponents. Most of the ammunition was being wasted on its supporters in private drawing rooms and public halls where friends, drummed up and harried by the ardent, listlessly heard the same old arguments.[14]

Having witnessed the militant suffrage movement in England led by Emmeline Pankhurst, Harriot Stanton Blatch saw no point in working with the established American suffrage organizations. She joined the Women's Trade Union League in 1905, where coming to know wage-earning trade union women and their independently wealthy or self-supporting middle- class allies made her realize the connection between organized labor and the enfranchisement of women. She established the Equality League of Self-Supporting Women, afterward the Women's Political Union, which had its first meeting in January 1907 in a "dingy little room" on Fourth Street just off the Bowery. Just one month later, the league was in Albany to enliven the annual futile hearings on suffrage by presenting as witnesses working women, such as Mary Duffy of the Overall Makers

Union, who informed the legislators that women like herself who lost their husbands could not stay at home, but had to work to keep their families together, that women "need every help to fight the battle of life," and that without the vote, "Bosses think, and women come to think of themselves, that they don't count for so much as men."[15]

Within a year and a half, the league's membership rose to 20,000, including divisions from the Typographical Union, Bookbinders' Union, and the Inter-Borough Association of Women Teachers. Trade unionists and WTUL members such as the Jewish capmaker Rose Schneiderman and the Irish former collarmaker and garment worker Leonora O'Reilly were members, along with passionate reformers like nurse Lavinia Dock of the Henry Street Settlement House and Greenwich Village radicals such as lawyers Ida Rauh, Inez Milholland, and Jessie Ashley.[16]

The league, in cooperation with the New York Collegiate Equality League, organized large public meetings; the first, at Cooper Union in 1908, honored the visiting English suffrage leader Anne Cobden-Sanderson, who spoke of the achievements of the Women's Social and Political Union, led by the Pankhursts, Emmeline and her daughter, Christabel. The success of that meeting led to others, and audiences thronged to hear the well known and admired Charlotte Perkins Gilman, as well as women who became well known and admired such as Jessie Ashley, Leonora O'Reilly, Lavinia Dock, Inez Milholland, and Rose Schneiderman.[17]

Under the leadership of Harriot Stanton Blatch, annual suffrage parades were initiated. The first of these, launched by the Equality League in 1910, stirred so much enthusiasm that other suffrage groups, at first reluctant to join, found in subsequent years that they could not afford to remain out of the parades, and participation in these events grew as the suffrage parades became New York's most colorful and dramatic public celebrations. The Woman Suffrage Party, under the leadership of Mrs. Carrie Chapman Catt, was launched in New York the same year as the suffrage parades, its organization built on the Tammany Hall plan of dividing the city into districts and precincts with leaders at each level. Catt, an educator and journalist from Iowa, had been active in NAWSA since 1890. She was instrumental in the launching of the International Woman Suffrage Alliance in

Figure 3: Harriot Stanton Blatch introducing Rose Schneiderman at
noonday street meeting at Wall Street. Reproduced by permission of the
Robert F. Wagner Labor Achives, New York University. Rose Schneiderman Collection.

Berlin in 1904 and later served as its leader. Her leadership of the
Woman Suffrage Party brought her recognition as the most effective
organizer in the suffrage movement, and at its annual convention in
1915, NAWSA drafted her to be its president.[18]

However, the growth of the suffrage movement in New York was
due as much to the efforts of rank-and-file women as it was to the skills
of these superb leaders. The suffrage parade of May 3, 1913—led by
Inez Milholland, mounted "on a splendid chestnut"—was again a
pageant of "bewildering color"; the women wore bright sashes and
carried banners bearing slogans such as "More Ballots: Less Bullets"
and "Let the People Rule: Women Are People." They marched eight
abreast for two hours from Washington Square up Fifth Avenue where
a crowd estimated at 500,000 had gathered to watch them; they passed
a reviewing stand holding members of the city administration (not

including Mayor William Gaynor, however, who a few days later enraged suffragists by claiming that only a few women wanted to vote and those who did were in need of husbands) and went on to a rally at Carnegie Hall. There the suffragists, including delegations from neighboring states as well as more representatives of occupations than had ever participated in a suffrage parade before, were addressed by Harriot Stanton Blatch, who praised the police force of 1,200 for providing the protection that had been lacking at the previous year's parade and then, while claiming she favored "lawful methods," paid tribute to the sacrifice of the imprisoned, hunger-striking, Emmeline Pankhurst and attacked the British government for its treatment of suffragists.[19]

Although the parade was the major suffrage demonstration, it was one of many suffrage events scheduled throughout the year. Weeks after the parade, for example, the Women's Political Union held a "cabaret-burlesque" at which Ruth St. Denis danced and Sarah Bernhardt sang; a suffrage leader from Albany, "General" Rosalie Jones, opened an "aeroplane carnival" by flying as a passenger from Staten Island cross-country to Oakland, California, dropping "Votes for Women" leaflets along the way; and in June various suffrage organizations banded together to speak each day for a week at the Park Theatre in Columbus Circle, an event that closed with actresses reading a letter of support from Lillian Russell.[20] Shortly after launching Heterodoxy, Marie Jenney Howe organized its first public forum, "Twenty-five Answers to Antis," at the Metropolitan Temple. Determined that the forum should not be like the usual boring suffrage gatherings, Howe, in her capacity as chairwoman, limited each of twenty-five speakers to five minutes in which to take up and "mop up" a trite objection to suffrage. The excitement was heightened by the five-minute rule that Howe rigorously carried out; the more absurd the anti-suffrage argument the speakers answered, the more colorful were their replies.[21]

Inspired by the actions of New York suffragists, suffrage groups across the nation sprang up to launch outdoor meetings, vigils, trolley car and automobile speaking tours, suffrage parades, and lobbying trips to state capitals. The new vitality in the movement resulted in numerous—sometimes rival—suffrage organizations at the grassroots level, formed around neighborhoods, colleges, trades, professions, and clubs. Working-class women, black women, young women, veteran suffragists, radical women, and upper-class women joined forces on the local level. Women in the Socialist Party campaigned for working-class support for suffrage in New York State. Black leaders and black women's organizations in increasing numbers supported suffrage, believing that the enfranchisement of women would deter the enforced disenfranchisement of black men by southern Democrats. National leaders in the WTUL worked more intensively for the franchise, on the grounds that women had to be able to protect their economic interests through political participation. In the second decade of the twentieth century, suffrage had become a mass move-ment, for, with its goal to grant women the same rights as men to express their differences from each other and from men, it harmonized the various strands of advocacy for women's rights. Moreover, through the vote, women would have equal status with men to obtain political recognition of their special contributions in their capacities as wives and mothers.[22]

In 1914, when suffrage organizations had been established in New York's other boroughs, the big May suffrage parade was replaced by a large rally in Union Square, to be followed by the dispersal of various organizations to hold open air meetings throughout the city. The calendar of suffrage events was even more crowded. In April, for example, the Women's Political Union opened a headquarters on Nassau Street and prepared to address the men of Wall Street for a month of noon meetings. In November, the WPU opened a "suffrage shop" at 663 Fifth Avenue for suffrage supporters, especially men, to speak each day on behalf of the cause.[23]

The year 1914 also marked the birth of feminism as an expres-sion of the women's movement's rising expectations. In February, the "first feminist mass meeting," on a program entitled "Breaking Into the Human Race" organized by Heterodoxy founder Marie Jenney Howe, was held at Cooper Union. A capacity crowd gathered to hear, among others, Rheta Childe Dorr speak on the right to work; Beatrice Forbes-Hale, author of the 1914 book *What Women Want: An Interpretation of the Feminist Movement*, speak on the right of a mother to follow her profession; Fola La Follette speak on the right to keep one's name; Rose Schneiderman speak on the right to organize; Charlotte Perkins Gilman speak on the right to specialize in home industries; Nina Wilcox Putnam speak on the right to ignore fashion; and Frances Perkins (later secretary of Labor under Franklin Delano Roosevelt), who declared, "Feminism means revolution, and I am a revolutionist."

Several days later, Charlotte Perkins Gilman began a series of six lectures on "The Larger Feminism" at the Astor Hotel. In the first of these lectures, Gilman asserted that woman was the original organism and that it was through the caring for their young, whose gradually expanded infancy involved a mother assuming many functions, that woman was reduced from a dominant to a subservient position because when woman learned to cook, man wanted to profit from her service, and therefore kept her dependent.[24]

The women who defined themselves as feminists were, by and large, advocates of radical trends and behavior in the labor movement, art, and politics. Although from privileged backgrounds, they considered themselves socialists or progressives who advocated the elimination of the exploitation of labor by capital. As socialists, feminism appealed to them because of the analysis of class oppression and proposals for the transformation of society that it shared with socialism.[25]

However, feminists were more rebellious than conventionally respectable suffragists and socialists, who clung to the ideal of womanly virtue. Feminists disconnected themselves from the women's movement's traditional ties to Christianity, abandoned claims to moral superiority defined through sexual "purity," and insisted instead on women's sexuality. They believed in frankness about sex and undermined the distinction between the virtuous and the fallen woman by openly acknowledging that sex drives were as much a part of women's nature as of men's. They advocated a single standard, one that did not insist, as earlier critics of the double standard had done, on male continence, but was balanced in favor of women's heterosexual freedom.[26] Feminism rejected the traditional abstraction of womanhood, a rejection necessary, according to writer, radical activist, and Heterodite Edna Kenton, "to realize Personality," to achieve self-determination through life, growth, and experience. Women, according to trade union supporter and suffragist Mary Ritter Beard, were not "the source of all evil," not "more deadly than the male"; women were "people of flesh and blood and brain," capable of "feeling, seeing, judging and directing equally with men, all the great social forces." Charlotte Perkins Gilman heralded the arrival of the feminist: "Here she comes, running, out of prison and off pedestal; chains off, crown off, just a live woman."[27]

Feminists rejected the ideal of submissive femininity that had been imposed on women by society and even reacted against the emphasis within the woman's movement itself on woman's nurturing functions and benign moral influence. Feminists stood for self-development rather than self-sacrifice or submergence in the family. They rejected the traditional emphasis on duties and presented demands for women's rights, urging, in the words of the Feminist Alliance led by Henrietta Rodman, "the removal of all social, political, economic and other discriminations which are based upon sex, and the award of all rights and duties in all fields on the basis of individual capacity alone."[28] They relied on the communication networks of the suffrage movement as a vehicle to propagate their vision of a more radical transformation of women's status.

Unlike the suffrage movement, feminism did not have members in countable numbers or clearly established goals, but its ideas and assertions spread from New York to other intellectual communities in the country, there to resound with or compete against the tenets of Marxism and Freudianism. The suffrage movement, with more members, and feminism, with a larger plan, were distinct yet overlapping and mutually influential. Feminists broadened the scope of the suffrage movement, while the suffrage campaign provided feminists a platform. Feminists within the suffrage movement upheld their individualism in creative tension with their political identification as a class. Heterodoxy members, self-described as "most unruly and individualistic females," exclaimed over the paradox: "What a Unity this group of free-willed, self-willed women has become."[29] The expanding vision of the feminists fueled not only the objections of the "antis," but inspired reservations in even the men who were close to these women. Hutchins Hapgood, who was supportive of suffrage but not so "greatly interested" in it as he was in "its further reaches into feminism," believed many of the Heterodoxy women "were moving toward the unknown hoped-for world of feminine predominance." Marie Jenney

Howe, whom he knew well and acknowledged to be a very effective organizer, seemed to Hapgood to "be curiously significant of the feminist movement," in her belief in the "vital lie" that men were conspiring against women. Because of her "suffrage and feministic poison," Hapgood claimed, Marie did not recognize her husband's love for her.[30] And Howe himself later acknowledged in his autobiography that he "spoke for women's suffrage without much wanting it" and "urged freedom for women without liking it."[31]

Despite opposition and ambivalence, the movement advanced with style and efficiency. The skill and effectiveness, as well as the diversity, of New York activists is colorfully described in a 1915 letter from Mary Heaton Vorse to her family about her co-workers in the Woman Suffrage Party, a coalition of "uptown rich ladies mingling with us poor wage slaves of the slum." If the Labor Party, Vorse asserted,

> had a couple of women in it with the slave-driving capacity of Mrs. Whitehouse and the extraordinarily able Mrs. Frank Cothren the chance of a social revolution happening within the next five centuries would be greatly increased, for believe me I have never seen any slave-driver able to crack the whip louder than that langorous southern beauty, Mrs. Whitehouse.

Vorse went on in her letter to contrast the discipline of suffragists with the inefficiency of *The Masses*'s editors, about whom she declared, "Gee whiz, but men are slipshod." After attending "a snappy and most businesslike meeting . . . of the Suffrage crowd," she went next to a meeting of the magazine's stockholders to find that the meeting place had been changed, the members were late and quarrelsome, and the meeting probably was not legal in the first place because Max Eastman had forgotten to advertise the meeting in the newspapers. And so they "dawdled on for an hour and a half," while the artist John Sloan "made monotypes of Isadora Duncan, now and then spitting a little venom over his shoulder at the world in general." Nothing happened during this meeting, leading Vorse to wonder "how their 'Masses' happens every month."[32]

In 1915, the efforts of Vorse and her sister suffragists were focused on the November suffrage referendum. The main event in the campaign was an October parade in which 25,430 marchers (according to the *New York Times* count; 50,000 marched according to the police chief, while the anti-suffragists counted 24,629 marchers) from dozens of organizations and all five boroughs again paraded up Fifth Avenue through the afternoon until darkness fell while an estimated 250,000 spectators cheered them on. However, even though the movement had burgeoned and had significantly increased its support—for example, Mayor John Mitchel, successor to the anti-suffrage Mayor Gaynor, and Governor Charles Whitman voted for suffrage—the referendum was defeated statewide by a vote of 732,776 to 544,457. After their defeat, defiant suffragists gathered promptly at Cooper Union for the largest suffrage meeting ever held in the city. To the cheers of "Victory! Victory!" along with pledges of $100,000 from their supporters, suffrage leaders vowed to continue the struggle. Carrie M. Catt, declaring that if she were to be born again, she again would give forty years of her life to the suffrage cause, told the audience that the strategy to gain the vote would change and the state organization would be reorganized along Congressional districts: the focus from then on would be on a Constitutional amendment.[33]

Although women's suffrage had drawn much support since the campaign had revived in New York, old obstacles to the franchise remained and new ones had risen. The revival of the suffrage movement in New York under capable leaders with a growing, diverse, and energetic rank and file had produced a backlash. In 1911, the National Association Opposed to Woman Suffrage was formed in New York. The anti-suffragists were uniformly women of means and social position who argued that women's place was in the home and claimed they did not need suffrage as their interests were well represented by their menfolk. Its leader, Mrs. Arthur M. Dodge, wrote numerous anti-suffrage articles and letters to editors, organized counter-demonstrations to suffrage, challenged the numbers of parade participants claimed by suffragists, and even accused suffragists of dressing immodestly in order to gain men's support.[34] The emergence of feminism as a rebellious demand for more rights than the vote provided the "antis" with a rationale for claiming that the demand for suffrage would lead to a demand for "sex independence," a state wherein "the male, preserved for one purpose only, will be permitted to drag out a subordinate and somewhat surreptitious existence, sneaking in and out of the back door . . . like a guilty plumber."[35]

The Socialist daily the *New York Call* had been consistently friendly to the suffrage cause. The newspaper had reported in 1912 that at that time, "the activities of women have become the most absorbing thing in the day's news." When the suffragists went to Washington to testify before the House and Senate, the *Call* reported the testimony of Jane Addams, Anna Howard Shaw, Inez Milholland, and others on behalf of a national suffrage bill; the ballot was necessary, they had urged, to guard the interests of the eight million women in the nation who must earn their daily bread, for as the Triangle fire had demonstrated, when women had been burned alive, "we went to the courts and tried to get justice, and . . . failed." The *Call* also demonstrated, in its account of the 1913 suffrage march in New York, that Inez Milholland's glamour transcended class divisions, for it reported that the "mighty" parade of 30,000 had been led by Milholland, "Socialist, suffragette and lawyer, mounted on a fiery charger."[36]

The *Call* aside, the popular media were not friends of suffrage. Editorials in the *New York Times* regularly berated suffragists. The leading women's magazine, the *Ladies Home Journal,* confined its fiction to stories about romantic love or maternal self-sacrifice and its nonfiction to advice columns on the order of "The Minister's Social Helper" and "The Young Mother's Guide."[37] The magazine's publisher, Edward Bok, flaunted his opposition to suffrage in a volley of anti-suffrage views from "representatives of the oldest and foremost families of New York" such as Mrs. Grover Cleveland and Mrs. Andrew Carnegie, as well as from prominent career women such as the writer Ida Tarbell, who feared suffrage would distract women from their "pressing civil duties" and engross them in "the political game."[38] The theme of suffragist profligacy appeared in the July 1912 issue of the *Ladies Home Journal,* in which the anonymous author of "A Man's Letter to a Man" claimed,

> I happen to know personally some of these suffragist leaders here in New York. I have dined at their tables and I have smoked with their husbands and if the women of the country knew these fashionable suffragists as I know them—and their game life and their past—they

might stop and wonder whether they're the kind of women whose lead they want to follow.[39]

The slightly more moderate *Good Housekeeping* devoted itself to the premise that housekeeping ought to be seen as a science, a position that Charlotte Perkins Gilman endorsed, but whereas Gilman saw scientific housekeeping as a means to liberate women from domestic chores in order to pursue careers and fulfill social responsibilities, the magazine would have women confine themselves to the role of informed consumer. *Harper's Bazaar,* while favoring women's suffrage and other progressive reforms, nevertheless rejected the demand for experience outside the home, deploring "the spirit of unrest in the drawing room" and urging women to seek the higher fulfillment of wifehood and motherhood.[40]

However, more powerful opposition to women's suffrage came from other interests. Within the liquor industry, where women's suffrage was seen as a prelude to Prohibition, brewers' associations worked behind the scenes to set up anti-suffrage organizations, buy editorial support for "educational campaigns," and financially support legislators so that they would vote against suffrage bills. Entrenched machine politicians also opposed woman suffrage, fearing that as members of the electorate, women would be insusceptible to bribes, more militant, and advocates of reforms such as the abolition of child labor and of machine politics itself. Anti-suffrage legislators masked their opposition with silly arguments such as one offered in Albany that women's suffrage would mean prostitutes could vote, to which Leonora O'Reilly responded that if the companion of a woman of the street could vote, she should be able to vote as well.[41]

Big business also fought tenaciously—if surreptitiously—against women's suffrage. Railroad, oil, meatpacking, and general manufacturing lobbies worked against suffrage whenever it came up for legislative action or referendum; they funded anti-suffrage organizations and sent "educational" material to newspapers. The vested interests were threatened by the federal income tax, authorized by the Sixteenth Amendment in 1913, as well as the Federal Banking System, the Tariff Commission, the Federal Trade Commission, and the new anti-trust legislation. Big business saw a new menace in the entry of independent and reform-

minded new voters into the body politic. Within the industries most
likely to be affected, there also was a feeling that women would use the
vote to improve the conditions of women workers.[42]

The racism and class bias underlying the fear that women's
suffrage would produce an electorate swollen by African-American,
foreign-born, and working-class voters was shared by suffrage leaders.
Despite her support for the Women's Trade Union League, Alva
Belmont gained a reputation for badgering maids that caused her to be
blacklisted by women in domestic service; she also weighed all the
goods delivered to her Newport mansion, Marble House, because she
suspected her servants of theft. Belmont became a ruling-class symbol
from whom working-class suffragists like Rose Schneiderman kept a
distance. Affluent NAWSA leaders Mrs. Norman Whitehouse and Mrs.
James Lee Laidlaw publicly deplored the condition of being "subjects
of men of alien races" who were illiterate and unable to speak English.
Carrie Catt maintained that the votes of Negro males were "purchas-
able" by office seekers and proposed a literacy test and a small property
requirement for immigrant men as prerequisites for voting. But the
core of New York suffrage activists did not share these views, having
worked too long building up a base among women of Chinese, Jewish,
and Italian backgrounds; having been sensitized through participation
in the Socialist Party and the Women's Trade Union League to the
needs of African-American and foreign-born working-class women,
these suffragists would not demand suffrage on the grounds that white
women should not be the political inferiors of immigrant and Negro
men.[43]

That this view of the essential sisterhood of women was not
shared by women nationwide was dramatically demonstrated in the
1912 contest for the national presidency of the Federation of
Women's Clubs. At the San Francisco convention, one candidate for
the office, Mrs. Philip Carpenter, along with her supporters, maintained that if women's clubs and federations meant anything at all,
they stood for the sisterhood of women, regardless of race, color, or
previous condition of servitude, and that the Negro woman should
have the right to vote as well as the Negro man. Her opponent, Mrs.
Percy Pennybacker of Texas, opposed women's suffrage on the
grounds that it would mean "giving the ballot to densely ignorant

negro women, a repetition of the grave error made in giving suffrage
to the negro man." Mrs. Pennybacker had solid support from
southern state delegates, but her argument was persuasive with state
delegates from northern and western states as well, and she won the
election.[44]

The outbreak of war in Europe in August 1914 and subsequent
reports of atrocities committed by Germans against the Belgians
inspired sympathetic society women to engage in a knitting bee for
Belgian children at the Plaza and to open a shop on Fifth Avenue to sell
articles for Christmas for the benefit of the Belgian people.[45] The war
diverted New York women from suffrage activism. Weeks after the war
began, 1,500 women dressed in mourning garb joined a "March for
Civilization" down Fifth Avenue from Fifty-eighth Street to Union
Square. The organizers had urged New York women of all classes to
participate in the demonstration and urged women in other cities to
hold demonstrations as well to demand a mobilization for the Hague
Peace Conference to be held in 1915. The parade caused a public rift
between the suffrage leaders Carrie Catt and Harriot Stanton Blatch—
Catt opposing the parade on the grounds that President Wilson was
doing all he possibly could to stop the war, Blatch maintaining that he
had not done all that was possible and should ask all the neutral
nations to join in mediation to stop the war.[46]

In November 1914, Crystal Eastman organized the Woman's
Peace Party of New York and invited as a speaker Emmeline Pethick
Lawrence, the militant English suffragist who had been imprisoned
and force-fed in London's Holloway Gaol. Until 1919, Eastman
presided over the Woman's Peace Party of New York, which was far
more militant than two other organizations she helped to create: the
national Woman's Peace Party and the American Union Against
Militarism. Eastman recruited other Heterodoxy members as leaders of
the New York WPP: Margaret Lane, Anne Herendeen, Katherine
Anthony, Madeleine Doty, Freda Kirchwey, Marie Jenney Howe, Agnes
Brown Leach. These women were militant suffragists and feminists
who were disrespectful of authority and not afraid of criticism. They
booed and hissed the preparedness advocates who addressed their
public meetings, which occasionally were broken up by violent
patriots, often in uniform.[47]

Because of their radicalism, Heterodoxy members were harassed and kept under surveillance during the war by the Bureau of Investigation, the forerunner of the FBI. Jo Baker remembered that the club had to shift its meeting-place every week to elude the surveillance. It was like a novel, except that Baker's "colleagues in treason were not sloe-eyed countesses, with small pearl-handled revolvers in their pocketbooks, but people like Crystal Eastman, Fannie Hurst, Rose Pastor Stokes, Inez Haynes Irwin, Fola La Follette, and Mabel Dodge Luhan."[48] Despite these obstacles, or perhaps because of them, Mabel Dodge recalled her fellow Heterodites as "fine, daring, rather joyous and independent women." During the war, Dodge recalled, when Fola La Follette, the daughter of progressive Wisconsin Senator Robert La Follette, was persecuted as "pro-German" because of her father's politics, people "snubbed her, cut her, and behaved like idiot barbarians." Fola stopped going out, but did go to Heterodoxy luncheons, for Heterodoxy was a "safe refuge," and its members were glad to see her. "Fola was Fola, as she had always been. She would come in looking somewhat pale and pinched, but after an hour in that warm fellowship her face flushed and her muscles relaxed. It must have been a comfort to come there."[49]

In the spring of 1915, an international women's committee issued a call for a women's peace congress to meet in neutral Holland. Heterodoxy member Mary Heaton Vorse went to the congress as delegate for the Woman Suffrage Organization of New York, representing 150,000 women, and as a correspondent on assignment from *McClure's* and *Century* magazines. The American delegation, which was the largest delegation of women attending the congress, was headed by Jane Addams and in Vorse's view, included, besides "many of the most forward looking women in America,"

> women who had come for the ride. . . . New Thought cranks with Christian Science smiles and blue ribbons in their hair, hard-working Hull House women, little half-baked enthusiasts, elderly war-horses of peace, riding furious hobbies.[50]

Ultimately, Vorse found the congress a futile gathering; although the more than 1,200 women assembled in The Hague hated the war, they were largely from neutral nations, and those from warring nations were not "the women who suffered the most." The decision of the congress, "as brave as it was futile," was to send committees of women to the heads of warring nations requesting them to end the war. The American delegation, with Jane Addams at its head, "plodded on its useless errand from one chancellor of Europe to another."[51]

Vorse returned to New York and worked actively for the November suffrage referendum, heading one of the five subcommittees of the Press and Publicity Council, the division of the Empire State Campaign Committee, whose members were responsible for producing pro-suffrage literature, newspaper releases, and advertising while also serving as speakers and organizers.[52] Many New York activists continued to oppose the war and campaign for suffrage, but the divisiveness among women over the issue of war reached a peak during the election year of 1916, when suffragists supported Charles Evans Hughes, who did not promise peace but promised suffrage. Wilson opposed war but also opposed suffrage; nevertheless, suffragists who had become peace activists, such as Jane Addams, Lillian Wald, and Crystal Eastman, supported Wilson. Eastman's support for Wilson separated her from women who had been her closest friends for many years; especially painful was the loss of the friendship of Inez Milholland, who was campaigning for Hughes when she was fatally stricken and had told her audience in one of her last speeches that there was no more important issue in the country than women's suffrage; that while some people might believe suffragists should "retire at this time," "Women First" must be their stand.[53]

Later that year the Democratic Party failed to adopt the suffrage plank and commit itself to pushing the amendment through Congress. Alice Paul and Lucy Burns, who had transformed NAWSA's Congressional Committee into a national organization, the Congressional Union (CU), had become impatient with the policy of non-partisanship supported by the older NAWSA women; it seemed to them that women were in that way acting as supplicants for suffrage. The failure of the Democrats to act on suffrage prompted Paul and Burns, still in their twenties and with experience in the English suffrage movement, to lead the younger, more militant and feminist suffragists in a campaign to defeat all the Democratic candidates for national office, including the president. As an envoy from the CU, Inez Milholland made a stump speech through the western states, reminding enfranchised women that the Democratic Party had the power to liberate women, but "have refused to put the party machinery back of the Constitutional Amendment." Milholland urged the "women of the west" to "let no free woman, let no woman that respects herself and womankind, lend her strength to the Democratic party that turns away its face from justice to the women of the nation" and to "refuse to uphold that party that has betrayed us."[54]

Carrie Catt viewed the Congressional Union's action to punish the party in power as a mistaken single-issue approach typical of the radical feminist wing of the suffrage movement. Catt's approach, her "Winning Plan," involved careful coordination of work in the states to provide a flow of letters and notices of mass meetings to every member of Congress with diplomatic lobbying in Washington. The Congressional Union sent smaller numbers in the lobbying effort, but they were as diligent as the NAWSA lobbyists—although, viewing themselves as "an army of young Amazons," they eschewed diplomacy in favor of undeferential confidence, a solid fund of information, and a refusal to be put off by bluster, rudeness, or political trickery.[55]

The CU members' flaunting of their youth contributed to the friction with NAWSA, but the older organization had more substantial reasons for its objections to the CU's tactics. NAWSA leaders believed that political expediency debased the cause of women's suffrage, which they held to be the inevitable result of the recognition of the changing social and economic needs of women. NAWSA had become the largest voluntary organization in the country; its two million members were effectively breaking down opposition to women's suffrage by following what it regarded as a "positive" program—in contrast to the CU's "negative" militant party politics—of education and argument by Democratic members to influence Democratic congressmen and Republican members to influence Republican congressmen and having NAWSA and through the steady pressure on President Wilson by NAWSA members of both parties.[56]

In 1917, the Congressional Union joined with its members in the full suffrage states—Wyoming, Colorado, Utah, Idaho, Washington, California, Oregon, Arizona, Kansas, Nevada, and Montana—to form the National Woman's Party and increased its militant tactics. After an unsatisfactory meeting with President Wilson in January, CU members picketed the White House, carrying banners that read, "Mr. President, How Long Must Women Wait for Liberty?" They were insulted and even assaulted, but they persisted; in March 1917, during Wilson's second inaugural, a thousand women marched in the rain around the White House. The entry of the United States into the war caused the protests to be viewed as unpatriotic, even though the NWP had voted not to take a stand on the war and reaffirmed their dedication to a single issue. The picketing continued without official intervention until June, but then arrests were made for obstructing traffic. Like the British suffragettes, the NWP women never paid fines, but received sentences of up to sixty days in the Occuquan workhouse, presided over by a brutal superintendent, on the outskirts of Washington.[57]

In August, following the government's suppression of *The Masses*, Dorothy Day decided to go to Washington with her friend Peggy Baird and join the suffragists in picketing the White House. The NWP members were by this time displaying banners addressing the president as Kaiser Wilson and accusing him of denying his countrywomen of rights he claimed to defend abroad. Men and boys mobbed them, but the police arrested only the picketers, and Day and Baird were taken with other women to the police station and after delays were sentenced to thirty days in Occuquan.

The women declared a hunger strike and refused to work. "Those first six days of inactivity," Day wrote, "were as six thousand years." After the inactivity and the nausea and dazedness of hunger, Day reported, "I lost all consciousness of any cause. I had no sense of being a radical, making a protest against a government, carrying on a nonviolent revolution. I could only feel darkness and desolation all around me." After six days, some of the women were force-fed, a painful process in which the women were stretched on a bed and held down by five people while a doctor inserted a tube in their nostrils, resulting in bleeding of the nose, sore muscles, and pain in the stomach because food had been dumped like a "lead ball" directly into it. However, the strike ended on the tenth day when their demand to be returned to City Jail was met. Their clothes were returned to them, their mail was given to them, they were served delicious meals, and within days they were taken in limousines to Washington to complete their sentences in relative comfort at the City Jail.[58]

NAWSA suffragists were disgusted by the NWP's White House picketing because they believed such tactics were indecorous and politically naive. Eager to immunize NAWSA from NWP's militant image, Carrie M. Catt, who years earlier had helped to found the Woman's Peace Party, summoned 100 members of NAWSA's executive committee to Washington in February for a preparedness meeting, from which was issued a pledge that, in the event of war, NAWSA's two million members would serve their country "with the zeal and consecration which should ever characterize those who cherish high ideals of the duty and obligation of citizenship."

Following the outbreak of war, NAWSA declined to comment on the treatment of the NWP picketers who went on a hunger-strike to protest conditions in the Occuquan workhouse; the organization's silence on the picketers' martyrdom brought sympathy and new support to NWP, especially since the party mounted a national publicity campaign; as fast as the women were arrested, their congressmen and senators were besieged by letters and telegrams from their constituents demanding that they visit the prisoners. When the International Socialist Party opposed participation in the Great War, NAWSA excluded Socialist colleagues from their speakers' platforms and gave little credit to Socialist Party contributions to the suffrage cause. During the final years of the suffrage struggle, the NWP's neutrality on the war and socialism brought socialist suffragists to its ranks, along with pacifist suffragists who were repelled by Carrie Catt's opportunism.[59]

In actuality, it was the efforts of both NAWSA and the NWP—the right and left wings of the suffrage movement—that ultimately brought victory. However, the turning point came in November 1917, when the suffrage referendum carried New York, the first eastern state to grant women the ballot. And the victory, after so long a struggle, was due to the activists in New York City, for in upstate New York, the referendum barely carried, and it was New York City's five boroughs that gave the referendum a lead of 70,000. In tribute to the 12,000 women who took an active part in the practical work of carrying on the election, the *New York Times* reported that the city's women were "more numerous, better organized, and more energetic" than they had been in any previous election. A strong organization of African-American women had worked in Harlem; Chinese women had campaigned in Chinatown; and Italian women, originally not enthusiastic about suffrage, had been converted during the campaign and had turned out in large numbers. Women of every race and class, of all political beliefs, and of all religious faiths had won the day for the state, and the democratic spirit of the New York City suffragists turned the tide for the rest of the nation.[60]

In January, 1918, the House of Representatives passed a Constitutional amendment for woman suffrage. The NWP stopped picketing, but when the Senate failed to pass the amendment in September, they returned, staging even more shocking demonstrations through the winter of 1918-1919—climbing statues, burning "watchfires" in front of the White House while Wilson went to Versailles, setting banners with his words on democracy on fire as these were announced from the Peace Conference. In June, 1919, the Senate finally passed the suffrage amendment, which was ratified in August 1920. American women won the right to vote, ironically, in the anti-suffrage solid South, when twenty-four-year-old Harry Burn, the youngest member of the Tennessee House of Representatives, obeyed the instructions of his suffragist mother "to be a good boy and help Mrs. Catt put 'Rat' in Ratification," and broke a tie to vote "yes."[61]

Chapter 6

The Great Movements: Economic Justice

ALTHOUGH WOMEN HAD BEEN ENTERING THE WORK FORCE of the United States in growing numbers since the 1830s, their presence in the work force was still a subject of debate, even within the suffrage movement, in the twentieth century. Charlotte Perkins Gilman was, of course, an advocate of women—even those who were mothers—in the work force, and therefore when the South African writer Olive Schreiner published *Women and Labour* in 1911, Gilman praised the book in *The Forerunner* for "its full and clear demand for industrial freedom and equality for women," and for showing, "with a terrible clarity," the "shallow folly of the idea that a woman cannot work because she is a mother."[1] The book's main topic is dependence— "parasitism"—a theme that echoed Gilman's own concerns about the greatest threat to women's progress. In *Women and Labour* Schreiner predicted that the then rapidly advancing technology that had eliminated the "crude, physical, human exertion" of affluent and middle-class women would, in fifty years, eliminate even the physical labor performed by working-class and poor women. Schreiner warned of the danger of abandoning the rapidly developing fields of work to men, for then modern women, like the parasitic women of Ancient Greece, would "slide into a state of more or less absolute dependence on their sexual functions alone."[2]

Implicitly refuting Socialist Party policy, Schreiner denied that the rights of male workers and the rights of women were parts of the same question, for the male labor movement had arisen mainly from the poor and manual-laboring classes, while the women's movement had developed almost exclusively among privileged intellectual workers.[3] The strain of dealing with a rapidly changing society would be less painful, according to Schreiner, if the two great movements, though working in harmony and cooperation, remained distinct, for, although men and women were alike in many ways, "the moment actual reproduction begins to take place, the man and woman enter spheres of sensation, perception, emotion, desire and knowledge which are not, and cannot be, absolutely identical." In most fields, women could contribute little that could be distinguished from what men contributed; nevertheless, Schreiner insisted, women must enter all fields—those where the differences between the sexes played a part and those where they did not—for woman's reproductive function endowed her with something radically distinct to contribute to the sum of human knowledge.[4]

The progressive vision shared by Gilman and Schreiner was countered by the work of one other important contributor to the literature of the women's movement in the early part of the century, Swedish-born Ellen Key. Key had begun writing articles in 1870 and later wrote several books on the position of women that brought her a wide following in Europe and the United States. In *Century of the Child*, published in America in 1909, Key declared her estrangement from the women's movement because it had ceased to be a struggle for the freedom "which enlarges the soul and heart" and had become instead "an egoistic self-concentrated campaign." She opposed women's rights advocates who urged women to enter all possible occupations, for "a low rate of wages and an overcrowding of all fields is the result." Key pointed out that many of the new fields of labor that had opened to women were low-paying and unpleasant; a woman who was forced to work "like a beast of burden to reach a minimum of existence" was not achieving freedom.

Like Gilman, Key opposed individualism because it led to social conflict, but unlike Gilman and Schreiner, who urged a separate women's movement as a way to ameliorate social conflict, Key argued that women's rights advocates, instead of opposing unions and strikes, should help working women to organize unions and support strikes where they were justified. Women could advance in the work force,

Key maintained, only by struggling in partnership with men to transform the whole society. She foresaw a future in which all people would work under healthy conditions for an adequate wage, but at that time she saw women's energy being drained by industrial occupations that impaired their development as human beings, wives, and mothers. Key held that a woman's responsibility was to the future generation; she must choose her husband well and then see that her children "were born in love and purity, in health and beauty," and in a home where as a mother, "the most precious possession of the nation," she could devote all her care to her children. Key further believed that in return for stopping all work outside the home and dedicating themselves entirely to the future generation, women should receive an allowance from society.[5]

In *Love and Ethics*, published in 1911, Key wrote that by entering industry, women would lose their femininity—that "very inward-turning quality which men love in women"—and their efforts to "navigate all the seas with men" would result in sexual relationships that were not harmonious but dull. The gain to society was nothing, according to Key, "if millions of women do the work that men could do better, and evade or fulfill but poorly the greater tasks of life and happiness, the *creation of men* and the *creation of souls*." To perform these tasks properly, women needed the same human rights as men, but women "must learn to know that their power is greatest in those provinces in which 'imponderable' values are created, values . . . capable of transforming humanity." The millions of American working women who leave the care of their children to a collective, Key wrote disdainfully, "only seem to be socially useful."[6]

In *The Woman Movement* (1912), Key softened her criticism of the suffrage movement; she supported suffrage because, in common with Gilman, she foresaw the "genius of social reform" enfranchised women would develop and "the new fresh current" they would introduce into political life. However, she again insisted on the importance of remaining within the home, maintaining that "woman retains her power over a man if she retains her womanly charm, created out of peace, harmony, and kindness."[7]

Gilman, of course, opposed this position. In a review of *The Woman Movement*, she wrote that Key's claim that "it is good for the husband, home, and child to have the entire devotion of a woman's life" ran counter to the new ideal that the "main devotion of life should be to Humanity." There was no more powerful deterrent to this new ideal, according to Gilman, than the institution that Key supported, "this ancient root-form of society, this man-headed, child-restricting, self-serving home."[8]

During the course of the Key-Gilman argument and long before it, women workers were performing low-paying and unpleasant jobs while more affluent yet sympathetic women served "humanity" through advocacy of better wages and working conditions. Women's activism in connection with labor issues had come to life in New York during the early 1880s through the creation of a women's federation in the German-American socialist movement. Party leaders recognized the potential benefit of the federation to party and labor success because its members could explain to workers' wives that shorter hours, higher wages, and better working conditions would benefit the whole family, for men would be better husbands and fathers, and children could enjoy a brighter future. Through conversations with friends and speeches at public meetings, women were seen as able to rally the entire neighborhood to the cause of labor and the Socialist Party.

In the mid-1880s, the federation became involved with working women outside Socialist ranks, assisting young women in their economic struggles and bringing them into the party. Working women's organizations were set up to build the eight-hour movement among younger working women, and within a short time these organizations formed a militant wing of the socialist movement. But the success of these groups was brief, for in the late 1880s, party leadership decided to close ranks and dissolve these separate organizations. A few women entered actively into the party after the dissolution of the women's organizations, but most women, unaccustomed to working alongside men, chose not to make the transition. Without women leaders, the majority of women were lost to political life.[9]

Women's participation in the Socialist Party reemerged in the twentieth century when the leadership of German-American women was broadened by participation of native-born women and recently immigrated militant Jewish women, self-confident younger activists eager to bring "party wives" into full participation in the regular local.

The Social Democratic Women's Federation, which had replaced the earlier women's federations, had the advantage of providing women access to the party press. Beginning in 1901, the German-American socialist newspaper, *New Yorker Volkzeitung*, published a regular half-page on Sunday devoted to women's issues, to which German-American women and Jewish women—who were denied access to the Yiddish press until 1916—eagerly contributed. The "For Women" columns were marked by distinguished writing; they attracted letters from women on matters—such as the difficulty of shopping on a tight budget—that their husbands considered trivial, and provided women an opportunity to be identified as political leaders.

While the constituency was broadened, the membership of the Social Democratic Women's Federation never grew large, for growth was limited by the aversion on the part of Socialist women to be identified with the "bourgeois" women's movement—for class consciousness always must come before gender consciousness—and by the opposition of German-American and Jewish Socialist men to participation of women in the workplace or in the party. Moreover, younger women, refusing to be limited by ethnic affiliations or patriarchal traditions, availed themselves of the opportunity to join American branches of the party.[10]

At this point, a core of women organizers relatively new to the Socialist movement emerged to assist party wives in making the transition into the local party branch. Native-born reformers from the settlement houses, college-educated professionals, and militant Jewish activists were recruited among the generation succeeding the old ethnic base to form an English-language women's contingent within the Socialist Party. Although they approached women as housewives, these organizers disparaged women's traditional roles within the home, while in contrast, organizers in rural areas and small towns took advantage of the network of clubs and organizations that were so much a part of the idealistic Christian Socialism characterizing women's culture in those regions. The drive to integrate women directly into the local party branch encountered resistance, for most women were considered unequal to work with men in a political setting. Because organizers in California and the Plains states were more cognizant of the value to women of their own sphere, the drive toward building a national Socialist women's organization emerged in those states, and a first national meeting of Socialist women was held in 1904.[11]

The movement toward a national women's organization was squelched by the party in 1908, when at the national convention, a Women's National Committee was established to address women's concerns within the party. A few stalwart militants recognized that assimilation into the party meant that their interests would not be addressed in mixed locals; Josephine Conger-Kaneko, who published *Socialist Woman* (later *Progressive Woman*) from her base in Girard, Kansas, warned that if men were unsympathetic, separate organizations were necessary for the "unsophisticated little woman" to gain leadership skills.[12] However, the militants were greatly outnumbered by party loyalists who readily surrendered the autonomy of separate organizations and supported the WNC.[13]

The growing participation of women in the garment industry gave Socialist women in New York hope that they could recruit working women into the party. However, while women workers attended lectures and programs sponsored by Socialist activists, few of them evolved into disciplined party members. The other goal of Socialist women, to organize women into trade unions, also failed because of lack of interest on the part of male union leaders in organizing women. Finally, Socialist women turned for a solution to women in the traditional New York women's movement who had envisioned a cross-class alliance. The organization that offered hope to Socialist women was the Women's Trade Union League.[14]

The WTUL was the idea of William English Walling, a young midwestern-born worker at University Settlement on the Lower East Side, where he had established ties with the local labor movement and had become sensitive to the needs of women workers. In 1903 he traveled to England to witness the work of the Women's Trade Union League, established in 1874, and was impressed with the effectiveness of the collaboration between upper-class and working-class women that had resulted in the integration of working women into established male unions. Later that year, Walling went to the American Federation of Labor (AFL) convention in Boston to see whether a similar organization could be organized in the United States.

AFL executives expressed little interest in the organization, but Walling's idea drew the enthusiasm of Mary Kenney O'Sullivan, who before her marriage to a Boston streetcar organizer had been a bookbinder in Chicago and, briefly, the federation's East Coast women's organizer. Together they invited women settlement workers and reformers from Boston to a series of meetings, and the Women's Trade Union League of America was established under two basic principles: commitment to an alliance between classes and allegiance to the American Federation of Labor.[15]

Walling returned to New York to begin organizing the city's branch of the WTUL. He and the small group of supporters who joined him devoted most of the league's organizing efforts to the increasing numbers of women who were entering the city's industrial work force, for, as the capital of the men's and women's clothing trades, New York employed more women workers than did any other American city. Following the principles of the English Women's Trade Union League, Walling set about recruiting women workers and "allies," women from the middle and upper classes who would provide services and financial support to the league.

Leonora O'Reilly became one of the league's most influential working-class members. Born into an impoverished Irish working-class family, O'Reilly began working in a shirt factory at the age of eleven. She had been frustrated by male unionists in her efforts to organize women shirtmakers, but nevertheless favored the league policy of cooperating with the labor movement. She also favored the idea of cooperation between working-class and upper-class women, having had the support in her organizing efforts of Lillian Wald and Lavinia Dock of the Henry Street Nurses' Settlement and having benefited from the friendship of Louise Perkins, a wealthy Boston teacher and reformer. Perkins had served as her mentor and had provided the financial support that enabled O'Reilly to leave factory work and complete a course in industrial education at Pratt Institute, which provided her with skills she used to help establish the Manhattan Trade School.

O'Reilly brought her friends Margaret and Mary Dreier, reform-minded daughters of a wealthy German-American businessman, into the league. Margaret became the league's first president in 1905, after the league established its headquarters in a tenement on the corner of East First Street and Second Avenue. When Margaret left New York following her marriage to Raymond Robins, a Chicago settlement house worker, Mary succeeded her as the league's president. The league drew the enthusiastic support of settlement house workers such as Lillian Wald and Lavinia Dock and suffragists such as Harriet Rodman, Rheta Childe Dorr, and Harriot Stanton Blatch. Helen Marot, a child-labor investigator, joined the league and became its secretary in 1906. The league's "allies," women such as Irene and Alice Lewisohn, daughters of the copper magnate; Carola Woerishoffer, daughter of a wealthy investment banker; Maud Younger; and Elizabeth Dutcher, were affluent and well-educated. Male reformers did not maintain interest and even Walling lost interest and went to Russia in 1905 to observe the revolutionary movement.[16]

The task of organizing women industrial workers was far more difficult than the women with trade union organizing experience and their idealistic "allies" realized. The garment industry, where the league directed its organizing efforts in the early years, maintained a pattern of occupational segregation; men were skilled workers—tailors and cutters—while women performed unskilled tasks—finishing, tucking, basting, filling, trimming—and the semi-skilled task of operating sewing machines. Furthermore, work in the garment industry, as in other industries, was seasonal. When the league began its work, only 10,000 of the city's 350,000 women workers were organized, principally in the garment, cigar-making, bookbinding, and printing unions, and of these, only the Bookbinders Local #43, a female local of the International Brotherhood of Bookbinders, had achieved stability and power.

The absence of women in the trade union movement was due in part to their immigrant status, which, together with gender, kept them out of the skilled occupations that were organized into the powerful American Federation of Labor craft unions. However, a more serious obstacle to organizing was the lack of serious regard for women as workers on the part of employers, the trade unions, and women themselves, who, typically young, single, Jewish or Italian, and living with their families, viewed their years in the labor force as an interlude before marriage, which they welcomed as a liberation from the oppressive conditions of the workplace. The patriarchal nature of the women workers' culture inhibited their participation in the trade union movement; before marriage a woman was under the authority of her father, who viewed a daughter's union activism as a deterrent to attracting a suitor, and after marriage, a woman was under the authority of her husband, who required her to devote herself to home and family.[17]

The lack of steadfastness on the part of women workers greatly frustrated league organizers, who devoted much energy to setting up meetings to which the few women who had promised to come failed to appear, or built small unions member by member, only to have them fall apart. These setbacks were heightened by the predominance in the early years of upper-class "allies," who, lacking experience in the workplace, set about organizing women workers by inviting them to Sunday "sociables" involving drinking tea, listening to music, and discussing unionism. These affairs left the young women uncomfortable, and the allies, despite their commitment to sisterhood, at times found themselves repelled by the working women, who seemed to them to be interested only in attracting men. Or, conversely, these upper-class league members often idealized work as a liberation from the confinement of idle gentility and did not appreciate the drudgery working women endured, nor did they understand that holding a job did not make a woman independent of her family.

Nevertheless, while class conflict always was a factor, the league did provide a network of support for working women and deep ties were formed between allies and workers, as was the case, for example, of Mary Dreier and Leonora O'Reilly.[18]

The league's great recruiting achievement in its early years was bringing to membership Rose Schneiderman, born in Poland in 1882 to Orthodox Jewish parents who emigrated to New York and worked in the needle trades. After her father's early death, Schneiderman left school at age thirteen to work, first as a retail clerk and later as a cap-lining worker. In 1903, Schneiderman and other young women organized the twelve women in their factory into a woman's local that, by 1905, had several hundred workers and was strong enough to win a Saturday half-holiday. Schneiderman's experience as a skilled organizer transformed her from a lonely, unhappy young woman into an eager participant in the intellectual and political activities of Lower East Side radical groups. It was the beginning, she later recalled, "of a period that molded my subsequent development."[19]

After attending WTUL meetings, Schneiderman was doubtful that women who were not wage earners could understand the problems of workers. But when Margaret Dreier offered her the league's assistance during a capmakers' strike in the winter of 1905 and the league's efforts led to favorable newspaper publicity for the strikers, Schneiderman changed her opinion, joined the league, and was shortly elected its vice president. In 1907, Irene Lewisohn provided Schneiderman with a monthly stipend that enabled her to leave factory work and devote herself to organizing for the WTUL during the day and attending the Rand School in the evenings. The league became central to Schneiderman's life, and she remained a member until it disbanded in 1955.[20]

In its early years, the league followed Margaret Dreier's policy of organizing women in the "most exploited trades": paper box makers, laundry workers, retail clerks, and waitresses. The league's lack of understanding of the difficulties involved in organizing these categories of workers inevitably led to failure. In 1906, the league changed its policy to supporting workers ready to take action against their employers and supported spontaneous strikes in the garment industry against oppressive working conditions, which included being abused or sexually harassed by factory foremen. However, despite the efforts of skilled organizers Leonora O'Reilly and Rose Schneiderman and league leaders Helen Marot and Mary Dreier—together with allies who walked on picket lines, organized boycotts, held street meetings, raised funds, and publicized the strikes—the league made little progress in organizing women into stable AFL craft unions, which were not suited to the needs of women workers and were not interested in admitting women workers to their organizations. Yet the WTUL remained committed to the principle of affiliation with the AFL, largely out of fear of being regarded as "do-gooders" without class consciousness.[21]

The spontaneous uprising beginning in 1909—known as the "Uprising of the 20,000"—of shirtwaist makers in the factories around Washington Square marked a turning point in the women's clothing industry and in women's unionism. The strike had originated in three shirtwaist shops—Leisersons, Rosen Brothers, and the Triangle Waist Company—and as it spread, workers began to flock to International Ladies Garment Workers Union Local 25, which called for a general meeting in November at Cooper Union. The crowd poured in early to listen to Samuel Gompers of the AFL, union officials, lawyers, and Mary Dreier of the WTUL, none of whom worked in shirtwaist shops. After two hours of speeches, Clara Lemlich, a twenty-three-year-old Ukrainian-born striker from the Leiserson shop, rose and made her way to the platform, where she made an eloquent impromptu address in Yiddish, concluding with a motion for a general strike that the electrified gathering unanimously supported.

In the days following the Cooper Union Meeting, 20,000 workers joined the strike. The manufacturers retaliated by hiring thugs to insult and beat the young picketers. During the thirteen weeks of the strike, over six hundred women, many as young as fifteen, were arrested; thirteen were sentenced to five days in the Blackwell's Island workhouse and several were held for a week or ten days in the Tombs prison. Nevertheless, in spite of being thinly clad and ill-nourished, the workers continued to picket through the winter months, and their courage attracted much press coverage and public sympathy.[22]

Meanwhile, Local 25, overwhelmed by the chaotic situation created by the strike's momentum, turned to the WTUL for help. League members joined strikers on the picket lines, assigned teams to observe the treatment of picketers and to prevent arrests, and recruited volunteers to act as court witnesses. Small manufacturers quickly met the strikers' demands: a fifty-two-hour work week, piece rate increases, the abolition of charges to the workers for the cost of materials used in manufacturing, and the elimination of fines. However, larger shops, formed into a manufacturers' association, refused to recognize the union and hired strikebreakers.

As both sides hardened their positions, violence against strikers increased and more arrests were made. The league appealed to upper-class women to support the strikers for sisterhood's sake. However, when J. P. Morgan's daughter, Anne, and Alva Belmont joined the WTUL and were elected to its board, the league's members were divided, especially when the strikers rejected the Manufacturers' Association offer to accept the contract's terms but without recognition of the union. The strikers' refusal of an open shop settlement alienated many supporters; Anne Morgan, for example, quickly resigned from the league, denouncing it as a "socialist organization." Although some Manufacturer's Association members settled independently, when Local 25 declared the strike ended in mid-February, more than 150 large firms had not settled.[23]

While the strike had not gained the workers recognition for their union, it brought the league another important organizer, Pauline Newman, whose origins, like Schneiderman's and Lemlich's, were in the Russian-dominated Jewish community. Born in Lithuania around 1890, Newman emigrated to New York with her family in 1901 and immediately went to work in a hairbrush factory; when she was twelve, she went to work in the Triangle factory.[24] Like Schneiderman, whose parents had encouraged her aspirations, and Lemlich, whose parents did not, Newman wanted to be educated. She and her Eastern European co-workers recreated the self-improvement efforts of the nineteenth-century Yankee farmers' daughters who labored in the textile mills of Lowell, Massachusetts. Newman later recalled, "I would invite the girls to my room and we took turns reading poetry in English to improve our understanding." Newman and her Triangle coworkers used as texts the novels of Charles Dickens and George Eliot, and the poetry of Percy Bysshe Shelley.[25]

Like Elizabeth Gurley Flynn, who was born in the same year, Newman joined the Socialist Party and, while Flynn was addressing street meetings in Harlem in 1906, Newman was exhorting her Lower East Side neighbors in English and Yiddish. And as Schneiderman had been nurtured by the trade union movement, Newman found her mentors among the older women in the Socialist Party, notably the former garment worker Theresa Serber Malkiel. After joining the WTUL in 1909, Newman became a close friend of Mary Dreier, but was especially close to the working-class activists Leonora O'Reilly and Rose Schneiderman, who shared her ambivalence about upperclass women. Newman and Schneiderman were close to O'Reilly until she died in 1927; they remained each other's very close friends until Schneiderman's death in 1972.[26]

The "Uprising of the 20,000" had a tragic coda in the Triangle Shirtwaist Company, one of the largest of the non-union firms, which occupied the three upper floors of an overcrowded ten-story building near Washington Square. On a late March afternoon in 1911, shortly after Local 25 renegotiated its contracts, a dropped cigarette ignited one of the large workrooms. Fed by the combustible fabric, the fire quickly became an inferno. Singly, or in twos and threes, women jumped from the windows; some bodies crashed through the firemen's safety nets or the frail horse blankets held by passing teamsters who had jumped from their carriages to try desperately to save them. Workers died at their work stations, or in the stairs to the exit, which the employers, fearing employees would leave early or sneak away with pilfered shirtwaists, habitually kept locked. Others died when the fire escape, blocked by iron window shutters, collapsed and spilled flaming bodies into a rear courtyard. A temporary morgue had to be set up on East Twenty-sixth Street and the East River for survivors to claim their loved ones among the 146 victims, 7 of whom were never identified. The Triangle owners, Isaac Harris and Max Blanck, were charged with manslaughter but acquitted, despite testimony from more than 100 witnesses about the crowded conditions and locked workroom doors.[27]

In the spring of 1911, in the wake of the Triangle fire and settlements resulting in disappointing contracts, the shirtwaist-makers' union wanted to go on a second strike with the aim of winning a protocol agreement, such as the male-dominated cloakmakers' union had won in a well-financed and organized strike in 1910. This agreement provided for improved conditions, standardized wage and piece rates, and a preferential shop clause requiring firms to hire union workers rather than unorganized workers. The WTUL, dissatisfied with the incompetent leadership of Local 25 and with other International Ladies' Garment Workers' Union (ILGWU) locals in the women's trades because of the contempt for women and denial to them of leadership roles, refused its endorsement when Local 25 called a second strike in October 1911. In this period, small unions in other trades—wrappers and kimono workers (ILGWU Local 50), children's dressmakers (ILGWU Local 58), and household linen workers (ILGWU Local 62)—repeatedly asked the international for permission to call general strikes in order to organize workers and win standardized agreements. But the international remained unwilling to allocate money to trades composed largely of unskilled women and refused to endorse general strikes or pay for organizers.[28]

The international, under its president, Abraham Rosenberg, resisted militancy from women and efforts to democratize unions. But with a growing militancy among shirtwaist-makers that resulted in the replacement in Local 25's officers by a more responsive and gender-balanced leadership and with a rising militancy among the unorganized, the ILGWU reluctantly conceded to demands and authorized a general strike in the household linen industry. The WTUL, for different reasons, reluctantly supported the strike, for, as Helen Marot declared, the league's mission was "to bring women into a position of responsibility in the trade," and in a general strike, men dominated and women had "no place and power . . . and mostly no voice."[29]

The strike, which lasted from early January until mid-February, 1913, brought, through the efforts of Local 62 and the WTUL, nearly five thousand women into the union. It ended with a contract specifying a fifty-hour work week, improved health and safety conditions in the workplace, a 10 percent piece rate increase, an industry-wide minimum wage of five dollars a week, and a preferential shop. However, it retained an institutionalized gender-based division of labor that allowed only men to fill the highest-paid positions, relegated women to the lowest-paid positions, and guaranteed higher wages to men in jobs open to both men and women.[30]

The uprising of the household linen workers marked the end of the general strike era. The Women's Trade Union League's efforts from 1909 to 1913 had resulted in gains for trade unions and improvements in the conditions of working women. But of the 72,500 women who were union members by September 1913, 63,000 belonged to unions in the garment and textile industries, 2,000 belonged to tobacco unions, nearly 3,000 women were members of printing and bookbinding unions, 3,000 belonged to musicians' and theatrical unions, and the rest were members of small organizations in marginal occupations as box makers, artificial flower makers, hair workers, leather goods workers, candy makers, and laundry workers. Women's strikes in these industries between 1910 and 1913 failed and working conditions remained unchanged.

The league's experience with the 1912 laundry workers' strike had been especially discouraging. The league enthusiastically had supported the strike with funds and publicity, and hearings held by the State Board of Mediation and Arbitration concluded that intolerable conditions and low wages had led to the strike and recommended that employers grant workers' demands for a fifty-four-hour week, a minimum wage of six dollars a week, safety guards on machinery, and union recognition. Nevertheless, the strike failed; when it ended on January 31, 1912, only six laundries recognized the union and agreed to pay higher wages. Other employers replaced the unskilled workers.

The WTUL came to the understanding that affiliation with the AFL burdened them with methods and ideology inappropriate for unskilled immigrant women and that, perhaps, unionization was not the best way to improve women's working conditions. The league's relationship with the AFL had been harmed when it was attacked by influential leaders in the federation and its affiliates as being dominated by socialists and upper-class dilettantes.[31] The perceived failure of suffragists to support the women's strikes drew bitter criticism from Elizabeth Gurley Flynn, who accused "rich faddists" for suffrage of being "women of the very class driving the girls to lives of misery or shame"; the suffragists, in Flynn's view, could have financed the strikes to successful conclusions, but chose instead to make the workers' cause "the tail of a suffrage kite" until "the points at issue were lost sight of in the blare of automobile horns attendant on their coming and going."[32]

The league's ambivalence about its mission caused internal tensions as well. The WTUL's conservative allies feared the radicalism of the Socialist members and the Socialists resented not having their work for the league sufficiently credited and not being defended by the league from AFL attacks. Tensions were heightened by the league's revisionist assessment of women workers. During the 1909 strike, Italian women did not strike in the same numbers as Jewish women did, and many of those who did strike returned to work before settlements were reached. The patriarchal nature of Italian family life made the women—who, when unmarried, turned their wages over to fathers and brothers and who, when married, left the work force— difficult to organize. After poor participation by Italian women in the

1913 household linen workers' strike, the WTUL ended its efforts to organize them.[33]

By contrast, the overwhelming participation of Jewish women in the strike of 1909 had demonstrated to the league that these women were committed trade unionists and had brought the organization two skillful organizers, Rose Schneiderman and Pauline Newman. As the league's organizer on the East Side, Schneiderman tried to build on the success of the 1913 general strike, but now encountered resistance from the Jewish women she was trying to bring into the union, for although they were less submissive than the Italian women, they also were less militant than the Jewish women of the general strike and accepted the tradition that marriage and family were their only acceptable options. Moreover, the strained relations between the league and the ILGWU created another obstacle for Schneiderman.

Because of these problems, the league's executive committee, acting in agreement with Helen Marot and the conservative American-born organizer Melinda Scott, decided to focus their organizing efforts on "American girls," a decision that angered the league's Jewish workers and was opposed by Rose Schneiderman and Pauline Newman. Both women left the league to work as ILGWU organizers, but the rudeness, disrespect, and discriminatory behavior of the Jewish men who dominated the unions drove them out, and they returned to the league and remained with it until it dissolved in 1955.[34]

By 1913, the league, which always had placed trade unionism before feminism, turned in another direction, placing gender before class and shifting its emphasis from women's needs as workers to their needs as women, and committed itself to working for protective legislative for working women and for suffrage. The dramatic change in the league's direction alienated young garment workers like Clara Lemlich, who had entered the WTUL in 1909, and the experienced women who had built the league like Helen Marot and Leonora O'Reilly; these women became disillusioned with the league and left.[35]

The league directed most of its efforts in the 1915 campaign for the suffrage referendum to gaining support from union men, for although organized labor publicly endorsed suffrage, the rank and file were hostile and heckled WTUL suffrage speakers when they addressed labor meetings. Despite a well-organized and well-financed campaign, New Yorkers defeated the 1915 referendum, statewide by 200,000 votes and in New York City by 89,000 votes. Only two of the city's thirty-one districts supported the referendum, one of which, on the Lower East Side, was Jewish. That immigrant workers opposed suffrage in the same numbers as native-born voters did not prevent the city's suffrage leaders from blaming immigrant workers for the referendum's defeat. Harriot Stanton Blatch's statement the day after the election that no women in the world are so humiliated as American women because "non-native born men" had the power to vote and pass laws "upon all the native born women of America" marked the wide breach that had arisen between the suffragists and the workers.[36]

Despite the rejection of workers by suffrage leaders, the WTUL continued to work for suffrage and protective legislation, at the expense of trade union organizing. League members were active in the Woman's Suffrage Party, devoting their efforts to winning labor support for a second state referendum as well as for a federal amendment. They also were active in the Congressional Union, which, in addition to endorsing a federal amendment, undertook a partisan campaign against the amendment's opponents. Prior to the 1917 referendum, the WTUL again made efforts to win support among unions in the city and upstate, this time encountering a far more favorable response. That the victory in the city was large enough to carry the state was due in no small part to the participation of immigrant communities among whom the league had labored for so long.[37]

The Mother-Teacher Struggle

Advocates did not limit their concerns for laboring women to factories; they strove to improve conditions of women in other work settings. In an article in *Harper's* in May 1914, Inez Milholland exposed the low wages and oppressive working conditions of female department store workers.[38] When the Maxwell Motor Company agreed to hire women to sell cars on an equal basis with men, Milholland celebrated their policy, and Crystal Eastman, Harriet Rodman, and other activists organized to persuade other automobile manufacturers to hire women to sell cars to women on the grounds that women drivers were more likely to buy cars from women on the sales force.[39]

Despite these early efforts, conditions for women in retail sales did not substantially improve until department stores were unionized in the thirties, and women still are not represented on a level with men in automobile salesrooms. However, one labor struggle that was concluded with some success in New York broke out in 1914 over the issue of whether women who were mothers could be teachers. Married women traditionally had been barred from teaching; during the entire nineteenth century, when the profession had become almost completely feminized with the development of the common school, married women were not permitted to teach, a prohibition in effect in more than 70 percent of the nation's schools until the 1930s. As late as 1950, married women were forbidden to teach in many major cities, including Boston.[40]

Charlotte Perkins Gilman was an early critic of the New York City Board of Education policy on married women teachers in a *Forerunner* essay in 1910. Women, she observed, taught at the lowest levels at lower pay, and married women were excluded from the schools—the exception being a married woman who could provide a doctor's certification of her husband's illness—because officials objected to them on the grounds that they might become pregnant and the children might notice their "condition." Gilman responded that woman is, by virtue of her motherhood, the original teacher. In Gilman's view, it is the normal and natural condition for women to marry, and they "would be no poorer teachers for that new relationship." Gilman argued further that all normal women should be mothers, "and as such, would be better teachers—not worse."[41]

In 1915, following several challenges—and responding to the need for more teachers to meet the expanding school population—the New York City Board of Education formally established and incorporated into its bylaws its policy regarding married women teachers. The policy required every woman who married while in service to report her marriage and the name of her husband immediately to the Superintendent of Schools. Failure to do so constituted neglect of duty and insubordination. However, married men were not required to report their marriages.[42]

The issue of whether a woman who became a mother should be suspended from service was challenged in 1914 when several teachers who had become mothers—Mrs. Lora Wagner, Mrs. Sarah Breslow, and Mrs. Bridget Peixotto—challenged their suspensions following the births of their children. The mother-teacher issue attracted fervent support from suffragists; Alva Belmont's remedy for the dispute was the establishment of a teachers' union that could strike if the school board refused to allow women to go on maternity leave and would, furthermore, enable women to be elected to the school board. Christabel Pankhurst, under indictment in England and arriving incognito in the United States, claimed that motherhood was an even greater service to a nation than that of a soldier, and stated that "a woman who is a mother is better qualified to teach other children." The case attracted even more attention when Henrietta Rodman, a public high school teacher and activist on many issues, allied herself with the cause in her capacity as vice president of the League for the Civic Service of Women. In challenging the board's policy, Rodman wrote a letter to the *Tribune,* a New York morning paper, in which her use of the words "mother baiters" so infuriated board superintendent William Maxwell that he immediately suspended her on the grounds of gross misconduct, insubordination, and discourtesy.

Rodman's allies quickly rallied to support her as well as the mother-teachers. A mass rally was held at Washington Irving High School at which Charlotte Perkins Gilman—Rodman's mentor—as well as other Heterodites, such as Fola La Follette and Marie Jenney Howe, were speakers in support of Rodman and the mother-teachers. Grace Strachan, a Brooklyn district superintendent who had led efforts to get the legislature to pass the Equal Pay Bill, nevertheless was hissed by the 400 assembled mother-teacher advocates when she expressed support for the board's policy.

However, Strachan's support of the board's actions echoed the puritanism of other New Yorkers who feared the prurient interest the sight of an obviously pregnant teacher would arouse in young children. A woman identifying herself as "A Mother" wrote in a letter to the *New York World* that when a young married woman was willing to "parade" before her pupils—especially boys—"it is time to quit." However, the conservative board's views were not shared by the

Figure 4: Henrietta Rodman. Reproduced by permission of the Schlesinger Library, Radcliffe College.

progressive mayor, John Mitchel, who believed that it was inconsistent to allow married women to teach but not to allow them the option of taking maternity leave and refused to accept the board's actions with respect to the fired mother-teachers as final.[43]

The issue of whether a married woman teacher in New York City should be deprived of the right to be reinstated after childbirth was settled in the courts in 1915, when Bridget Peixotto won her case, which ruled that married women teachers had the legal right to the benefit of a leave of absence for childbirth and that such leave should not be construed as neglect of duty. The courts further enjoined the Board of Education from filling a position with a new appointee during a teacher's maternity leave, requiring the board to replace the teacher with a substitute until the expiration of her leave. The Peixotto case led to the formalization by the board of maternity leaves, requiring a woman to apply for and accept a two-year leave of absence for maternity as soon as she became aware of her pregnancy. Failure to report her pregnancy and file an application for maternity leave was deemed neglect of duty and an act of insubordination.[44]

The policy of the New York City Board of Education with respect to maternity leaves preceded by many years the policies of most cities in the United States, which refused to employ married women or reinstate married women to duty after they had children. A study by the National Education Association found that female teachers were discriminated against more than any other female wage earners; in most cases a female teacher's contract was cancelled when she married, but when a male teacher married, his salary was increased. During the Depression, married women teachers were especially vulnerable, for taxpayers demanded that they be dismissed to provide jobs for unemployed men. Nevertheless, the board's policy did not resolve the controversy in New York City. Married teachers, particularly those with children, were regarded with disapproval, for it was assumed that they were neglecting their families. On the other hand, they were considered less committed to the profession and were blamed for failing to assume their responsibilities or to continue their studies, or else for being absent from the classroom too frequently because of family obligations. Single women teachers, on the other hand, were blamed for using the profession as a stopgap prior to marriage if they were young or branded as embittered neurotics if they were older.[45]

Moreover, the mandatory maternity leave, reduced to eighteen months in 1937[46] with provisions for extension if the mother so wished, or reduction after a thorough investigation if a woman claimed economic need, remained onerous, for it subjected a woman to aggressive inquiries from an unfriendly principal looking for an excuse to banish her from the classroom or charge her with insubordination. However, the policy remained in force until 1973, when the Board of Education changed its bylaws to bring itself into compliance with the Equitable Employment Opportunity Commission's ruling that maternity leave was solely a matter to be decided by a woman and her physician.[47]

The mother-teachers of 1914 were able to return to their class-
rooms after their maternity leaves ended; Henrietta Rodman, however,
was tried in secret before the Board of Education's Committee on High
and Training Schools for writing an open and satirical letter—a charge
to which she responded that she had not sworn away her right of free
speech when she became a teacher—and was suspended from her
position for eighteen months. However, Rodman, who, in the course
of the controversy had revealed that she was a married woman with
two adopted daughters, did not suffer greatly from the suspension.
The debate had enabled her to publicize the view she held in common
with her mentor and defender, Gilman, that women with children
would rather work at their professions than do housework. She also
enhanced her reputation as an activist, for her defiance of the school
board was championed by Floyd Dell in *The Masses,* and her promul-
gation of Gilman's view that the professionally staffed "feminist
apartment house" liberated women from the burden of housework was
the subject of a lengthy interview in the *New York Times.* Of even
greater consequence was the reimbursement of her lost salary by the
Teachers' League of New York City.[48]

CHAPTER 7

The Great Movements: Birth Control

THE STRUGGLE FOR BIRTH CONTROL was a conflict between, on one side, a coalition of activist "new women" and poor, mostly immigrant, women who desperately needed to limit their families and, on the other, the joined forces of nineteenth-century puritanism and twentieth-century nativism. The major representative of the prudery confronting working- middle- and upper-class women's needs and aspirations was Anthony Comstock—after whom "Comstockery" became a synonym for prudery—a Yankee Civil War veteran whose obsession with sin and vice gained support during the conservative backlash following the war. With the backing of the Young Men's Christian Association, (YMCA), Comstock in 1869 helped secure the passage in New York of a law prohibiting traffic in contraception and abortion. In 1873, again with the prestigious backing of the YMCA, he successfully lobbied Congress to pass the broad but unclearly defined federal obscenity act with which his name is associated. The act expanded existing legislation to prohibit the sending of certain materials through the mails. These included:

> Every obscene, lewd, or lascivious, and every filthy book, pamphlet, picture, paper, letter, writing, print, or other publication of an independent character and every article or thing designed, adapted, or intended for preventing conception or producing abortion, or for any indecent or immoral use; and every article, instrument, substance, drug, medicine, or thing which is advertised or described in a manner calculated to lead another to use or

apply it for preventing conception or producing abortion, or for any indecent immoral purpose.[1]

The original statute produced similar anti-obscenity, anti-contraception, and anti-abortion legislation on the state level throughout the nation; however, most states exempted physicians, and some of the states, even pharmacists, from legal prohibitions. Under pressure from the medical profession, in 1881 the New York legislature passed legislation to enable physicians to prescribe contraception for use in combating the spread of venereal diseases. Comstock thus was restrained from interfering with doctors in his home state, but was free to persecute nonprofessionals who challenged him—and these he pursued zealously, particularly sexually flamboyant females.[2]

The nativism that obstructed the desires of women to control their fertility was based on two perceived perils. One was the fear that the Asian nations were uniting to form a "yellow wave" that was rapidly "moving eastward over the Pacific Ocean and lapping the shores of America." The response of political and military figures who saw inevitable conflict with Asia urged a strengthening of the navy in order to preserve peace through "the white man's supremacy."[3]

This fear was compounded by the concern that the birthrates of immigrant families were rapidly outstripping the birthrates of "American" families; that the descendants of "Pilgrim Fathers" were dying out; and that "race suicide" would be the result. That this phobia fed opposition to birth control and feminist aspirations was demonstrated typically in an essay by Dr. Max G. Schlapp, a professor of neuropathology at Cornell Medical School, who argued that modern women were leading to the deterioration of the human race as reflected in the increase of insanity, criminality, divorce, and a decrease in childbirth rates. Suffragists, Dr. Schlapp charged, had their prototypes in Greece, Rome, and Egypt just prior to the fall of those civilizations; women who devoted energies to pursuits outside the home in disregard of "a natural law" that demanded they conserve their energies for childbirth and childrearing were abnormal; and the terrible result of "unsexing the female" was a falling birthrate in Europe and the United States and a rising birthrate in Japan.[4]

The sociologist Elsie Clews Parsons responded to the conservatives' concern about the falling "native birthrate" in a witty essay in the June 1915 issue of *The Masses*. Were the "race suicide croakers," Parsons asked, willing to eliminate the distinction between legitimacy and illegitimacy, or to support the aspirations of women they considered desirable mothers to pursue the careers for which they had been educated in addition to rearing children. Parsons had wit and reason on her side, but those were not weapons that could defeat the forces of bigotry and prudery that prolonged the struggle for the right of a woman to decide how many children she wanted and when to have them.

Like suffrage, the struggle had begun at an earlier time, but woman's right to control her fertility did not come until long after she had won the right to vote. Emma Goldman credited a number of nineteenth-century trail blazers, citing in particular Moses Harmon, his daughter Lillian, Ezra Heywood, and Ida Craddock as pioneers in the battle for "free motherhood." Hounded by Comstock and facing a five-year prison sentence, Craddock, according to Goldman, took her own life.

Goldman added birth control to her series of lectures after returning from the Neo-Malthusian Conference, held Paris in 1900 to discuss population limitation. She did not discuss methods of birth control in her lectures because, she claimed, the question of limiting offspring represented only one aspect of the social struggle and she did not care to risk arrest for it.[5] However, when no interference from Comstock and his supporters resulted, Goldman grew bolder, and she gradually began including a discussion of contraceptives in her lectures, particularly at her Yiddish meetings on New York's Lower East Side. In 1916, the Comstock forces caught up with Goldman; a Carnegie Hall protest meeting followed her arrest and a banquet at the Brevoort Hotel was held on the eve of her trial in April, which concluded with a sentence of a one- hundred-dollar fine or fifteen days in the Queens County Jail. Goldman, of course, chose the latter option.[6]

Margaret Sanger met Emma Goldman after she and her husband, William, had moved in 1910 with their two sons and a daughter to New York City and established themselves in an old-fashioned uptown railroad apartment that became, because of William Sanger's commitment to Socialism, "a gathering place where liberals, anarchists,

Socialists and I.W.W.'s could meet."[7] Sanger did not like Goldman's ideas or her bullying manner of persuading people to her views, but she admired her frank and flamboyant insistence on woman's sexual liberation.[8] Sanger's involvement with birth control began with an invitation from Anita Block, editor of the woman's page of the Socialist Party newspaper the *Call* to substitute for a speaker unable to keep her engagement to speak to a group of young Socialist women. As a trained nurse, Sanger felt qualified to speak on health, which led to questions from the women about their marital relationships. Block urged Sanger to write her answers to their questions in a series of articles for the *Call.* Her first series, "What Every Mother Should Know," was followed by a second series, "What Every Young Girl Should Know," both of which were published in the weekend edition of the *Call* in 1912 and 1913 until one Sunday when Sanger found that her article had been replaced by an empty box headlined "What Every Girl Should Know—Nothing! by order of the U.S. Post Office." The article, which had dealt specifically with venereal disease, had been banned by Anthony Comstock, but after the *Call* challenged the action and negotiated with local officials, the censored column was published several weeks later.[9]

Sanger in these years was her family's main breadwinner—William Sanger's radical politics having lost him his position as an architect—by working part-time with Lillian Wald's Visiting Nurses Association on the Lower East Side. Sanger had accompanied strikers' children to New York City during the 1912 Lawrence textile workers' strike; she had been active that same year in the strike of New York laundry workers, an experience that made her aware of the differing concerns of men and women on strike together, for while the men were mindful of economics and politics, the women thought mainly of their too large families. Watching groups of women lining up outside the office of a five-dollar abortionist struck Sanger's conscience. Ultimately the sad, futile death of Sadie Sachs forced her to recognize the fatal effect of women's inability to limit childbearing and she abandoned nursing to "seek out the root of evil."[10]

Late in 1913, the Sangers sailed for Europe. After a stop in Glasgow where Margaret was to report on municipal housing for the *Call,* they traveled to Paris, where William Sanger hoped to establish himself as an artist and Margaret continued the research on contraception she had begun in New York. Through meetings with French labor organizers who advocated state-supported policies of family planning, she learned of the tradition, rooted in the anticlericalism of the French Revolution and the Napoleonic codes mandating equal division of property among children, by which French peasant women passed on birth control secrets from one generation to another, thus defying the church and maintaining the integrity of family property.

Leaving her husband in Paris, Sanger returned with her children to New York in the winter of 1914, conceiving on board the ship from France the idea of a magazine to be called *The Woman Rebel*, with working women as its target audience and the defiance of Comstock's prohibition against the dissemination of information on sexuality and contraception as its purpose. She approached the members of Heterodoxy with her plan, but they were not responsive. She struggled to sustain *The Woman Rebel*, as Heterodite Charlotte Perkins Gilman continued to struggle to sustain *The Forerunner*, raising money from advance subscriptions produced through advertisements in radical journals, putting it together on the dining room table of her uptown apartment, and sending forth in March a maiden issue under the slogan borrowed from the Wobblies, "No Gods, no Masters."[11]

The issue was dominated by Sanger's bitterness at other women activists. Max Eastman's editorial in *The Masses* expressed disappointment at the debut issue of *The Woman Rebel*, declaring that it fell into the "most unfeminist of errors—the tendency to cry out when a quiet and contained utterance is indispensable." Eastman was repelled by Sanger's attacks on other feminists for not having gone so far as Sanger or for going in a different direction; nevertheless, he promised to stand by her in her fight. Several months later, when Sanger was prosecuted for publishing *The Woman Rebel*, Eastman kept his promise to her. When Emma Goldman was prosecuted for distributing birth control information, Eastman threw *The Masses's* support to her as well.[12]

Sanger's biographer Ellen Chesler has argued that the women of Heterodoxy turned Sanger down perhaps out of reluctance to associate themselves with her avowed radicalism in politics and social behavior, or because they were skeptical about her lack of education and erratic emotional behavior. However, the women of Heterodoxy included women who were themselves regarded as radicals; many of the women had supported the women's clothing industry strikers in the "uprising of the 20,000." In the same year that Sanger asked for their support, Henrietta Rodman had been suspended from her own teaching position for protesting the suspension of mother-teachers and Crystal Eastman had formed the Woman's Peace Party of New York, which included other Heterodites among its leaders and remained active and militant throughout the First World War. Moreover, members of Heterodoxy later formed a committee called the National Birth Control League, dedicated to reforming the federal and state Comstock Statutes. If they were reluctant to support Sanger initially, they perhaps had sensed that instead of working with them in partnership, Sanger would expect her supporters to follow her lead unquestioningly, for this was the style that marked the organization she eventually established—which later emerged as Planned Parenthood.[13]

Margaret Sanger and Emma Goldman had in common a commitment to a woman's right to sexual pleasure. Goldman frankly relished the "intoxicating joy and bliss" of "the great life-giving force." She openly advocated free love and opposed "binding people for life," claiming that "constant proximity in the same house, the same room, the same bed" revolted her.[14] Sanger was more discreet, but no less enthusiastic about the joys of sex. Mabel Dodge recalled that Margaret Sanger was the first person she had known who set out to rehabilitate physical pleasure; she was an "advocate of the flesh" who believed that attitudes toward sex had been "infantile, archaic, and ignorant," and that the conscious attainment of the pleasures of sex would make previous relations between men and women "seem stupid beyond words in their awkward ignorance." Dodge was much more interested in Sanger's ideas on sex than in her efforts to establish clinics for the poor and was spellbound one night at dinner in her apartment when Sanger, sitting serene and quiet, "unfolded the mysteries and mightinesses of physical love," which had never before seemed "as a sacred and at the same time a scientific reality." Sanger taught

> the way to a heightening of pleasure and of prolonging it, and the delimiting of it to the sexual zones, the spreading out and sexualizing of the whole body until it should become sensitive and

alive throughout, and complete. She made love into a serious
undertaking—with the body so illumined and conscious that it
would be able to interpret and express in all its parts the language
of the spirit's pleasure.[15]

In addition to a commitment to the right of a woman to sexual
gratification, Goldman and Sanger had in common, despite their
advocacy of women, a dislike of their sex. In the early stage of her
career, Sanger was scornful of women who did not rally unquestioningly to her crusade and later in her career was imperious to women
who did not perform according to her exacting demands.[16] Goldman
infuriated women who came to her lectures on feminism with her
"critical attitude toward the bombastic and impossible claims of the
suffragists" and by her claim that woman "is naturally perverse" for
inconsistently keeping men dangling "between the idol and the brute,
the darling and the beast, the helpless child and the conqueror of
worlds." In Goldman's view woman would achieve liberation only
when she had learned to be as self-centered and determined as man
was, and "as willing to delve into life . . . and pay the price for it."[17]

Goldman and Sanger began in the birth control movement as
allies. After the inaugural edition of *The Woman Rebel* appeared, to
which Goldman had contributed an article on the Neo-Malthusian
theme that women had been degraded into breeding machines in order
to serve the interests of the state, Goldman sold subscriptions while
she was on a lecture tour and wrote Sanger from Chicago with glee that

> most of the women are up in arms against your paper; mostly
> women, of course, whose emancipation has been on paper and not
> in reality. I am kept busy answering questions as to your "brazen"
> method. They would not believe me when I told them that you
> were a little, delicate woman, refined and shrinking, but that you
> did believe in the daring and courage of woman in her struggle for
> freedom.[18]

In June, Goldman wrote Sanger from San Francisco that the Post
Office's actions to hold up the distribution of *The Woman Rebel* had
turned the publication into "the best seller of anything we've got."[19]

However, publication of the magazine ended with Sanger's arrest in August on four criminal charges carrying a maximum sentence of forty-five years. Sanger arranged for her son Grant and daughter Peggy to be cared for by Caroline Pratt, founder of City and Country School, and her partner, the labor activist, Helen Marot (Sanger's son Stuart was in private school) and fled the country to avoid prosecution and imprisonment, but not before writing a birth control primer, *Family Limitation*, finding a printer brave enough to undertake the job of setting it in type, and supporters brave enough to distribute clandestinely 100,000 copies.[20]

Bearing new birth control information gathered during her European travels, Sanger returned to New York to face trial the following year, spurred by concern for her estranged husband, who had returned from Paris following Margaret's indictment and had been entrapped by a government agent into providing her with a *Family Limitation* pamphlet. Arrested, tried, convicted, and presented with a choice between a one-hundred-fifty-dollar fine and a thirty-day prison sentence, William had chosen to go to jail. Another factor in Sanger's decision to return was the encouragement she had received from radical friends who persuaded her that the political climate was turning in her favor. Elizabeth Gurley Flynn urged her to go on a national lecture tour in order to generate interest in her trial. Another hopeful sign was the death, two weeks after William Sanger's trial, of Anthony Comstock.[21]

But Sanger's return also was followed by the sudden death on November 6, 1915, of her daughter, Peggy; the loss devastated Sanger and subjected her to fits of remorse for the rest of her life. Emma Goldman, on a birth control lecture tour, wrote Sanger from Chicago, enclosing a money order for forty dollars and pledging to send all further money from lectures on birth control to Sanger, all of which was not enough, Goldman assured Sanger, "to express my affection for you and my devotion to the thing we both love."

With respect to Peggy's death, it was, Goldman believed, "impardonable" for Sanger to blame herself or hold herself responsible for something that could not have been in her power. The letter's next sentence, however, reveals either tactlessness on Goldman's part or the ambivalence of her feelings for Sanger: "No doubt the child would have been given better care in your home, but whether that would have saved her life is mere speculation." Goldman went on to express her deep feelings for Sanger's loss, along with the advice that "you owe it to yourself and the work you have before you to collect your strength."[22] Goldman followed that letter the very next day with one from St. Louis expressing alarm because she had heard "our good friends" were urging Sanger to plead guilty, which, according to Goldman, would be an "impardonable error," for Sanger had friends all over the country and she had "aroused interest as no one ever had." All that had been gained would be lost if Sanger declared herself guilty. "Don't do it," Goldman admonished.[23]

Sanger was by then well aware of how much support she had gained, and Goldman's advice was superfluous. Media coverage of birth control, not only in the *New York Times* but in national news magazines, had increased dramatically. As word of her work spread, Sanger received thousands of letters each year from women, almost all of them poor, desperate to learn how to keep from bearing more children. Eventually, Sanger published several hundred of these appeals, including a number from men, chosen by Sanger because they were typical of certain types of "enslaved motherhood in America." The repetition of the letters, Sanger informed her readers, builds the unity "of this tragic communal experience." The litanies run on:

"I have six children in school and two under my feet, am milking five cows, sell from seventy-five to one hundred pounds of butter. . . . Tell me how to keep from having another. Don't open the door of heaven to me and shut it in my face"; "I am the mother of nineteen children, the baby only twenty months old. I am forty-three years old and I had rather die than give birth to another child"; "I would rather die than have another one, for my husband is a sufferer from gonorrhea"; "I have six living children and they go to work early in life. . . . Were I to become pregnant again I would . . . die before I would have another running around half clothed"; "Our doctor seems not to want us to have any definite information. He says 'The only way' to keep from having children is to live in different parts of town.' Whereupon he laughs heartily at his own joke."[24]

Figure 5: Emma Goldman speaking at Union Square in 1916. Margaret Sanger is seated at her right. Reproduced by permission of the Bettman Archives.

This testimony either reminds or informs us for the first time of what women endured before birth control became legal and accessible. But Sanger's correspondents were powerless women, and in her time of travail, her cause was embraced by daring feminists—the women Goldman scorned—who for years had insisted that suffrage was but one item on the agenda of women's emancipation.[25]

Knowing the case against Sanger was weak—for the debate she had initiated had since been discussed in major newspapers and periodicals—the government twice postponed her trial. Each adjournment only served to increase Sanger's celebrity, and on February 14, 1916, all charges against her were dropped. Sanger used the opportunity her sudden fame had given her to lecture nationwide on birth control; despite her reluctance to speak in public, she was very successful, and she gained advocates for her cause on each of her 191 speaking engagements.[26]

Sanger's prominence challenged Goldman's position as the pioneer of the birth control movement, and the "older sister" role she had played with Sanger was transformed into a rivalry. Arrested for distributing birth control information, Goldman defiantly went to jail in April, 1916. Her coverage of her experience in *Mother Earth* made no mention of Sanger, while Sanger, for her part, never acknowledged her debt to Goldman's influence and support. However, Goldman removed herself from the competition when she, along with other radicals, turned her attention to the question of American involvement in World War I. Sanger, having witnessed the loss of effectiveness by activists who overextended themselves to too many causes, remained committed solely to the issue of birth control, a position that allowed her to function during the political repression accompanying and following America's entry into the world war.[27]

On October 16, 1916, Sanger opened America's first birth control clinic in the Brownsville section of Brooklyn. The poor women of the community responded to the handbills, printed in English, Italian, and Yiddish, advertising the benefits of contraception over abortion. However, Sanger was entrapped as her husband had been, when, on the ninth day of the clinic's operation, a police agent purchased a birth control pamphlet, *What Every Young Girl Should Know,* and returned the next with three vice squad plainclothesmen to arrest Sanger and her assistant, Fania Mindell. Sanger's sister, the nurse Ethel Byrnes, who had not been present in the clinic on the day of the sale of the pamphlet, subsequently was arrested and was the first of the three women to be tried for dispensing contraception information. Sentenced to one month's imprisonment, she went on a hunger strike and was force-fed. Granted a pass by Governor Charles Whitman to visit her sister in prison, Sanger became so concerned by Ethel's deteriorating physical condition that she agreed on her sister's behalf to the terms Whitman had offered and she had previously rejected: in return for a pardon, Sanger pledged for her sister that she never would break the law again.

During this period, the members of National Birth Control League, calling themselves the Committee of 100 and including stalwart Heterodites Mary Ware Dennett, Rose Pastor Stokes, Crystal Eastman, and Elsie Clews Parsons, came to Sanger's support. When

Ethel Byrnes was sentenced to prison, the Committee of 100 called a protest rally at Carnegie Hall, attracting 3,000 supporters and raising $1,000. The group's chair, Gertrude Pinchot, who earlier had given the Sangers money for their children's education, and committee member Juliet Barrett Rublee were wealthy women, representatives of the class to whom Sanger would increasingly turn for support in the years when repression forced her radical allies from positions of influence, when the movement itself had been driven from the headlines by the war and into quietus during its aftermath, and later, when a more formidable foe than Anthony Comstock—the Catholic Church—would vehemently and unremittingly oppose her cause.[28]

Fania Mindell and Margaret Sanger were tried in January 1917. Called first by the prosecution, Mindell was found guilty on obscenity charges and given a $50 fine, which Gertrude Pinchot paid. Sanger also was found guilty and given the choice of a $5,000 fine or a prison sentence. Sanger chose prison and was given a thirty-day sentence, which she served at the Queens Penitentiary for Women. She emerged from jail a hero; the group of friends and supporters who greeted her included representatives from the Women's City Club of New York and the Committee of 100.[29] Sanger reported in her autobiography that the group who gathered for her "coming out party" sang the *Marseillaise* while the women prisoners looked on from their cell windows.[30] Later the National Birth Control League honored her at a luncheon at the Plaza Hotel and then formed a corporation to provide her with support and to get federal and state amendments to laws that would enable physicians and nurses to provide birth control.[31]

However, the entry of the United States into the war at this time resulted, with assistance from the Wilson administration's propaganda machinery, in a wave of militaristic fervor and xenophobic intolerance of dissenters. The Federal Espionage and Sedition Acts threatened suppression of all speech, press, and assembly that could be described as obstructing the war through fines, imprisonment, and even deportation in the case of foreign-born perpetrators.[32] Teachers opposed to the war were labeled "disloyal" and suspended from their jobs; the internment of "enemy aliens" was proposed, and a "hunt for spies in every part of the United States" was launched.[33] The hysteria deepened following the Bolshevik Revolution in Russia, and that "red scare" led to further political repression, the extent of which most Americans recognize only dimly, if at all, perhaps because the wave of political repression that came later had a label: McCarthyism. Seventy-five left-wing journals and magazines—including *The Masses*—were suppressed in a single year. American radicals were targeted for persecution. The IWW effectively was wiped out as meeting halls around the country were raided and hundreds of its leaders, including Bill Haywood, were arrested, convicted of crimes, and imprisoned. Elizabeth Gurley Flynn and Carlo Tresca, who at the time were no longer affiliated with the IWW or other radical groups, were harassed and arrested by federal agents, though never convicted of crimes. Emma Goldman and Alexander Berkman were imprisoned and then, as convicted traitors, were forced into exile.

Sanger made a pragmatic decision to focus on birth control, thereby eluding the persecution that befell her radical friends, although her continued association with them brought her under the surveillance of the Lusk Committee, which was authorized by the New York State Legislature to pursue subversives. When she joined the Amnesty of Political Prisoners, formed to protest the Berkman and Goldman arrests, she came under the surveillance of federal agents, and from then on her activities were tracked by the Federal Bureau of Investigation, the permanent outgrowth of the wartime surveillance activities, which maintained a file on her associations with alleged subversives.

Although she continued to revere dissident heroes like Eugene Debs and Bill Haywood and send small contributions to support radical causes, she no longer was interested in utopian dreams of building a better world. By the end of the war, few of her radical friends remained in positions of influence or leadership, and those who did were as out of sympathy with her goals as she was with theirs. She was not active in national political movements[34] or interested in revolutionary movements abroad, except as they provided economic and personal freedom for women, including "the knowledge which will enable them to have as few children as they themselves consider consistent with their health, their desires, their opportunities for economic development, their economic resources, their ability to rear and educate."[35] After the war, she pursued and won a constituency for birth control among business leaders, professionals, and academics. Hutchins Hapgood, in one of his mean-spirited descriptions of the leading women of the era, described Sanger as "a pretty woman" whose husband was "a sweet man who lacked ego and ambition" and seemed more interested in their children than she:

> at any rate, Mrs. Sanger seemed to grant little value to her husband, and perhaps it is no accident that when the birth-control movement in America gradually transferred itself from the revolutionary class to the respectable middle class, the able and ambitious Mrs. Sanger should become head of the movement; and that well-to-do ladies of leisure . . . should aid her in her work.[36]

Pragmatism was necessary, for Sanger's movement-building lasted her lifetime, and though it drew thousands of adherents, from dedicated volunteers to skillful administrators and medical professionals, the struggle for a woman's right to determine how many children she shall have and when she shall have them, is much alive in the United States and other so-called developed nations, and beginning or burgeoning in so-called undeveloped nations, and still is linked with its principal mover and shaker, Margaret Sanger.[37]

CHAPTER 8

The New Woman in Love

THE ACTIVIST WOMEN OF THE TEENS revealed their personal lives in autobiographies they later wrote; however most of them screened more intimate and sometimes painful aspects of their emotional and sexual lives from their memoirs, and only access to the archives they left to be read after their passing has enabled readers to understand more fully the double nature of their struggles.

Emma Goldman, the flamboyant advocate and practitioner of "free love" whose frank discussion of her affairs in her autobiography "revolted" Dorothy Day, nevertheless kept the most deeply private and erotic side of her life hidden when she wrote about the public side of her life in her autobiography. Because of the chance discovery in a Chicago guitar shop of Goldman's letters to Ben Reitman by Candace Serena Falk, we know the torment and ecstasy Goldman experienced in the great love affair of her life with a man ten years her junior, a gynecologist-turned-activist known as "the King of the Hobos" who from 1908 to 1917 was the manager who widened her audience and increased the circulation of Mother Earth and the lover who kept her as "helpless as a shipwrecked crew on a foaming ocean."[1] Six months after beginning her relationship with Reitman, Goldman wrote him,

> You have opened up the prison gates of my womanhood. And all the passion that was unsatisfied in me for so many years, leaped into a wild reckless storm boundless as the sea . . . can you then imagine that I could stay away from you?[2]

Every night when they were separated, Emma and Ben wrote letters in which they expressed their passion, evading the laws against obscenity in the mails through a barely disguised code for sexual language. After a long night of work on *Mother Earth*, Emma wrote,

> Good night, or, rather, good morning, dear. It's 5 A.M. Even if I am tired and weary and love hungry for my no account lover, I should show him [Willie] some things if he were here. Come close and see two actually big M[ountains] and a little bright-eyed t[reasure] b[ox]. Your mommy.[3]

Reitman was well established as a ladies' man when Goldman met him and continued to have affairs during their relationship. Goldman extolled the virtues of free love in her lectures on "Marriage and Love," but could not convince Ben that free love was different from promiscuity. "Your love is all sex," Goldman charged; her love included sex, but also "devotion, care, anxiety, patience, friendship, it is all."[4] She tried to forget her pain by throwing herself into her work, but her effort was futile, and she was caught in an exhausting cycle of withdrawal and engagement. "Hobo! Hobo! cried my soul," she lamented in one of her many letters,

> Why did you ever enter my life, if you are to be out so much? Foolish question, is it not? . . . You came to me like a stroke of lightning, kindling my soul and body with mad passion, as I have never known before. Ever since you have consumed me, sopped me up into your blood, and when you go away, you leave me weak and nerveless. Yet when you stay, you cause me tortures of Hell.[5]

Ben's letters to Emma express his loneliness and dependence on her, and a heart "full of love for Mommy," but the pattern of their relationship did not change; Emma continued to yearn, to pour out her passion, and to hurl accusations. Three years after they began their relationship she wrote that she never would be able to overcome her repulsion when he shattered the faith that had begun to take root: "Your escapades, your promiscuity, tears my vitals, fills me with gall and horror and twists my whole being into something foreign to myself." They finally grew apart when Ben began to tire of being "a mere office boy" and lost interest in his work with Emma, who, in turn, became disillusioned with him. Reitman returned to Chicago, resumed his medical practice, and established a home and family with Anna Martindale, a labor activist.[6]

Goldman had scorned marriage and family as a prison, not "so large as the factory," but with "more solid doors and bars." She proclaimed love as "the strongest and deepest element in all life, the harbinger of hope, of joy, of ecstasy"; love that was free was an "all compelling force" that could not possibly "be synonymous with that poor little State and Church-begotten weed, marriage."[7] She had scorned women's quest for suffrage as a futile and tragic pursuit, but she would find, especially during her years of aging in exile, that she could not elude the tragic impact of the double standard. Her passion never abated, but while men of advanced years could find female sexual partners, heterosexual women of advanced years were sexually invisible.

Having some time earlier decided that her husband, Edwin, was "a wet blanket," Mabel Dodge fled to Paris with John Reed following the financially disastrous Paterson pageant.[8] After she began her affair with Reed, "nothing else in the world" had any longer any significance for Dodge. One can sense the influence of Margaret Sanger in Dodge's discovery of the "elixir of love" she contained within herself. Her power, she thought, "emerges at the source, that is, my sex, and rises, rises, through my belly, through my solar plexus, through my heart and to my head—and all these I have dedicated to that Power that uses me for its own purposes."[9]

Love was her vocation, Dodge told herself, and yielding was her destiny. Dodge claimed that, like most "real women," she longed for the "strong man" who would take responsibility for her and her decisions while she lay back and floated "in the dominating decisive current of an all-knowing, all-understanding man."[10] At the same time, Dodge aspired to achievements in "that world where men *do* things in order to prove themselves powerful to themselves," and a spirit of competition sprang up between Dodge and Reed.[11]

Max Eastman captured this dilemma in the novel he later wrote about John Reed's involvement with the Paterson strike, *Venture.*

Eastman expressed approval of Dodge—Mary Kittredge in the novel—for knowing how to love John Reed—Jo Sinclair—well and to encourage him in his work. However, Eastman's traditional view of women emerges in an ironic passage about Dodge/Kittredge: although consenting to be "a mother-premise to Jo's lively experiences, she did not put all her heart into that time-honored female role." She "redoubled her application to the egotistical adventure of becoming a learned woman," throwing herself upon the social sciences like a "wild mountain cat—tearing them to pieces and devouring the shreds," rather than learning them in systematic fashion, mastering Marxian vocabulary, which she uttered with "bloodthirsty conviction," and astonishing Jo and herself with her commitment to the workers' cause.[12]

That, despite an enormous self-absorption beyond the means or energy of most women, Dodge did not arrive at an understanding of herself is evidence of how badly women were served by the Freudian view that love was their true destiny. Dodge's efforts to force her strong ego into the role of love goddess led to turbulence in her relationships with Reed and later with Maurice Sterne and left her with a sense of defeat. She viewed her many projects as substitutes for love; in her lengthy memoirs, Dodge stated that having "so many pages to write" was a sign of her "unluckiness in love."[13] A greater unluckiness, perhaps, was denying the truth that another Freudian advocate, Floyd Dell, eventually recognized: that seeking the joys of expression was as normal and healthy for women as for men.[14]

Emma Goldman and Margaret Sanger were, of course, practitioners of the "Power" before Dodge's self-discovery, but many women, well known and not so well known, actively were pursuing sexual freedom. Although the spirit of sexual freedom was not limited to its borders, Greenwich Village was unquestionably the "free love" center of New York City and probably the nation. There the spirit of Comstockery and the vestiges of Victorianism were vigorously overthrown, replaced by what the critic Randolph Bourne described as "Human Sex," egalitarian relationships between men and women where friendship was as important as sex, and sex was not confined to marriage. Gossip about affairs fills the histories of the era and biographies of its leading figures. According to Dodge, Reed left an affectionate schoolteacher, Rose, to begin an affair with her.[15] She had met Reed at the apartment of another teacher, identified as "B.," who, Hutchins Hapgood explained to her, taught in the morning at a public high school where she instructed her students to respect the flag and honor the government and at night slept with Bill Haywood when he was in New York. "B.," whom Hapgood identified as Bea Shostac, was, in his estimation, one of many "brave young American women" who were adapting themselves to this way of life and were "thus doing their share towards a final disintegration of our community."[16] School-teacher "B." apparently had to wait her turn for nocturnal visits from Haywood, for he was widely accepted as the lover of Jessie Ashley, the daughter of the president of the New York University Law School, the sister of its dean, and a wealthy lawyer in her own right who had adopted the workers' cause and became Secretary of the IWW.[17] While other suffragists were discreet about the question of "free love," Ashley openly proclaimed that she did not believe in marriage, or even much care for children. Ashley and Haywood are described as

> the oddest combination in the world—old Bill with his one eye, stubby, roughened fingernails, uncreased trousers, and shoddy clothes for which he refused to pay more than the minimum; Jessie with her Boston accent and hornrimmed glasses . . . was one of the most conspicuous of the many men and women of long pedigree who were revolting against family tradition. . . . A Socialist in practice as well as in theory, she spent large portions of her income getting radicals out of jail. . . . Nevertheless, [at] her appearance at strike meetings . . . class tensions rose up in waves.[18]

Contemporary photographs of the young women activists on plat-forms speaking of their causes like passionate goddesses on pedestals to largely masculine—and no doubt frequently sexually aroused—audiences attests to the magnetism of these women, whose iconic quality we know in later decades as the property of rock and film stars. Of course, radical women in love stirred the public's curiosity. During the waiters' strike of 1913, when Elizabeth Gurley Flynn's lover, Carlo Tresca, scuffled with police attempting to arrest him, a copy of Elizabeth Barrett Browning's *Sonnets from the Portuguese*, with an affectionate inscription from Flynn, dropped from his pocket, with the result that the next day Flynn was embarrassed to see their pictures, "with copies of the book cover, marked sonnets, dedication and all, reproduced in the New York papers as a hidden IWW romance!" The strike leaders were delighted, however, because the publicity helped advertise their cause. By this time Flynn had joined Heterodoxy and contact with these remarkable women had softened her former bitterness against suffrage; when Tresca became her lover, they lived according to the code followed by feminists: "not to remain with someone you did not love, but to honestly and openly avow a real attachment."[19]

When Flynn and Tresca parted in 1925—after Flynn discovered that Tresca had sired a son by her sister, Bina—there was no question that Flynn would remain committed to political struggle; indeed, the dedication that led her to part from Tresca on a moment's notice to go in aid of an imprisoned Wobbly had been a cause of friction and no doubt allowed him to rationalize his unfaithfulness to her.[20] However, when Dodge and Reed ended their affair in 1914, Dodge not only said "good-by forever" to Reed, to "the gay, bombastic, and lovable boy with his shining brow; [but] to the labor Movement, to Revolution, and to anarchy."[21] John Reed later married Louise Bryant, who had left her marriage to an Oregon dentist to join him in the Village.[22] The code of living with someone until one no longer loved that person was expressed for that era in the metaphor of love as a candle burning at both ends in the well known quatrain by Edna St. Vincent Millay— with whom the *Masses* editor and novelist Floyd Dell was, for a time, in love "to the point of distraction"; for her part, Millay was, in the spirit of that age and place, seriously attracted to John Reed.[23]

In a period of intense activism, politics made bedfellows, espe- cially since the young people—Dell, St. Millay, Reed, and Bryant— were so physically attractive. In his autobiography, William Carlos Williams recalled that at a party in his Greenwich Village apartment, Bryant wore a white silk shirt that hung over the curve of her buttocks "like the strands of a glistening waterfall." She was wearing nothing under it, Williams concluded, for the shirt followed "the crease between her buttocks in its fall. No fault there."[24] Bryant had reported to Sara Bard Field that prior to her marriage, people in Portland had gossiped about her and Reed and predicted that Reed would not marry her. Bryant scorned the idea that marriage, as "that most diabolical law of all laws—could *purify* anything." On the contrary, according to Bryant, their relationship was "so free": "We don't interfere with each other at all, we just sort of supplement, and life is very lovely to us—we feel like children who will never grow up."[25] In their marriage, Reed and Bryant tried to adhere to their philosophical belief in free love, but in reality, each was tormented by the other's infidelities.[26]

Hutchins Hapgood observed at the time that the women of Greenwich Village "were not victimized in any way." Indeed, according to Hapgood, a man was at a disadvantage in relationships, for a woman was in full possession of what the man used to regard as his "rights." A man's "property" had been taken from him, "and no matter what his advanced ideas were, his deeply complex, instinctive, and traditional, nature often suffered." Hapgood revealed a noble-savage view of Village women, maintaining that the freedom there made the observer "see a little more clearly some of the typical relations between men and women" and "brought out into sharper relief the greater naturalness of woman's instinct." In the Village, woman "shows herself as indeed a part of nature. She remains herself, as does nature, in the recurring years, often with a new lover, leaving not even a memory of the old." Woman, in Hapgood's view, was like the rotation of crops, the force of gravity, the ebb and flow of the sea, with the "power and primitiveness of earth," and he warned of woe "to the more artificial male, dependent on the unconsciously remembered past and on willful desire to maintain the impossible structure of civilization" if he got in her way, for he would be opposing a force of nature.[27]

However, Floyd Dell had a completely different view of the New Woman in Greenwich Village; "girls" wanted to be married, in his view, not only for conventional reasons, but also because they felt guilty and miserable about sex relations outside of marriage. Women could justify their "sacrifice" of themselves for love if they pitied their lovers. Dell maintained that any "tenth-rate free verse poet could find a capable and efficient girl stenographer to type his manuscripts, buy his meals and his clothes, pay his rent and sleep with him; the maternal emotion sufficed instead of a marriage ceremony."[28]

Dell had observed the "victim" type of women Hapgood claimed did not exist in Greenwich Village; however, the writings and personal papers of the activists who defined the culture of that time and place testify to large egos. Although they made errors and were fools for love, they were women of purpose, not women who willingly would sacrifice their own goals for those of unproductive men of small talent. One feminist, Florence Wooston Seabury, presented a view of Village women in love that was far more light-hearted than the view of either Hapgood or Dell. In a mock anthropological study called "Marriage Customs and Taboo Among the Early Heterodites," Seabury asserted, "Three types of sex relationships may be observed, practiced by those who call themselves *monotonists, varietists,* and *resistants.*" According to Seabury's categories, "Most of the *monotonists* were mated young and by pressure of habit and circumstance have remained mated. The *varietists* have never been ceremonially mated but have preferred a succession of matings. The *resistants* have not mated at all."[29]

The atmosphere of Greenwich Village in the teens was robustly heterosexual, especially after the introduction of Freudian theory. However, Heterodoxy members included conventionally married heterosexual women, a number of whom kept their maiden names after they married, divorced women, "free lovers," and a large number of women who never married, including women who formed with other women loving partnerships that put the lie to Henry James's portrait of a doomed "Boston marriage" in an earlier generation of unsympathetically presented suffragists. "The Feminist does not find all of life in a love affair," Marie Jenney Howe wrote in 1914. "She is able to be happy though unmarried. She does not adjust her life according to the masculine standard."[30]

At a 1912 rally of the Woman Suffrage Party on the Lower East Side, Rose Schneiderman listened as an immigrant audience was addressed in Italian by a speaker with the unlikely name of Maud O'Farrel Swartz. Greatly impressed, Schneiderman introduced herself to Swartz after the rally and the two women began a twenty-five-year partnership. Swartz had been born in Ireland, one of fourteen children of an impoverished flour miller. Unable to care for his children, Swartz's father placed her in the care of nuns. Swartz grew up unhappily in German and French convents until, at the age of eighteen, she became a governess for an

English family living in Italy. Four years later she emigrated to New York. Her language skills made her a sought-after governess; however, the beautiful, auburn-haired young woman repeatedly was sexually harassed by her male employers. Finally, she found work as a proofreader in a printing plant for eight dollars a week. In 1905, at the age of twenty-six, she married a man named Lee Swartz. The marriage was unhappy but brief; Swartz left her husband but never divorced him and continued to carry his name.

Because their personal papers have been lost or destroyed, the degree of intimacy between the women cannot be known; however, they did share a personal and political partnership. Swartz, who never had become a union member, joined a union after meeting Schneiderman. In 1916, Swartz left her job to become secretary of the New York WTUL; after Schneiderman was elected president of the National WTUL the following year, the two women ran the organization together. Swartz's administrative skills and Schneiderman's skill in persuasion made the pair a powerful force in the national league and its New York branch. However, probably because of her conservative upbringing, Schneiderman needed to be regarded as respectable, and she put constraints on her relationship with Swartz. Although she and Swartz were involved for more than a quarter of a century, she never lived with her, choosing instead to keep a home with her mother and to involve herself with the lives of her siblings. She never would reveal anything more specific about her feelings for Swartz—than to say that "she was a wonderful companion."[31]

In 1917, Schneiderman's good friend and colleague Pauline Newman, assigned to organize a WTUL branch in Philadelphia, met and immediately was drawn to Frieda Miller, a Wisconsin miller's granddaughter and research assistant at Bryn Mawr College. Longing to do something more "socially beneficial than write an academic dissertation," Miller left her job at Bryn Mawr to become secretary of the new Philadelphia WTUL branch. Their working partnership paralleled that of Schneiderman and Swartz in New York: Newman was the organization's forceful spokesperson, and Miller served as administrator and policy developer. But Newman was far less restrained in her personal relationship with Miller, and the romance of shared struggle drew Miller to Newman. The two women lived together; however, Miller had reservations about committing herself to a woman and had been involved in an affair with a married man. In 1922, she became pregnant and the affair ended.

By this time the postwar reactionary fervor had made the work of the pair more difficult, and, tired of the constant struggle in Philadelphia, they resigned their posts and went to Europe to travel before attending the Third International Congress of Working Women in Vienna. Miller and Newman came to an agreement that they would continue to live together and raise the child as their own. After the baby was born, they returned to New York, rented an apartment in Greenwich Village, and lived as a family, explaining that the infant was an orphan Miller had adopted and had named Elisabeth. Although living forthrightly with Newman, Miller shared with Schneiderman enough need to be regarded as a respectable woman to keep the facts of her child's conception and paternity secret; the fiction was maintained, and Miller did not reveal to Elisabeth the circumstances of her birth until her daughter was seventeen years old. Miller and Newman remained partners for life.[32]

Another of the extraordinary partnerships between women was that of charter members of Heterodoxy Katherine Anthony and Elizabeth Irwin, who, in Inez Haynes Irwin's euphemistic phrase, "kept house together." Anthony, author of "a generous line of brilliant biographies," was, in Irwin's view, "a wise woman with a philosophic and delicious sense of humor." Elizabeth Irwin (no relation) she described as a "warm, earth type," and "an intelligent iconoclast." Elizabeth's "crowning achievement" was establishing The Little Red Schoolhouse. Begun as an experiment sponsored by the Public Education Association in 1916 at Public School 64 in Greenwich Village, the program emphasized what has become a given in modern pedagogy: the importance of the child's state of mind when that child comes to school. A proponent of what was labeled "progressive" education, Elizabeth Irwin claimed that the greatest enemy to growth and learning was fear, and that when the methods of a kind of teacher who "has inherited a certain technique" are examined in the light of mental hygiene, "they begin to look as the stock and the ducking stool looked to people who abandoned these instruments about one hundred years ago." Later the program was established at Public School 41.

In 1932, the program was discontinued because of opposition from conservative Villagers, supported by unfavorable testing results reported by the Board of Education and economic limitations imposed by the Depression. The program's supporters at first fought to maintain it, but then directed their fund-raising efforts to establishing a separate school, a goal that was reached in the fall of 1932 with the opening of the Little Red School House. The progressive method adopted at the school did not, Irwin insisted, mean that a child did not strengthen weak points, for each day a half hour was devoted to a child's weakest subject. The children went on trips and afterward made charts about the places they had visited. By reading the charts they had created, the children, Irwin explained, "build up a vocabulary that means something to them." Thus word recognition is made easy to them. Under the Little Red Schoolhouse system, when children begin to learn to read, "they read with a sweep." The eye does not settle slowly on each word, but sweeps across the page, "taking in the meaning of a whole sentence or a paragraph." The same real-world method of learning was applied to arithmetic.

In 1941, the Elizabeth Irwin High School was established and both institutions continue to thrive in Greenwich Village. Anthony and Irwin adopted several children, and, like Newman and Miller, lived together in the Village as a family.[33] However, their living arrangement, though recognized and, to a degree, accepted in the Village, was in their life- time still considered irregular and even deviant beyond the borders of that small community. In the 1942 edition of *Twentieth Century Authors*, Anthony writes only of herself, concluding her comments with the statement, "I live in New York in the winter and in summer at Gaylordsville, Conn." The editors list her works, provide critical commentary, and include the statement, "Miss Anthony is unmarried," a description that perforce masks the intense and full nature of the family she and Irwin together had established.[34]

Still another of these productive partnerships of activist women was that of Helen Marot and Caroline Pratt. Marot, as has been explained, was a WTUL activist, then a labor reporter for *The Masses*, and then editor of *The Dial* until she retired. Pratt was an educator of the progressive philosophy that inspired Irwin, but her vision of learning centered around the symbolic play of children. She was not concerned, as the educational philosopher Froebel was, with developing ideals and spiritual truths, nor, as was Maria Montessori, with developing rational order to the external world, such as isolating categories of causality, time, space, seriation, classification, and number. Pratt interpreted the play of children in a pragmatic way similar to Irwin's method: developing ideas that came out of children's experiences, putting the ideas to work, and judging them by the results. Play, she insisted, was work for children, and they must be allowed to work as hard as possible at their "jobs" before they begin learning from secondhand sources.[35]

Born in Fayetteville, New York in 1867, Pratt received her teacher training at Columbia Teachers College, but found the training inadequate when she began working at the Normal School for Girls in Philadelphia. She took courses at the University of Pennsylvania and correspondence courses from the University of Chicago. She spent a summer learning manual training at a school in Sweden, but largely through self-education and the students, whom she regarded as her teachers, she began developing her own approach to teaching. This approach began with the principle that children, like all workers, must see their labor end in a finished product. [36]

While in Philadelphia, she met Helen Marot and assisted her in an investigation of the custom tailoring trade. Later the two women moved to New York, Marot to work with the WTUL, and Pratt to work in a private school and in settlement houses—all the while holding on to a vision of a school as "a community of children who could in their own way, through the child activity which we misguidedly call play, reproduce this world and its functioning." In 1914, with financial support from a friend and WTUL member, Edna Smith, Pratt set up her school in a three-room apartment in Greenwich Village. This school had six students, much of whose education was gathered according to Pratt's vision—from visits to the local bakery, the neighborhood pushcarts, the docks, and the freight trains and from exploring the connections between commercial enterprises and the river traffic and freight trains that brought produce to the city. In 1921, the school, which had been growing rapidly, moved into its present buildings on West Twelfth Street, where, as the City and Country School, it has flourished ever since. Pratt knew and worked closely with Elizabeth Irwin when she was associated with the Bureau of Educational Experiments (later known as the Bank Street College of Education) and later when the Associated Experimental Schools of New York City united in struggle during the Depression years.

The partnership between Marot and Pratt continued until Marot's death in 1940, and when Pratt came to write *I Learn from Children* about eight years later, she dedicated the book to Marot, "whose spirit still lives."[37] The partnerships of Schneiderman and Swartz, of Newman and Miller in the labor movement, and of progressive educators Irwin and Pratt with Anthony and Marot demonstrate how important women were to one another, how they provided each other with the emotional support that enabled these visionaries to accomplish so much.

Of course, some of the activists had conventional monogamous marriages, complete with frustration and conflict. Hutchins Hapgood cited the marriage of Marie Jenney Howe and Frederic Howe as an instance in which "suffrage and feministic poison" were responsible for Marie's inability to recognize the depth of the love her husband had for her. Nevertheless, Hapgood found their marriage inspiring because "when the man and woman involved are of superior character, despite conflicting temperaments, emotional conflicts, and frustrations, they can keep the marriage alive."[38] A contrasting view of the Howe marriage was recorded by Mabel Dodge. Acknowledging that Howe, in his capacity as Immigration Commissioner, "made Ellis Island bearable for thousands where before it had been purgatorial" and indeed "tried to make it hospitable and a temporary home," he was in his own home

> one of those husbands who seem to be perpetually engrossed in thought and never on the spot. When he wrote his autobiography and his wife read it, she exclaimed, "Why Fred, were you never married?" He had neglected to mention this small fact.

In Mabel Dodge's view, it was Marie Howe's "loving wit [that] helped her accept the sterility of her domestic life."[39]

Another marriage that had its share of difficulties was that of Elsie Clews Parsons, who, after receiving her doctorate in Sociology from

Columbia University, was married in 1900 to Herbert Parsons, a Republican congressman from 1905 to 1911, and afterward a party leader. Her insistence on independence extended to nonconformity in behavior and dress; her habit of wearing sandals on Park Avenue, for example, caused her husband embarrassment, and her absences from home made him lonely. For her part, Elsie was hurt by Herbert's lack of interest in her ideas, experiences, and work. "From the very beginning of life together," she wrote in response to a complaining letter from him, "it was a great distress to find you indifferent to so much that mattered most to me." Her husband did not read her books nor wish to discuss them with her. The frequent absences from home he complained of were part of an attempt to keep herself from being miserable because of his companionship with another woman; likewise her own occasional flirtations, rare "as so few men are able to work up an interest in me or I in them," were also merely distractions. Despite their lack of compatibility in so many areas, Elsie had not been unhappy in "our *institutional* companionship," and regarded their relation as "the chief thing in the world to me."[40]

However, marriage to a man who respected an activist's autonomy could bring happiness. In 1900, Charlotte Perkins Gilman, whose attempts to fulfill the conventional ideal of wife and mother during her first marriage to the artist Walter Stetson caused her to lapse into mental illness, married her cousin, Houghton Gilman, and recorded in her autobiography that they "lived happy ever after." Gilman's husband, a not very successful attorney, was an easygoing, kind man who supported his wife's determination to "prove that a woman can love and work too" and was not threatened by her celebrity. With confidence in the love of a man who respected her, Gilman went on to produce *Concerning Children* in 1900; *The Home: Its Work and Influence* in 1903; *The Man-Made World: or Our Androcentric Culture* in 1911; numerous poems and nonfiction articles that appeared in feminist and mainstream periodicals; six novels; and seven volumes of her magazine, *The Forerunner,* containing articles, essays, and poetry. By the time of her death in 1935, she had countless lectures and the equivalent of twenty-two volumes of published work to her credit.[41]

Inez Haynes Irwin also had a happy second marriage. She met Will Irwin in 1904; in 1916, after her divorce from Rufus Gillmore, she married Irwin and lived until 1948 in the house they had bought on West Eleventh Street. Inez Irwin regarded the thirty-two years of marriage to her second husband as "one long adventure" overlaid with conversation. Yet her marriage was conventional in the sense that although Irwin published forty books—thirteen novels, ten books for children, five volumes of short stories, and twelve histories, including the history of the National Woman's Party—her love for her handsome, tall, broad-shouldered husband took precedence over her work. "Sometimes I think I might have been a better writer," she wrote in her memoir, "if I had not known Will Irwin. He was so good, so noble, at the same time so electric, so fascinating . . . that I was more interested in him than in my work."[42]

Although Irwin claimed to have succeeded in making a "complete feminist" of her husband, her role in the marriage was traditional in that she placed her husband's professional interests before her own. A contrasting model of a marriage based on the feminist ideal of complete equality between partners is revealed in the correspondence between Inez Milholland and her husband Eugen Boissevain. Milholland and Boissevain, an importer and native of Holland, had been introduced through a mutual friend and married in London in July 1913; they then traveled through Europe together until October when Inez returned to New York and her husband remained in Europe on business matters. It also appears, from the contents of the first section of the correspondence, which began on Inez's voyage home, that her parents and sister, Vida (nicknamed "Tub"), were in Europe with Eugen. Each day during the voyage back to New York, Inez wrote her husband one or two brief notes, containing gossip about her fellow passengers, concern for his health, accounts of her shipboard flirtations and conquests ("I played [tennis] marvelously, so that the whole ship gathered to watch. . . . We won amidst plaudits"), expressions of her love for him and references to their lovemaking ("what happy times we have had. I remember everything—our laughter, tears, quarrels, moments of contemplation and delight. . . . Whenever I think of you, I think of your head on my heart, your arms folded tight about me").

Inez expanded these short shipboard notes into a long letter she wrote from her office after she had returned to work, where, she reported to Eugen, her colleagues expressed a "crude disappointment" that she had not made a "world-stirring match." The major portion of this letter is an account of the men aboard the English ship, the *Olympic*, who were attracted to her. One "adorer," Sidney Brooks, the "well-informed, amiable, and unexciting" American correspondent for the London *Times*, did not "declare his passion," but followed her about "with admiring eyes." Another man, identified as Whitehorn, an English businessman, had fallen in love with her, but when he learned she was married, gallantly recovered and told Inez to tell her husband that he had "for a wife the most perfect possible specimen of womanhood." Although flattered by Whitehorn's praise, Milholland found "these old worshipful ways of men so unsatisfactory after our perfect comradeship."

Her most serious involvement was with a man identified as Beresford, a "clean-shaven, beautifully built Englishman" with whom Milholland came close to having an affair. When she confided to Beresford that if they made love, she would tell her husband everything, he was filled with admiration for "the marvelous thing" Inez and Eugen had between them. Nevertheless, Milholland's letters reveal an unsparing examination of her motives for her attraction to Beresford. At one point, Inez confides, she had decided to use diversions to keep from seeing him, but then realized that was an unsatisfactory solution because it felt artificial; restraining her feelings only made her more eager for something forbidden and she was likely to exaggerate its importance. Milholland wrote her husband that one reason she wanted to make love to Beresford was her desire to tell her husband "the worst." The joy of knowing that he knew everything ("the trust it evidenced was a joy all the time") made her exultant. She demanded the same honesty from Eugen, inquiring at one point about his "best beloved." "You thought I didn't know about that, did you? Well, I do. Have known about it all along—so don't try to keep anything from me in the future—see?"

She saw Beresford several times in New York, and they became more friendly than infatuated; besides, Inez declared, she had "too big a role to play in the life of this nation's life" to waste time in "frivelling or flirting." Yet Inez, between honeymoon and wifehood, was flattered by the attention of a "train of fascinated Englishmen" who accounted for the "immediate and overwhelming success" she had never had before. This long letter reveals the complex struggle to create a feminist identity. Milholland's frankness about her numerous admirers is a covert, yet conventional, challenge to Eugen: he must love her because other men, including a man to whom she is attracted, find her desirable. Yet, she despises the triviality of flirtation as a means to establish her independence. She holds out to Eugen a vision of the new marriage they can create together; she writes of a friend who is happy for her because she "has found someone who is really her equal," and of another friend she loves because, unlike her colleagues, he loves Eugen and has described Inez and Eugen as "a marvelously matched" couple, a "great and noble thing," and has prophesied they "will start a new race and a new social order in America." Inez assures her husband that "New York shall follow us."[43]

While Milholland's letters to her husband are filled with fascinating self-disclosure and self-analysis, much else was going on in her life during the autumn of 1913. In addition to her legal work, she was writing articles for newspapers and magazines; writing and delivering speeches; going to meetings; renting and furnishing an apartment at 247 Fifth Avenue ("I had no idea housekeeping meant getting so many things"); and attending the theater and parties with a wide circle of friends that included the William Randolph Hearsts and Alva Belmont, as well as the newly elected mayor, John Mitchel, with whom she "turkey-trotted" all night at the Knickerbocker Hotel during his victory party over the Tammany candidate. Because her letters to Eugen are filled with her social activities and references to past and future lovemaking, one does not realize the extent of her pro bono legal work and political activism—on behalf of prisoners and prison reform and against capital punishment and racism—until one reads the documents in the latter part of the collection. Of course, Milholland's strong ego is always present in her letters, but at the end of this period of correspondence, Milholland's boastfulness flags and her love for her husband resounds. She reports to him her pleasure in the messages from her parents praising him and in the desire of friends to meet the man about whom they have heard so many good things. This section of letters closes with Milholland expressing her deep desire to begin their marriage:

I adore you. . . . I depend on you so. I want your judgment in every
way. I trust you, I respect you, I need you, I worship you. . . . Come
to me soon. Nannie can't wait for you much longer. And we have
such a pretty home all ready for you.[44]

In the spring of 1915, Milholland went to Italy under assignment from
a Canadian newspaper, entered the war zone as correspondent, and
wrote a series of articles with a pacifist viewpoint that caused her to be
declared persona non grata by the Italian government.[45] Her letters to
her husband in this period were infrequent, but one from Brescia
including comments about male attention again produces a boastfulness; she reports to Eugen that at a dinner given by journalists, she and
another woman "were the whole cheese" and that he could not
imagine "the fun and excitement of being the only women."[46] Eugen's
letters to Inez of May and early June correspond with Floyd Dell's
description of him as the "adventurous man of business" with a
"romantic zest."[47] He boasts that the lift boys in his Broadway office
building are "wildly excited" about her and that his business partner
declared, "Got, she is the greatest woman dot effer wass." He was
proud, as Inez was, that people were beginning to understand something of their love, and thus, after "cheap jokes about marriage," they
had an opportunity to know "what a union can be under some
conditions." Eugen also had matured through their love; he writes of
the time in 1913 when he was waiting to return to the United States
and thought he knew what love was. He had thought of himself as "an
old warrior" in the game of love; in the one and one half years since,
his love had become "greater, stronger, finer, more passionate, and
(strange to say) more sensual," as different from his earlier love as "a
violin solo is to the mighty burst of harmony of the whole orchestra."
He confides to Inez his money-making plans, one of which includes
getting orders for goods from the Romanian government—but along
with expressing his concern about making money, he expresses the
wish that he not worry his "gallant sweetheart" with his propositions.

He also sends Inez lively gossip about her family and friends. He
reports receiving a tempting offer from Max Eastman to go with him
to Europe for six weeks, but deciding to build up his business instead
and get things for "Nannie" when she returns. After accompanying

Max to one of the tumultuous *Masses* meetings he reports that Art Young likes Inez a lot. He writes that Inez's sister, Vida ("Tub"), has often been in the company of Frederic Howe, causing their worrying mother to lament that the relationship with Howe could spoil Vida's "prospects" for marriage. He writes that Vida is giving her mother "some foundation" for her "mid-Victorian talk," which, as he listened to it, made him wonder at how little her parents had interfered with her and "think with pride of how different my girl managed her affairs to Vida." He is pleased that her mother has begun to understand how much he loves Inez, but of her father—who had begun, after a cabled report from her had appeared in the *World Tribune,* to approve of Inez's Italian venture—he writes that "his paternal, schoolmaster, clergyman attitude towards you makes me sick." At the end of May, he saw Max Eastman off to Europe and wanted very much to go with him, but thought it was better to stay at home, fight their debts, and "wait for Nannie to come home from the wars."[48]

However, in mid-June, Eugen's romantic zest was considerably dampened when he received a letter from Inez informing him that she had been unfaithful to him. His letter to Inez begins, "I got at last a letter from you—and so you have a new lover." Eugen struggled to maintain the ideal of the "new man," yet, as the letter reveals, was too much in pain to fulfill his aspiration to be liberated.

> I know I'll understand all when you tell me. When you are in my arms, at rest, home. Your letter was incoherent. I only know how passionate you were and that he spent several nights with you. The picture of you undressing, preparing your body for this strange man, opening the door for him, taking him in your arms, he entwining his limbs around you, and you telling him that you love him, giving yourself, throbbing in passionate abandon, that picture torments me, and clouds my vision. It isn't jealousy. For jealousy is bitter & I feel tender and sweet. I only want to understand and I want to get out of this numb suffering, this coldness, and Nannie, I feel so utterly alone. I'm trying to have an affair, like you have. Someone you know, and whom you admire (more than I used to do, in fact), has told me she loves and wants me to live with her. So far I cannot understand how I can take her naked body in my

arms. I like her and she is very pretty. But I cannot do it. . . . If I am able to do it, I fear it means that my love for you would be ending. At present I feel as if I would do anything to get rid of my aching and loneliness. Maybe I'm just jealous of you that you can do it & I cannot.[49]

Finally, yielding to hurt pride and desperate jealousy, he urges her to cable him whether she was sure of her love for him, or whether she had taken another lover and was "giving one of these men a baby." But the next day, in better spirits—or perhaps less under the influence of the spirits he had drunk the night before—Eugen wrote again, informing Inez of his disappointment that Crystal Eastman and her husband, Wallace Benedict—"Bennie"—were divorcing, proving that perfect love was difficult. "Let us show the world," he urges, "what complete love is. You are a naughty little hussy, but you are . . . still clear-brained and rather wonderful in your own dirty way. And although you do not deserve the love of a good man, still you've got it. It's up to us to show what love can be." Other letters followed, in which Eugen admitted that he had been jealous, but he could not be jealous any longer, for a "physical fascination" with another man could not replace the happiness of sharing everything with him; Eugen was confident that no man could take Inez away from "the lover you have made happy" and "given the best years he has known."[50]

The tone of most of Inez's letters to her husband in this period are gloomy because the spirit of war made "happiness seem sinful and dead in the world." She wondered how it was possible ever to leave Eugen and longed again for the splendid relationship they had together. Milholland was uncharacteristically filled with self-doubt and fear, blaming herself for not proving to the world that she was its equal yet reassuring herself that "if I can do something valuable and worthwhile I think I shall find peace, perhaps—and faith again." On her way home, she wrote more cheerfully, "Oh we have so much in store for us and I'll bring you a baby when I get home."[51] Milholland was torn between love for her husband and the need to meet the heroic vision of herself she wished to present to the world—to be the Amazon that Max Eastman had named her in a poem he wrote during their short engagement. Because of this conflict, she was home for only a brief time before she was again traveling. She set off for Europe in December on Henry Ford's "Peace Ship," but found the experience futile; the women among whom she traveled never asked for her opinions, which when offered were not accepted, although "in the end they inevitably come to the thing I have been advocating in the beginning." Milholland found the waste of time and energy caused by unnecessary obstacles presented by the women of the Peace Ship "appalling," and she left the group to return home in January 1916.[52]

Inez and Eugen's love achieved a maturity and depth that is revealed in the letters they wrote to each other in the spring of 1916, when Eugen was on a trip to New Orleans, Los Angeles, and San Francisco to develop clients for his business. During these months, Inez searched for a house to rent for the summer in the area near her parents' home in Harmon, New York. The plan was never realized, but Inez's search for a "love nest" led to reflections on her three-year marriage. "I have a sense of freedom that I have never had before when you and I have parted before," Inez exulted,

> I am so supremely happy in our love. I keep picturing happy summer scenes in the grass and in the pretty places I visited today. With you, oh, I want to have such a wonderful spring. Having you in the house will make it additionally exciting. I shall feel as if I were making a rendezvous all the time with you; not being together just by being married but because we want to.

Again, Inez wrote of her desire for a child that she so often had expressed before. Referring to friends, a couple who were expecting a baby, Inez vowed, "We'll beat 'em yet, won't we?" Of their marriage she wrote, "I read everything I can lay hands on about married people, and compare them to us—and I swear our love must always be full of color. We must study, of course, how to keep it warm and thrilling and take pains."[53]

Eugen's letters to Inez are, as always, full of expressions of love. From New Orleans he writes, "You are my wise, wise wife, and my laughing loony bachante! . . . I prefer to think of you as my bedfellow, rather than my goddess! but Venus was a goddess, and not a Comstockian goddess at that." When the plan for a summer house fell through, he writes that he didn't "care a hoot in hell about the house"; "I want you, Nannie, and all the rest is of no interest to me." From Los Angeles he writes that it was "wonderfully smart" of Inez to scent her letters, for the smell intoxicated him; her letter containing her reflections on their marriage thrilled him; "you have," he replied, "the power to drive my blood crazy with passionate love, just by saying I love you." When she wrote of her plans to go on the suffrage speaking tour in the western states, he encouraged her to go and hoped he would be able to send money: "I hate and loath the idea of you not doing what you want to do on account of money. It makes me feel like one bad cent." He also saw the western trip as an opportunity for them to meet so that he could take her to some of the places he had visited, especially Venice, California with its beautiful beach on the Pacific, and "lots of healthy, fit, and fine-figured young people."

He wrote of his pleasure about her involvement with "Negro cases" and of his agreement with the judge who told her she would be a good trial lawyer. However, the major focus of his correspondence is a desire to crown his efforts with significant business success. The many contacts he has made and agreements to do business have made him exultant that he and Inez are "climbing out of their troubles." "Eugen is a rotten money provider, so far," he confessed, blaming himself for not having given Inez anything else but "love and a lot of it." "But soon," he promised, "I'll give you more than that, and take your worries away—the worries which are fetters to my high, soaring Inez Milholland."[54]

The confident expectation that his business finally was becoming successful no doubt quieted the concern aroused by a letter from Inez's mother expressing her fear that Eugen was not providing a proper environment for her daughter nor "the things she never missed until she had to do without." "You have a glorious woman," Mrs. Milholland gratuitously reminded Eugen, who needs a proper environment to make her a "complete success." Mrs. Milholland promised to do her part, but she could not bear for her daughter to be poor and warned Eugen, "I must *be sure you* [sic] are in deadly earnest."[55]

However, Inez did not seem troubled by financial worries, although it seems from the accounts of household expenses and concerns about payments that she was the principal breadwinner. Her last letters to Eugen, written while she was on a suffrage tour in the western states held in connection with the presidential candidacy of Republican Charles Evans Hughes, include a query about the absence of any mention of business affairs in his letters. She instructs him not to keep back unpleasant facts, reminding him, "Really, I'm afraid of nothing. I adore you." Clearly, Inez Milholland was perfectly mated. Eugen was a man of progressive sympathies; his letters reveal his approval of Inez's work on behalf of blacks accused of crimes and his detestation of anti-semitism and racism. However, his most important qualities with respect to his sympathetic championing of his wife were his appreciation of her splendor, his support for her activism, and his willingness to struggle with painful emotions in order to strive for an ideal of unselfish love. He admired his wife and was proud of her. (Eugen Boissevain's attraction to outstanding women resulted in his marriage, some years after Milholland's death, to Edna St. Vincent Millay. After Millay's death, the correspondence passed to her sister, Norma, from whom it was purchased by the Schlesinger Library.) But even Eugen's patience had limits. He had encouraged her to go on the tour that ended with her unexpected death, but in April he wrote, "Now don't you dare leave New York when I return. Not for suffrage, nor for peace, nor for criminals."[56]

Inez had considered, then decided not to go on the suffrage tour, for she was just "getting into the running in law" and did not want to come back to "bills, bills, bills, with nothing to show" for her labor. However, her father, who was as ambitious for his daughter as her mother was, became furious when she refused to go because he saw the tour as an opportunity for her to become a national figure.[57] In contrast to this reaction, Eugen had written that he was glad Inez had decided to stay in New York, for there would be other opportunities; a "personality like yours cannot be forgotten, and it wants but a little to make it burst out nationwide."[58]

In October, Inez changed her mind again, and with her sister, Vida, she set out on the journey that would end with her death. She was ill even before she left New York, suffering weakness, heart palpitations, aches, and pains. She saw doctors on at least three occasions, all of whom diagnosed her illness as due to "poison" draining into her system from her tonsils and advised her to have an operation. She was also extremely anemic, but, on each of these visits to doctors, insisted on a gynecological examination to assure herself that she was capable of conceiving the child she wanted so much to bear. She was assured on this issue but the various medications prescribed (including arsenic and strychnine), while helpful at times, did not stop her throat from hurting or abate her weakness. She was in almost constant pain but kept up the hectic "pack-and-go" pace of the tour. Proud of her body, an excellent athlete, Milholland refused to recognize the precarious state of her health, and thought all her ills would be remedied through a tonsillectomy during a Christmas visit to Holland. The doctors who examined Milholland failed to realize that she was suffering from aplastic anemia—her bone marrow was failing to produce the components of blood cells. If recognized in time, the ailment might have responded to the transfusions that came too late to save her.

Her letters to Eugen about her experiences during this time are as full of colorful details as were her letters from New York just three years earlier. Of the Republican sponsors of the tour, she observed, "They are a rather 19th Century lot. Hopeless—But give us a vote and we'll bounce 'em." In Pocatello, Idaho, she attended a revival and reported to Eugen that it was worse than listening to the evangelist Billy Sunday and made her despair of American spirituality. "These people," she declared, "are desexualized . . . and the best among 'em take to drink, and the worst to revivals." She reported warm receptions for the suffrage speakers in Idaho, Wyoming, Oregon, and Washington, and people who came to meetings or thronged the railway stations during stops often demanded that Inez speak to them. When she was not ill, she was pleased by her success, and with her characteristic confidence, she claimed, "Oh, I could carry any state if only I had time." The letters are full, as always, with outpourings of love for her husband; the last letter closes, "I cannot live without you."[59]

Milholland collapsed in Los Angeles—a city she had been looking forward to visiting because her husband had been there—and died on November 25. Of the many expressions of hope for her recovery that poured into the hospital while Milholland was dying, one of the most poignant was from William M. Sealy, a Sing Sing prison inmate, whom

Milholland had represented in the appeals process. Sealy assured Inez that he had not forgotten her and her "loving sister Vida who payed [sic] us a visit and sang for us in our Chapel." He wished, he wrote, that he could send flowers.[60]

The many tributes to Milholland after her death included one from the NAACP expressing a "sense of irrepressible loss" over the death of one of the "apostles of equality."[61] One of the cases that engaged Milholland intensely during the last months of her life concerned Charles Stielow, an upstate farm laborer of limited intelligence who had been convicted of murder and sentenced to die in the electric chair. The papers in Milholland's collection reveal the effort she made to unearth evidence that Stielow had been pressured by police into confessing to the crime; she lobbied hard for Stielow, writing letters to legislators and even to the wife of the pro–death penalty governor, Charles Whitman. The case was on Milholland's mind often when she was on the western tour; she died before Governor Whitman commuted Stielow's sentence to life imprisonment.[62]

The letters of condolence to Eugen include poignant notes from Crystal Eastman. One invited him to come to her Waverly Place home "any time for meals and any other time—without sending word, the way Max does," and wrote of her desire to hold a service where friends of Inez could pay tribute to her. The second letter expressed gladness that Max would be with Eugen and included a postscript referring to Eugen's possible resentment over the rift between Crystal and Inez: "If you don't want to see me at all—just want Max—I'll absolutely understand. I understand it all."

Years after Milholland's death Max Eastman presented a disillusioned view of Milholland, writing that, for all her radical opinions, she lived a "function-attending, opera-going rich girl's life," and that her home was always full of a succession of men who included millionaires, bounders, labor fakers, and the ilk. Eastman apparently had forgotten the tribute he had paid, during a visit Inez and Eugen had made in the summer of 1915, to the success of their marriage.[63] Eastman's posthumous judgment was unfair; the correspondence and personal papers of Inez Milholland reveal her dedication to her work on behalf of the causes that engaged her. She was an extraordinary woman, a stellar figure before she had entered her thirties. Her papers leave the reader without doubt that her confidence in herself was merited, and that the faith her parents and husband had that she would become a national leader would, had she lived, been realized.

CHAPTER 9

Arts and Letters

INEVITABLY, SO MANY TALENTED WOMEN living through such interesting times left their legacy in creative expression. One notable example of this achievement was the creation of the Provincetown Playhouse, begun as a lark by Mary Heaton Vorse, Susan Glaspell, and their husbands and friends during the summer of 1915. One evening, as Vorse and her husband, Joe O'Brien, her friend Neith Boyce, the novelist, and her husband Hutchins Hapgood, and Susan Glaspell and her husband George Cram—"Jig"—Cook, together with the writer Wilbur Daniel Steele and his wife, were sitting around a driftwood fire on the beach, Cook attacked the widespread commercialism of the American theater; the trivial quality of such Broadway hits as *Peg o' My Heart* would never attract the sophisticated Villagers, nor could the Villagers, Cook believed, create works that would be acceptable to a Broadway audience. Even a new little theater in the Village had rejected *Suppressed Desires*, a play Cook and Glaspell had written that satirized Freudianism. Boyce had written a play called *Constancy* that spoofed the love affair of John Reed and Mabel Dodge.

The group's complaining was followed by a mutual agreement to put on the plays themselves, and so they presented the two plays, first in the Hapgood home and later, in response to a demand from Provincetown visitors, in the vacant fish house on the wharf Vorse owned. The enthusiastic audience brought chairs from home and came down through a downpour to the lantern-lighted wharf to enjoy the performances. For Vorse, the fun and success of the Provincetown Players was a respite from witnessing industrial strife and the futility of efforts to stop an inevitable war. It was also a peaceful prelude to another personal tragedy, for her husband Joe became ill and died in October.[1]

Mabel Dodge was in Provincetown that summer, recovering from her involvement with John Reed through a new relationship with Maurice Sterne, whom she married the following year. Hutchins Hapgood, who had been her good friend but was no longer part of the center of her world, ascribed to Dodge "a great power for good and evil in the way of subtle propaganda." After surrounding herself with a new group of followers, Hapgood recalled, Dodge tried to instill her little group with "dislike and suspicion for all those outside the group." The target of her hostility was Mary Heaton Vorse, who became "quite a witch" to the members of the Dodge group. Hapgood approached each of the members of the Vorse group, told them what he thought "was subtly going on," and the "spell was broken."[2]

In the summer of 1916, Vorse returned to Provincetown and the group, expanded to include Louise Bryant and John Reed, planned a new season. The first bill reprised *Suppressed Desires* and introduced Boyce's *Winter's Night* and Reed's *Freedom*. Searching for new material, Glaspell met the anarchist Terry Carlin on Provincetown's main drag, Commercial Street, and asked him if he had any plays to read to them. He said he did not, but his roommate, Eugene O'Neill did. O'Neill came to Glaspell's home that evening and read his one-acter *Bound East for Cardiff*, based on his experience as a seaman. Vorse recalled that no one who heard that play reading would forget it, nor would they forget Glaspell's reading of a one-act play, *Trifles*, about the conspiracy of two farm wives to suppress evidence of the murder by another woman of her abusive husband. The O'Neill play went into immediate rehearsal, sharing billing with Wilbur Steele's *Not Smart* and Louise Bryant's *The Game*.

In July, Vorse left the group in response to Elizabeth Gurley Flynn's letter to join her on the Mesabi Range,[3] but the group remained to bring to fruition a project that all of Provincetown was interested in—a project that, Hutchins Hapgood recalled, "was really something of a Renaissance." It lifted the pall hanging over them and gave them hope.[4] Susan Glaspell marked the summer of 1916 as a splendid season: "We swam from the wharf as well as acted there; we would lie on the beach and talk about plays—every one writing, or acting, or producing. Life was all of a piece, work not separated from play."[5] Another O'Neill play went into rehearsal, and the success of his plays inspired the group, led by Jig Cook, to bring the plays to New York. With raised donations, they found a stable on MacDougal Street, right next to Polly Holladay's restaurant. Converting the building into a theater required much money, most of it raised by John Reed.

The first bill, O'Neill's *Bound East for Cardiff,* Bryant's *The Game,* and a farce by Floyd Dell called *King Arthur's Socks,* went into rehearsal in November.[6] The production of O'Neill's *The Emperor Jones* at the Provincetown Playhouse put the theater "on the map." Inevitably Broadway beckoned; Glaspell understood and sympathized with the ambition of the players and playwrights who wished to answer the call, but her husband saw success as evidence of spiritual failure and refused to join in "cashing in" on a dream. Glaspell became caught up in Cook's dream of living in the ancient classical past and went with him to Greece in 1922.[7] However, she continued to write plays, one of which, *Alison's House,* based on the life of Emily Dickinson, won the Pulitzer Prize in 1931.

The happy experience of the Provincetown Players, which launched Glaspell's playwriting career, was not representative of the prodigious amount of writing on very serious matters by women activists. Lack of money and staff—or, as in the case of Margaret Sanger and Emma Goldman, an abundance of government repression—shortened the life of publications, but the positions on questions of injustice were daringly ahead of their time. For example, *Four Lights,* the newsletter of the New York Woman's Peace Party, editorialized in 1917 against one of the worst wartime atrocities in this country: the race riot in East St. Louis, in which scores of black people were beaten and killed:

> Six weeks have passed since the East St. Louis riots and no public word of rebuke, no demand for the punishment of the offenders, has come from our Chief Executive. These American Negroes have died under more horrible conditions than any noncombatants who were sunk by German submarines. But to our President their death does not merit consideration.

Our young men who don their khaki are thus taught that, as they go out to battle under the flag of the United States, they may outdo Belgian atrocities without rebuke if their enemy be of a darker race. And those who guard our land at home have learned that black men and women and little children may safely be mutilated and shot and burned while they stand idly by.[8]

The pathbreakers who singlehandedly and consistently produced philosophical essays were, of course, Emma Goldman and Charlotte Perkins Gilman, each of whom published a monthly periodical—Goldman with assistance from others, Gilman singlehandedly—for years. Others also found ways to interpret and express their experiences and ideas; for example, Mary Heaton Vorse would be so moved by the 1912 Lowell textile workers' strike that she made a vow—one that she kept—to devote the rest of her life to write of the workers' cause. Suffragists and war opponents created publications to communicate their ideas. Still other women contributed poetry, fiction, and essays—usually on a one-time basis, but occasionally with regularity—to the era's most flamboyant radical magazine, The Masses. From March 1906 until June 1917, when the government suppressed it, Emma Goldman published Mother Earth, which she filled with taboo-breaking essays; three of these reflecting Goldman's views on women—"The Traffic in Women," "Marriage and Love," and "Woman Suffrage"—were included in a collection, Anarchism and Other Essays, she published in 1911.[9]

In "The Traffic in Women," Goldman cited women's economic and social exploitation as the cause of prostitution, for women were not valued for the merit of their work, but only for their sex; therefore it was only inevitable that they should pay with sexual favors for their right to exist. In New York, she pointed out, one out of every ten women worked in a factory, earning $6 per week for forty-eight to sixty hours of work, but the majority of these women were out of work for months, leaving them with an average annual wage of $280. Was it a wonder, she asked, "that prostitution and the white slave trade have become such dominant factors?"

Goldman attacked the double standard as a contributing factor to prostitution: "Society considers the sex experiences of a man as attributes of his general development, while similar experiences in the life of a woman are looked upon as a terrible calamity, a loss of honor and of all that is good and noble in a human being." It was inevitable, Goldman observed, that a young woman forced to work for long hours in factories, lacking home and comfort, would seek relief in a sexual relationship, and then, having strayed from what she believed to be the traditional path of virtue, would think "herself a complete outcast, with the doors of society closed in her face." Goldman urged that prostitution be recognized as a product of social conditions, that hypocrisy be swept away, and that more humane treatment of prostitutes be adopted.[10]

"Marriage and love have nothing in common," Goldman proclaimed in "Marriage and Love"; and while in some cases love continued in married life, Goldman maintained, it did so in spite of marriage. Goldman viewed marriage as primarily an economic arrangement, differing from the ordinary life insurance agreement only in that it is more binding and exacting. If a woman's premium is her husband, she pays for it, according to Goldman, "with her name, her privacy, her self-respect, her very life, 'until death doth part.'" Yet marriage was a failure, Goldman asserted, for "every twelfth marriage ends in divorce."

Goldman decried the prevailing contradiction that it was "indecent and filthy for a respectable girl to know anything of the marital relation," but that once the marriage vow was spoken, something that formerly had been filthy now must be considered sacred. Of course, then a woman was "shocked, repelled, outraged . . . by the most natural and healthy instinct, sex." Moreover, she then must look upon housework as her career, and, Goldman asserted, it mattered not whether the husband was a brute or a darling, for after marriage a woman "moves about in his [sic] home, year after year, until her aspect of life and human affairs becomes as flat, narrow, and drab as her surroundings." Thus, Goldman concluded, marriage made a parasite of woman, incapacitating her for life's struggle and paralyzing her imagination. Goldman looked forward to a time when men and women would unite in "oneness," not that "poor little State and Church–begotten weed, marriage."

"Free love?" she queried rhetorically and defiantly:

As if love were anything but free! Man has bought brains, but all the millions in the world have failed to buy love. . . . Man has chained and fettered the spirit, but he has been utterly helpless before love. High on a throne, with all the splendor and pomp his gold can command, man is yet poor and desolate, if love passes him by. And if it stays, love has the magic power to make of a beggar a king.[11]

In "Woman Suffrage," Goldman echoed Charlotte Perkins Gilman's description of the home as an oppressive institution. Gilman claimed that everything that a woman has must come to her through a small gold ring; Goldman called the home "a modern prison with golden bars." But Gilman proposed a range of solutions to free women from their chattel condition; Goldman focused on suffrage, taking on the argument of the most conservative suffragists that suffrage need not change their status as homemakers, wives, and mothers. Goldman scorned this view of suffrage because it only served to strengthen "the omnipotence of the very Gods that woman has served from time immemorial." Goldman surveyed the countries in the world and the states in America where women had suffrage and concluded that women's right to vote had not significantly changed conditions, especially for poor women, for women still did not receive equal pay for equal work. Although she acknowledged that suffrage was no longer "a parlor affair" detached from people's economic needs, she nevertheless continued to maintain a grudge against Susan B. Anthony for urging women to be strikebreakers during the 1869 printers' strike. She approved of the effort on behalf of working women by the Women's Trade Union League, but dismissed the league members as a small minority among the idly rich suffragists. Goldman valued class before gender; she viewed the middle-class woman, in "her exalted conceit," as being unable to see how enslaved she was—not so much by man as by her own silly notions and traditions. Suffrage was not the path to liberation, according to Goldman; woman's "development, her freedom, her independence, must come from and through herself." A woman must assert herself as a "personality" rather than a "sex commodity"; she must refuse to give the right over her body to anyone; and she must refuse to bear children unless she wants them. Goldman's formula for women's empowerment reveals how removed she was from the condition of the women she spoke of with such compassion.[12]

At the time Emma Goldman's ideas were attracting attention, Charlotte Perkins Gilman, far friendlier to women, found that the market for what she had to say was growing smaller. However, still being driven to produce manuscripts faster than she could sell them, she began in November 1909, a monthly magazine, *The Forerunner*, publishing in each issue sections of serialized novels, short stories, poems, articles, reviews, and essays, all of her own writing and all dealing with the position of women and the need for widespread social change. The magazine never drew the 3,000 dollar-a-year subscribers Gilman needed to sustain it, and after supporting it by doing extra writing and lecturing, Gilman reluctantly stopped publishing it.[13]

Inez Haynes Irwin was not impressed by her poetry or fiction, but her editorials, she believed, "voiced the true Charlotte."[14] In one of her characteristically spirited essays, part of a series of essays titled "Our Androcentric Culture: or the Man-Made World," Gilman took on "Masculine Literature" in the March 1910 issue, asking what "fiction has to offer concerning mother-love, or, for that matter, father love, as compared to this vast volume of excitement about lover-love," a love that lasted only for two or three years in life. Unfortunately, women new to the field of fiction seemed to Gilman to follow masculine canons because all the canons were masculine. *Uncle Tom's Cabin*, she reminded her readers, appealed to the entire world, "but if anybody fell in love and married in it, they have been forgotten." The art of the future was at that very moment being reborn, Gilman asserted, and the humanizing of women opened up five distinctly fresh fields of fiction. One subject was the young woman who is being called upon to give up her career for marriage; a second was the middle-aged woman who wants not more love but more business; a third was concerned with the interrelation of women with women; a fourth dealt with the interaction between grown children and their parents; and a fifth was the full-grown woman who confronts the demands of love with the high standards of conscious motherhood.[15]

In another essay critical of "Androcracy," Gilman asserted that suffrage was necessary, first, because "a dependent and servile woman-hood is an immovable obstacle to race development," and second, "because the major defects of our civilization are clearly traceable to the degradation of the female and the unbalanced predominance of the male," which are responsible for "that wholly masculine phenomenon—war."[16] Gilman, who had begun her magazine at the age of fifty, made one of the early arguments against what has become known as "ageism" by insisting that fifty is the age when woman's "humanhood" begins, and that women of that age could constitute a valuable class of workers—distributing or selling goods, keeping shops or restaurants. They could learn new sciences and languages and enjoy the thirty years remaining to them.[17]

Gilman was a giant, achieving an intellectual leadership in her era that has only begun to be appreciated since the "second wave" of feminism. However, writing that expresses a wider range of women's experiences in this period can be found in *The Masses,* a publication so thoroughly associated with its editors—Max Eastman, Floyd Dell, and John Reed—that the volume of contributions by women only recently has begun to be acknowledged and appreciated.

The earlier version of *The Masses* had suspended publication when its editor and publisher, Piet Vlag, no longer could find money to support it; his proposal to merge the magazine with Josephine Conger-Kaneko's *Progressive Woman* was rejected by the magazine's collective because they wanted their publication to emulate sophisticated European publications like *Simplicissimus, Jugend,* or *Gil Blas,* not a socialist feminist magazine.[18] Art Young's counter-proposal was to invite Max Eastman, a Columbia University instructor and graduate student whose principal credential for the position was that he had organized the Men's League for Women's Suffrage in New York. The group agreed, and an invitation was sent to Eastman: "You are elected editor of *The Masses.* No pay."[19]

Under Eastman's leadership, the magazine no longer published the didactic essays by party activists examining the flaws of the capitalistic system and offering conventional socialist solutions to problems; Eastman pledged to readers in the December 1912 issue that henceforth *The Masses* would be a *"popular* Socialist magazine of pictures and lively writing."[20] Poetry, which Eastman introduced into *The Masses,* was an area in which women became significant contributors. Between December 1912, when Max Eastman became editor,

and November-December 1917, when the last issue was published,
over ninety women—the number is difficult to determine because
poems were published anonymously or simply with the author's
initials—contributed poems to *The Masses*. Their poems made a slow
beginning: only one poem by a woman appeared in January 1913; the
February, March, April, and May issues had no poems by women (but
usually one, three, or five poems by men); thereafter, none, one, or at
most, two poems by women appeared in each issue until 1916, when
in some issues three, five, six or even ten poems by women were
published, on a par with or exceeding the number of poems by men.
By 1917 most of the poems were by women; an issue might have five,
seven, or even twelve poems by women (the final November-December issue had twenty-one)—clustered in narrow columns under the
heading, "Orchids and Hollyhocks."

The poetry includes contributions from women who were known
then or later for poetry or other kinds of writing. The February 1915
issue included a poem by Freda Kirchwey—who later became editor of
The Nation—entitled "To A Soapbox Orator," about the futility of
trying to influence pleasure-seeking Saturday night crowds ("What
does it matter? What do we care / Your words come hot and urgent and
wise, / But—it's Saturday night—and a dime to spare").[21] The January
1916 *Masses* contained "Joe," a tribute by Susan Glaspell to Joe
O'Brien, Mary Heaton Vorse's husband, who had died of cancer in
October 1915 (". . . I want to sit over a drink with you and talk about
the I. W. W. and the damned magazines and the Germans . . .").[22] Two
early poems by the poet, novelist, and translator of Russian literature
Babette Deutsch were published: "Ironic," a poem urging the "fireless
poor" to strike, in the June 1917 issue,[23] and "Extra," about the impact
of war news on American domestic tranquillity, in the November-
December issue of the same year.[24]

Amy Lowell's career was well established when two of her poems
were published—"The Poem" in the April 1916 issue ("It is only a
little twig / With a green bud at the end / But if you plant it / And
water it / And set it where the sun will be above / It will grow into a
tall bush . . . "),[25] and "The Grocery" in the June 1916 issue. "The
Grocery" is a long poem mostly in dialogue between Alice, the
daughter of a grocery owner, and Leroy, a local ne'er-do-well she

once loved. Still without means or prospects, Leroy tries to dissuade Alice from her plan to leave their small New England town to go to Boston; he wants her to make up, telling her she "ain't been half so kind to me / As lots of fellers' girls." Alice responds that his own words have killed her love for him; telling him, "you've took away my home, I hate the sight o' the place," she leaves him, slamming the door as she departs.[26]

However, the careers in poetry or other kinds of writing for most women began and ended with *The Masses*. The majority of them published a single poem in the magazine; a smaller number published from two to four poems. Those who can be considered regular contributors are Louise Bryant, Sarah N. Cleghorn, Mary Carolyn Davies, Lydia Gibson, Helen Hoyt, Florence Ripley Martin, Jean Starr Untermeyer, and Elizabeth Waddell, each of whom published from five to twelve poems, except for Gibson, who published twenty-seven. The poems were usually about love, nature, and family life—themes also prevalent in poetry by men. But that a significant number are political is evidence of women's enthusiastic response to the opportunity the magazine provided them to enter new areas of consciousness, to reflect on their experiences and the major events of the era, and to respond passionately—if not always with eloquence, in created extensions of emotions usually proscribed to women, such as anger, scorn, or outrage.

The women's love poems reveal the impact of the new sexual freedom that liberated them, but at the same time brought new burdens. Under the "Orchids and Hollyhocks" heading, poems flaunting sexuality streamed down the back pages like trellises enclosing bowers of delight, intimately juxtaposed with numerous ads for books on female sexuality authored by various, often European-educated, authorities.[27] "I love thy body / It is good to me," Helen Hoyt exulted clumsily in "Gratitude," one of a group of her poems published in the August 1916 issue.[28] Hoyt had been even more explicit in "Return," one of a group of her poems published in the September 1915 issue:

Sometimes,
When we are quite together,
Full of love,

Contented,
With hearts far off from speech,—

Then sometimes,
Strange soft noises begin to come through our lips:
Breathing from us
Out of our throats:
Murmurings that make no words,
And yet they have a meaning more than words.
. . . .[29]

Hoyt's group of poems includes one that is perhaps even more intimate than poems about lovers or lovemaking—"Menaia," a tribute to menstruation:

. . . .
Always returning,
Comes mystery
And possesses me
And uses me
As the moon uses the waters.

Ebbing and flowing
Obedient
The tides of my body move;
Swayed by chronology
As strict as the waters;
Unfailing
As the seasons of the moon and waters.[30]

Hoyt's poems on lovemaking and her poem on menstruation can be seen as defiant expressions of rebellion against Comstockery, but they also make use of the opportunity provided by preoccupation with Freudian psychology to confront masculine squeamishness about women's bodies.

In July 1917 Margaret Hunt Hetzel declared in "Aprille's Love Song," "You come to me across the wet meadows, / All youth in your

footsteps, / All youth and all age in your eyes that sing low to me."[31]
In the November-December 1917 issue, the speaker in Nann Clark
Barr's "You" addresses her lover:

> First you were a great storm,
> Swooping upon me with white wings;
> Battered and breathless under the wings I lay,
> There was terror in the night,
> Darkness and the light of snow;
> And the wind of you was a roaring in my ears.
>
> Now you are the broad sky,
> Still and clear beyond the clouds;
> You are over me always, height of the air I breathe,
> The earth changes under my feet,
> The wind fades but the sky remains,
> When I die, the last that I see will be the sky.[32]

And on the same page, Alice May Richards saluted "The Lips of My
Lover":

> To the lips of my lover, my eyes give heed,
> His whole soul-life in their lines I read!
> Rebellious, full, the nether one tells
> Of a wayward spirit that in him dwells,
> An eager, tumultuous, ardent child,
> By all the warmth of life beguiled!
> It calls to the mother love, half divine,
> That dwells in me, and it makes him mine.
>
> Close pressed on its warm rebellious mate,
> The other lies firm and grim as fate,—
> Firm in the cause of the poor and the weak,
> Grim on the tail of the strong and the sleek!
> It tells of a spirit austere, aloof,—
> Of stern Puritan sires, the proof!
> It calls to the pulsing woman in me,
> It makes me his—till the end shall be.[33]

The giddy, taboo-breaking expression of the delightful discovery of sexuality celebrated in these poems nevertheless springs from a traditional view of sexuality—much in accord with Freudian theory—that women's sexual pleasure derives from the power of the male and that fulfillment comes through the call of the male to a woman's maternal instincts. However, the poems also express a feminist insistence on the frank enjoyment of sex and a rejection of prudery. In the July 1917 issue, Flora Shufelt Rivola's "The Mothers' Meeting" mocked women who defended "all the old conservative repressed ideals for women" and who called children's sexual curiosity evil.[34] Nan Apotheker's "In the Hallway" in the September issue of that year begins with the lament, "My poor little sister— / Why must she always meet her lover in the hallway—Starting at every sound she hears / In the midst of her sly, sweet kisses."[35] Earlier that year, in the February issue, Apotheker had projected a defiant enjoyment of sexuality onto a working-class woman. In "Bohemia—From Another Angle," Rosa, who "used to pick olives in Italy," now lives in Greenwich Village with her lover—"You hear that?"—Giuseppe, who "works in a gang on the railroad"; Rosa has no wedding ring, but she and Giuseppe live on bread and cheese and dream their "fire-tipped dreams."[36]

Poems expressing—freely if awkwardly—enchantment with sexuality are tempered by poems revealing awareness that sexuality might not be wholly compatible with emancipation. Helen Hoyt, who championed sexuality in "Gratitude," "Return," and other poems, also wrote poems about the confinement of love. For example, in "To Love On Feeling Its Approach," she wrote in the September 1915 issue that

Love is a burden, a chain,
Love is a trammel and tie;
Love is disquiet and pain
That go slowly by.

O why should I bind my heart
And bind my sight?
Love is only a part
Of all delight.

Let me have room for the rest,—
To find and explore!
Love is greatest and best?
But love closes the door.
And closes us off so long from the ways
And concernments of men;
And owns us, and hinders our days.
O love, come not again!
. . . . [37]

The politics of sex in pre–World War I Greenwich Village required that one must grant one's partner the freedom one demanded for oneself. Maintaining this ideal required courage, and brave Greenwich Village women discovered that a sexual revolution can bring pain as well as pleasure. Lydia Gibson's "Not Years" (August 1917) records a stoic sense of diminished expectations:

Not years, not the close dear daily living, not the savor
Of life I ask you; nor the flavor
Of day-by-day; nor hand covering hand with haste;
(These are to others; these we shall not taste)
But surely, maybe silently, before age overtakes us
Before the sweet fine strength of our bodies is laid waste—
Two days or three
Without question, without past, without future
Somewhere in the hills, somewhere in sight of the sea.[38]

Living up to the ideal of the emancipated woman had its price as Nan Apotheker revealed in "Morning After Thought" (January 1917):

Me! Me! I shrieked . . .
Flaunting the red ribbon of my personality
Before his kind, bewildered eyes . . .
When he stood alone in quiet places
I sought him out and dragged him to the light—
All the while talking loud, above the revelers' shouts

See—see—am I not flamboyant . . .
Aren't my little comments wise and clever—
Can't I turn a phrase brilliantly . . .
And please regard my bold, challenging person . . .

Me! Me! I shrieked.

How could he know—
That it was only a slim, wistful ~~ ~e in me
Crying out for a quiet moment of understanding—
Groping humbly for a bit of contact with his soul.[39]

The bittersweetness of brave bohemian love and the turmoil caused by the freedom to remain unbound are reflected in Louise Bryant's poems. "Dark Eyes" of the July 1917 issue ("Dark Eyes / You stir my soul / Ineffably / You scatter / All my peace . . .")[40] probably refers to Eugene O'Neill. But the rueful ending of her June 1917 poem, "Lost Music" ("Oh, my love, / Let us go back / Through all the ages behind us / Until we find the music / That was in your laughter"),[41] which probably refers to John Reed, who was known for his good nature,[42] reveals the turmoil that could result when partners insisted on unfettered love.

If the new ideal of love had its bright and dark sides, women's poems in *The Masses* reveal the same ambivalence about traditional marriage. A frequent statement in the poetry is discontent with the confinement of domesticity. Hortense Flexner's "The Fire Watcher" in the September 1913 issue cites the passivity of ancient women rather than the curiosity of Eve as the cause of women's downfall and the root of modern women's oppression. Addressing a "Mother of Ages, brooding in the dusk," the poem demands

O why for us,
The weary after-keepers of the hearth,
Did you not heed the call of wind and bird,
Tread the red embers cold and take your way,
Alone and free,
That all the misery of the faggot load,

The guarding of the flame by those who wait,
Had never been?[43]

Another poem protesting the confinement of domesticity and
expressing the search for empowerment is Jean Starr Untermeyer's
"Deliverance" (October-November 1915). In the poem, a woman
"haunted by ghostly shapes" thinks she will at last see "the sun
without his veil" when she marries a man who makes her "a bright
palace of words," but after living in "a bright dream," she finds her
old fears, the "dread presence" again within her. She has a child and
for a time believes he will be the fire to burn away the mist," but his
flame "only danced like a butterfly," leaving her at last to the
recognition that she must be the source of her liberation and to
acknowledge that the "cleansing flame" of deliverance must be the
fire of her own heart.[44]

Untermeyer's poem had its origins in an epiphany experienced
when Edna St. Vincent Millay visited her home in the fall of 1912. As
she listened to her husband, the jewelry salesman, poet, and *Masses*
editor Louis Untermeyer, converse with Millay and listen to her
poetry, Jean Starr Untermeyer perhaps realizing that Millay had
achieved a status in her husband's eyes that he did not grant to his
wife, felt words erupting from her like a "hidden volcano" and
"Deliverance" was the result. She continued to write poems in secret
until her husband discovered them accidentally one day while
searching for concert tickets; Louis Untermeyer praised his wife's
poems and launched her career by publishing them in *The Masses*
and submitting them to other magazines. Her first volume of poems,
Growing Pains, published in 1918, marked the beginning of a long
career.[45]

Another poem, Margaret Haughawout's "Wyrd," (March 1917)
reveals a rueful view of marriage; while sitting in a boat withher
adoring husband of many years at the helm, a woman confides,

He is a stranger to me
And the sunset and the canoe
shooting the little while caps
And the wild birds screaming over my head

Are my kinfolk
I said yes to him in a moment when
The pathways of the stars had crossed.[46]

Flora Shufelt Rivola's "Mother" (May 1917) reveals the limitations imposed in marriage by class as well as gender. The poem's speaker describes herself as a "mountain girl," one of the "poor mountain whites"; she married at sixteen, without courtship or romance, to "a bloke like my father and my brother," who asked her to "mate up with him" as "an animal might seek his kind." Knowing no other kind of life, the mountain woman married a man to whom youth and love meant nothing.

But this mountain woman has a sister, Sue, twelve years younger, who goes to college where she has a suitor, a professor at the school, who has taught her, "with his fine manner and easy grace," to be a lady. From the books Sue has brought her, the woman realizes the mother she might have been, the father she might have given her daughter, and vows: "The callous on my hands shall / grow thick with toil / That she may go to college and be a lady".[47]

What the mountain woman seems not realize is that a husband who has taught his wife to be a lady may not be an ideal husband.

Another bleak view of marriage is to be found in the poems of Claire Bu Zard. "Comfortable" (September 1917) reflects a wife's disenchantment with marriage: "My husband has a happy brain / He never teases it with problems that are hard to solve; / He never prods or even tickles it; / But lets it rest in quiet and peace before the fire."[48] However, something much stronger than disenchantment is expressed in Bu Zard's "A Question" (June 1917) in which the poem's speaker asks

Did you ever lie in a man's arms and hate him;
And mend your children's clothes
And look out across the front lawn
And wonder dully what you'd get for lunch?

Did you ever walk along the boulevard
On a hot afternoon

Wheeling a baby,—
A pretty golden haired baby
That you'd like to paint
But couldn't,
And it cried and had to be fed,
And you hated it?

Did you ever serve dinner to a silent man
Reading a paper;
And after washing up the dishes
Sit alone and twist your wedding ring
And hate it?

And plan your next day's work while
Taking down your unkempt hair
And wonder why you looked so old and
Wrinkled and so bent
At thirty?

And did you ever go to bed and wait,—
And wait—
And dread the arms you waited for,—
Those hot and selfish arms of the man
You lived with,
Cooked for, claimed to love,—
and hated?[49]

A lighter statement of the idea that domesticity is soul-stifling is presented in Mary Carolyn Davies's "College" (July 1916):

First I became
A Copy of a Book
Then I became A Copy of a man
Who was also a Copy of a Book. Now
I would not know
What I am
Except that I have

On my wall
A framed paper
Which explains it fully.[50]

These anti-marriage poems were offset to some degree by poems
that supported Floyd Dell's claim that women were not comfortable
with the new morality, felt guilty, and yearned for marriage. In "A
House With Green Blinds" in the January 1917 issue, Virginia Brastow
declared

> I want a white house with green blinds
> And a roof all painted red,
> With alder trees to shade it,
> And the blue sky overhead.
> . . . .
> I never knew a house like this,
> But I can see it plain—
> Some homesick girl of long ago
> Must live in me again.[51]

And in Jeanette Eaton's "Rebellion" in the August 1917 issue, the
poem's speaker proclaims:

> . . . .
> Success is mine, quoted at market rate
> But I am stifled with a bitter cry,
> I scorn my fruitless body and my fate.
> Daughter of pioneers, I hate my barren years,
> When heart and soul and blood long for a mate!
> . . . .[52]

However, the majority of poems in which women reflected on
their situation in society are forward-looking rather than reactionary,
hard-eyed rather than sentimental. Such a tone, certainly, was what
The Masses welcomed—and when, additionally, the opportunity to
write on subjects unacceptable elsewhere was offered, the result was a
poem like Lydia Gibson's "Lies" in the October 1913 issue, which

presents a bleak image of prostitution: "Under the shadow-spreading trees / They walk, the slender silhouettes, / Night-hidden, but for outlines hard. / Slow-stepping, wanly mad to please, / While heart-deep, endless Hunger frets.[53]

Three themes dominated women's politically conscious poetry: feminism, anti-militarism, and class struggle, with the themes not infrequently merged in a single poem. The campaign for suffrage was an obvious subject for feminist poetry. Ruza Wenclaw mocked President Wilson in "The 'New Freedom' for Women" (March 1917); he had been called the "greatest president since Lincoln," but the woman forced to sell her body to feed it gets not a Lincoln to free her but "only a man from the South" who tells her, "You can afford a little while to wait."[54]

Sarah N. Cleghorn's "The Mother Follows" (December 1913) reflects the two principal reasons for endorsement of suffrage by Socialist feminists: they believed poor and working-class women needed the empowerment of suffrage, and they believed women would use it to improve society and not as a means to seek personal power. The central figure in Cleghorn's poem is a tenement mother fearful of the dangers posed to her children by the neighborhood saloons and brothels, but especially by their work in a factory:

> She follows the young things to the mill
> And rashly seeks to guard them still
> From fenceless cogs that whirl and thrust
> And fill the air with lint and dust.
> The pay is small, the hours are long,
> The fire escapes are none too strong—

The mother's efforts to protect her children are met with the rebuff, "Go home and take care of your children." Aroused at last to demand suffrage, she wears upon her breast "A button with the bold request: / 'Let me take care of my children!'"[55]

A principal problem confronting women who wrote political poems was to avoid shrillness. Satire was one approach, but often the result was coyness or an undermining flippancy. And just as often, there was, of course, shrillness. Poems expressing opposition to the entry of the United States into the European war presented a stiff challenge. Among poems with a satirical approach, Elizabeth Waddell's "Them and Their Wives" (November 1914) mocked the consorts of "Emperors, War Lords and Czars," all of them "pious and dutiful, mostly unbeautiful, Kirching and Kindering wives," stout anti-suffragists with "the bovine bourgeois" sort of "good squaw graces" that monarchs are blessed with in wives.[56]

Usually, however, the tone of anti-war and anti-militarism poems was serious, even self-righteous. Sarah Cleghorn accused her country in "And Thou, Too, America" (June 1916) of emulating Germany—whose acts of war it had condemned—through using money to "invest in tools for killing men" rather than to "save the little children of the poor."[57]

Another scornful anti-war poem, Mary Carolyn Davies's "To the Women of England" (April 1916), mocked the women of that nation who had humiliated men they believed were shirking military service; while the women of England now were left to weep for their "blind, legless, broken, dead men," American women guiltlessly could dance and shop, for, Davies claimed, "We have never—yet—pinned a feather on a boy and killed him."[58]

In Babette Deutsch's "Extra," a poem published in The Masses's last issue, a woman sitting in a comfortable apartment where "soft lamplight falls / Upon piled cushions and pale-tinted walls" hears the "shrilling roar" of newsboys in the streets shrieking "like guns" headlines about war; about "tired workers tramping to and fro"; about "children vainly fretting to be fed"; or,—in a reference to striking Lowell textile workers— "Amazonian" women "[C]rying for bread, / And roses, too." The woman's solution to these cries of torment from the world is to seek "Promethean laughter" and the "conquering fires / Of unappeasable desires," for these, she concludes, are the only measures one can use against the futility of "divine insanities" that "[q]uicken men's raptures and men's agonies."[59]

The women's poems expressing class consciousness are usually written from the point of view of sympathetic onlookers. In Elizabeth Waddell's "The Job," (February 1916) a young couple learn of the husband's rehiring on the day when the "long winter was over and the works that were shut down had opened their doors." The couple laugh aloud, hug each other, take their baby from his crib and swing him; the poet reports that she never has seen joy as pure or beautiful as that of the young couple over their good news of a job.[60]

Florence Ripley Martin's "The Dream" (June 1916) describes a woman who buys a costly silk dress, but afterward dreams of "a ghostly crowd of girls with eyes too large and bright" whose childhood has been sacrificed to the manufacture of pretty garments and never can wear the dress again.[61]

Elizabeth Waddell's "For Lyric Labor" (September 1917) reports the complaint of a young Italian-born woman working in the garment industry that her situation "wouldn't be so bad if they would only let us sing at our work." The poem's speaker responds in terms that the young woman may find confusing, thus revealing the distance of sympathetic middle-class women from the realities of working-class life: she assures this "child of the Renaissance and little sister of Ariosto and Raphael" that the singing workers of Italy are one of that nation's treasures and promises her that one day in this country every tower will be raised with "mirth and music."[62]

Margaret E. Sangster's "Proportionately" in the final issue of *The Masses* reveals the stirring of feminism and class consciousness in the mind of the poem's speaker as she listens with growing skepticism to an assured conservative:

> He was young,
> And his mind
> Was filled with science of economics
> That he had studied in college,
> And, as we talked about the food riots,
> And high prices,
> And jobless men,
> He said—
> "It's all stupid and wrong,
> This newspaper talk!
> Folk have no business to starve;
> The price of labor always advances,
> Proportionately

With the price of food."

"Any man," he said
A moment later,
"Can earn at least two dollars a day
By working on a railroad
Or in the street cleaning department!
What if potatoes do cost
Eight cents a pound?
Wages are high, too . . .
People have no reason to starve."
I listened to him prayerfully (more or less),
For I had never been to college,
And didn't know much about economics,
But—
As I walked to the window
And looked out over the veiled, mysterious lights
Of the city
I couldn't help thinking of a little baby
That I had seen a few days ago;
A baby of the slums—thin and joyless,
And old of face—
But with eyes of the Christ Child—
A baby crying for bread—
And I wondered . . .[63]

In Hortense Flexner's "The Winds of Spring," a young woman factory workers addresses her audience directly, declaring that on a day when the winds of spring blow into the factory, the workers "may not stop nor lift an eye,"

But I know for all the whir of the wheels
And the clack of the loom's gaunt frame,
That the winds are calling, calling away,
From the factory's gray-faced shame,
Are tugging like tiny hands at my skirt,

And singing in tears my name.[64]

A warning is given in Margaret French Patton's "The Sound of the Needles," in which the poet questions whether the current needle-clicking, stitch-counting absorption of women knitting garments for wartime signifies an approaching revolution: "Do murderous thoughts like molten ore / Through ravaged brains and bodies pour?"[65] Another warning is given in Marguerite Wilkinson's "The Food Riots," which hints at the possibility of class warfare caused by the widening gap between the haves and have-nots. The poem describes the plight of the poor who cannot benefit from a rich autumn harvest and full markets; the poem concludes:

> . . . poor is the people
> Whose women must cry,
> "We work, but we starve—
> Give us food or we die!
> Give milk for our babies
> And meat for our men
> And bread that our bodies
> May labor again!"[66]

Like a number of political poems, Mary Field's "Names" refers to a specific event, the "pure milk" campaign—the mobilization in which Mary Heaton Vorse, among others, volunteered to see that milk, unadulterated by greedy distributors, was distributed to poor women at "milk stations" around the city.[67] Field's targeting of philanthropists, however, seems rather unfair, for wealthy women like Mrs. J. Borden Harriman raised funds—as did Vorse—to support these milk depots, with the result that infant mortality dropped significantly.[68] In Field's poem, a rich man raises the price of milk a penny a quart and through the summer months "made five thousand more than he ort,"

> He made five thousand more a year,
> And they called him "a wonderful financier."
> The babes in the slums went up to God—
> 5000! It startled the nation.

The charities puzzled. They wondered why
And began an investigation
Of what caused the babies to wither and faint,
And they called the cause "the summer complaint."
Then the rich man gave 500 bucks,
500 bucks he gave,
To relieve the scourge of summer complaint,
And the babies' lives to save.
With 500 bucks he headed the list,
And they called him a "great philanthropist."[69]

A poem referring to a specific personality is Sarah N. Cleghorn's
"Comrade Jesus" of April 1914, in which Jesus is presented as a
socialist worker, a vision sustained frequently in Art Young's drawings
and cartoons, most notably in his cover for the December 1913 *Masses,*
where Christ's face appears on a poster announcing that "the working-
man of Nazareth will speak at Brotherhood Hall on the subject of the
rights of labor." Cleghorn's Easter poem links Jesus with the labor
movement by casting him as a Haywood-like figure; it concludes: "Ah,
let no Local him refuse; / Comrade Jesus hath paid his dues. /
Whatever other be debarred, / Comrade Jesus hath his red card."[70]

Rose Pastor Stokes, one of the few *Masses* contributors with
experience as a worker, contributed two poems based on her experience in the 1912 New York waiters' strike and the 1913 textile workers'
strike in Paterson, New Jersey. In "A Waiter," a man watching people
eat food he can only dare but smell thinks the diners he serves "chatter
on, not dreaming we are thinking and waiting for a time . . . / Just
waiting."[71]
In November 1913, after the Paterson strike had resulted in an
unsatisfactory contract, Stokes captured the workers' simmering anger
in "Paterson":

Our folded hands again are at the loom.
The air
Is ominous with peace.
But what we weave you see not through the gloom,
'Tis terrible with doom.

Beware!
You dream that we are weaving what you will?
Take care![72]

One of the most shocking atrocities to occur on American soil in the
years before World War I is alluded to in "Chivalry" by Elizabeth
Waddell, whose poems frequently addressed political themes. The
poem's first stanza runs:

Georgia is the State that burns men alive for the honor
of its women—when it isn't for the alleged
stealing of livestock.
The age of consent in Georgia is ten years.
This is Chivalry.[73]

The stanza refers generally to Georgia's history of brutality to
black men and specifically to the lynching of a Jew, Leo M. Frank. In
August 1913, Frank, a Brooklyn-born supervisor at the National
Pencil Company in Augusta, Georgia, was arrested for the murder of
Mary Phagan, the thirteen-year-old daughter of dispossessed share-
croppers who worked in a factory. Frank was tried, convicted, and
sentenced to be hanged. Some trial witnesses afterward recanted their
testimony; others spoke of bribery attempts or intimidation by police.
A subsequent investigation by a private detective hired by a defense
committee pointed to James Conley as the actual murderer. Conley, a
black man employed as janitor at the factory, had testified that he had
acted as Frank's accomplice, and he was tried and convicted as an
accessory to murder and imprisoned for a year.

The case inspired anti-semitic boycotts of Jewish-owned businesses
in Georgia; nevertheless, people in that state spoke on Frank's behalf.
Around the nation, appeals for clemency came from newspaper editors,
state legislators, clergymen, leading congressmen, prominent businessmen, and women's organizations. Before leaving office in June 1915
Governor John M. Slaton commuted Frank's sentence to life imprisonment, an act that enraged the anti-Frank faction. Slaton declared martial
law when a mob menaced his home, and two regiments had to guard
him at the inauguration of his successor. In August 1915 a well-

organized mob broke into the Georgia State Prison Farm at Milledgeville where Frank was being held; they overpowered the superintendent, two guards, and a "trusty," seized Frank, dragged him to a car, drove him one hundred miles to Marietta, near Mary Phagan's birthplace, and hanged him from a tree. The *New York Times* reported that a "closely packed mass of men all but mad with excitement and hate" surged around the body before it was cut down and that afterwards. an onlooker ground his foot into Frank's face, distorting the features.[74]

A poem that reveals the bigotry patriotism can mask is Martha Gruening's anti-war "Prepared," in which the speaker declares, "As long as I can hang a Jew and burn a nigger / Or ride a labor agitator on a rail . . . why shouldn't I shed my blood and the blood of my neighbor / To guard these inherited rights against any alien invader?"[75]

A poem that the federal government cited in its campaign against the *Masses* for its anti-war position was Josephine Bell's tribute to Emma Goldman and Alexander Berkman. Though she despised both feminists and feminism, Goldman had become a feminist hero after being prosecuted for distributing birth control information. In 1917, Goldman and her longtime comrade, Alexander Berkman, were arrested and convicted under a recently passed espionage act for their opposition to the war.[76] Bell's poem in the August 1917 issue concludes:

> Emma Goldman and Alexander Berkman
> Are in prison tonight,
> But they have made themselves elemental forces,
> Like the water that climbs down the rocks:
> Like the wind in the leaves:
> Like the gentle night that holds us:
> They are working on our destinies:
> They are forging the love of nations:
> But tonight they lie in prison.

Bell's poem was cited as one of the texts in violation of the congressional act under which her heroes, Goldman and Berkman, had been imprisoned. However, when Judge Augustus Hand read Bell's poem at the *Masses* trial, he rhetorically asked the defense lawyer,

Morris Hillquit, "Do you call that a poem?" and ruled with respect to Bell, "Indictment quashed."[78]

Although Eastman had been reluctant at first to take on the editorship of *The Masses,* he soon found he loved the job. Later, another man with feminist credentials, Floyd Dell, became his trusted lieutenant. However, the man who became the star of *The Masses* was John Reed, a 1910 Harvard graduate and journalist who had recognized the potential of the magazine in its first issue and eagerly joined the collective. For the next five years, hardly an issue appeared without one and usually several contributions from Reed in the form of stories, poems, essays, and reports of labor strife, revolution, and impending or actual war.[79] Despite the matey, masculine quality of their leadership, the *Masses* editors were popular with feminists. "Max Eastman, Floyd Dell, Art Young and the rest are genuine warm-hearted Feminists," declared Alice Carpenter, Zona Gale, Marie Jenney Howe, Anna Strunsky Walling, and Vira Boardman Whitehouse in a letter in the February 1916 issue; they asked each woman reader to contribute five dollars as a New Year's gift to the magazine. "In cartoon, in verse, in editorial, in story THE MASSES has stood for us all along the line as no other magazine in America has," the endorsement continued. "When we fight for professional opportunities, for scientific sex knowledge, there stands THE MASSES, always understanding, always helping!"[80]

The Masses's good reputation among feminists was due to its vigorous and unqualified support for suffrage. In one of his early editorials, Eastman had proclaimed, "The question of sex equality, the economic, social, political independence of women stands by itself, parallel and equal in importance to any other question of the day."[81] In this and subsequent pro-suffrage editorials, Eastman took the position one would expect from a man claiming to have grown up in a household "run on feminist principles." Both his parents were ministers, his mother, Annis Ford Eastman, having been "the first woman ordained in the Congregational Church of New York."[82] His sister, Crystal, was a lawyer; his fiancee for a time, Inez Milholland, was a lawyer, as was his wife, Ida Rauh, whom Eastman credited with completing the political education founded on the principles of Marxism.[83] As editor, Eastman enjoyed the opportunity to emulate his

parents' role, "pounding up . . . weekly exhortations to the conscience."[84] These editorials were intended by Eastman to impose
"scientific idealism" on Marxian politics; nevertheless, he acknowledged, "notwithstanding its supposedly scientific framework, there
was plenty of romantic rapture in my revolutionism."[85]

This romantic rapture often was aroused by a suffragist leader who
appealed to Eastman's self-confessed tendency to hero-worship.
Emmeline Pankhurst, under indictment in England for criminal
conspiracy, inspired Eastman to write, "she will stand in history
among the heroes of human Liberty."[86] He supported Margaret Sanger
when she was prosecuted for distributing birth control information
and eulogized Inez Milholland after her untimely death. However, a
careful reading of Eastman's editorials reveals that the basis of his
support for suffrage was that he saw it as a means of removing women's
deplorable shortcomings. Preparing for citizenship, he believed,
would give girls something to think about besides clothes. As enfranchised women, they would not need to satisfy their ambitions by
participating in "the insane procession of fashionable buffooneries on
the public highways."[87] He argued that if women were permitted to
embark on a life of adventure and achievement, they would abandon
the preoccupation with trivialities and no longer grow up to be mere
drudges or "parlor ornaments" and "silly mothers," for the "heroic
race" needed to fight the struggles of the future depended upon
increasing "the breadth of experience, the sagacity, the humor, the
energetic and active life interest of mothers."[88] However, in an early
editorial, Eastman had qualified his support for suffrage by predicting
that it would benefit everyone without changing the social order:
"citizenship means a bigger world for women; that's all it means. It isn't
a political reform. It's a social reform".[89]

This darker side of Eastman's suffragism—his contempt for
women in their present condition—was probably connected to the
unhappiness he was experiencing in his marriage. He admired his
wife's intelligence, beauty, and talent, but thought she "did not know
what regular hours of work meant." To Eastman, Ida Rauh was a
dilettante, taking up sculpting, for example, and then abandoning it in
order to work with the Women's Trade Union League. Although Rauh
was respected as one of the league's founders and early leaders,

Eastman termed her activism as "this spasmodic, irresponsible, ideal-istic fooling with the labor movement."[90]

In this state of frustration and confusion, Eastman was unlikely to invite women into his workplace, for even as a suffrage orator, he had been more comfortable with male than female audiences. On ideolog-ical grounds, he had banished from the magazine the midwestern Socialists—Josephine Conger-Kaneko, Lena Morrow Lewis, May Wood Simons, Lida Parce, and Ida Crouch Hazlett—who had been a strong presence under Vlag's leadership. He did not invite into his confidence two women—Vorse and Irwin—who had played an impor-tant role in preserving *The Masses*. At the crucial meeting that settled Eastman's and the magazine's future, he had formed the impression of Vorse that she was "pale and fragile, and although abounding in energy, had a permanently weary look."[91]

Nevertheless, Vorse remained a loyal supporter and was on the magazine's editorial board for the five years of its life under Eastman's leadership. Because of the activities in that period of this weary-looking woman—pursuing writing assignments in Europe, including a series on Maria Montessori, in 1913; giving birth to a son by her second husband, Joe O'Brien, in January 1914; setting up her apart-ment as an organizing headquarters for unemployment demonstra-tions during the winter of 1914-1915; returning to Europe in 1915 as a war correspondent; going to Provincetown on her return where she helped establish the Provincetown Players; nursing her husband through a terminal illness; and, although again being left a widow with young children to support, going to Minnesota when Elizabeth Gurley Flynn asked her to report on the strike by miners on the Mesabi Range—she was able to contribute only four short stories and one article to the magazine.[92] Irwin wrote several insightful essays for the magazine during the Eastman era, but her short stories did not again appear in the magazine, and after June 1913 her name was not listed among the editors.

The man who became Eastman's trusted lieutenant, Floyd Dell, also came to *The Masses* with feminist credentials. A native Iowan, Dell had come to New York after working as a editor for the "Friday Review" section of the *Chicago Tribune*.[93] Before leaving Chicago, Dell had published his first book, *Women as World Builders,* a collection of

essays reprinted from the "Friday Review" on feminist leaders, including Charlotte Perkins Gilman, Jane Addams, Emmeline Pankhurst,
Olive Schreiner, Isadora Duncan, Emma Goldman, and Ellen Key. His
purpose for writing the book, Dell admitted, was to betray a secret:
historically having been what men wanted them to be, women now
were responding to men's weariness of subservient women and were
emerging as "that self-sufficient, able, broadly imaginative and healthy
minded creature upon whom we have set our masculine desire."[94]

Dell's writing for *The Masses* reflects this blend of feminism with
masculine self-interest, along with a fascination with female psychology. In "The Nature of Women" (January 1916), Dell confided that
even though he was a feminist, he always had believed that men were
innately more creative than women, and that even if women were free
to pursue their interests, that pattern was likely to continue. However,
Dell acknowledged himself convinced by the extensive studies on
newborns undertaken by the sociologist and Heterodite Leta Stetter
Hollingsworth that demonstrated there was no inherent difference
between males and females, and he cited in his essay another study by
Hollingsworth that disproved the myth that women were incapacitated during menstruation.[95]

Male self-interest was baldly apparent in "Feminism for Men"
(July 1914). Here Dell pointed out that men's freedom was limited
because of their obligation to support wives, but women's economic
independence meant men's loss of control, and men preferred power
to freedom. Keeping women in boxes for which they paid rent cost
men the companionship of their wives, who, limited for achievement
to a new dress—"not the same kind of achievement as a home run"—
became dull. If men only would relinquish their power and privilege,
they not only would be free of an economic burden, but also their
wives once again would become be as exciting as sweethearts, who
listen to and learn from men about politics, poetry, sports, and many
other subjects. "Feminism," Dell declared, "is going to make it
possible for the first time for men to be free."[96]

Early in Eastman's tenure, the man appeared who brought an aura
of romance not only to the magazine but to the age. When the
December 1912 *Masses* appeared, John Reed, a 1910 Harvard College
graduate working part-time as a reporter for *The American* recognized

the importance of the revived magazine and called Eastman, asking him to read a short story he had written. Although resentful of Reed's intrusion, Eastman agreed.[97] The story, "Where the Heart Is," tells of a dance-hall hostess who yearns to travel. Her savings take her as far as London; thereafter a series of wealthy and aristocratic men support her journeys through France, Germany, Belgium, and finally Brazil, where, bored with this way of life, the young woman returns to New York and resumes her life among her friends and customers at the dance hall.[98]

Eastman was titillated. Believing that Reed was "writing about a significant phase of American life that no other magazine would dare to mention unless sanctimoniously," Eastman published the story in the very next issue and invited Reed to contribute humorous or dramatic stories or comments as often as he could.[99]

With this triumvirate, assisted by numerous other male contributors, writing about all facets of women's lives in addition to local, national, and world affairs, the number of women contributing to the magazine under Eastman's leadership was, not surprisingly, lower than the number of women contributing to the earlier *Masses.* During Eastman's five-year tenure, twenty-one women contributed stories (the actual number of women submitting stories is impossible to know); most of them had only a single story published. Mabel Dodge had three stories published, two anonymously; Mary Heaton Vorse had four stories published; and Helen Hull and Adriana Spadoni had five stories published. Mary Heaton Vorse was the only writer well known when *The Masses* published her fiction, and, as in the case of the poets, only a few women—Vorse, of course, Mabel Dodge, Elizabeth Hines Hanley, Mary White Ovington, Adriana Spadoni, and Helen Hull—continued their writing careers.

The political themes found in the poetry also appear in the short fiction, although anti-militarism, so frequent in the poetry, is addressed in only one story, Marie Louise Van Saanen's "The Game," (May 1916) in which the son of a woman who has forbidden him to play war games is killed when a returning veteran teaches his son how to shoot.[100] The dark side of love in an age of new sexual freedom, explored in a number of poems, is explored more fully in Eileen Kent's "Moon Madness" (May 1917). A young woman waiting for her lover realizes he will not come to her. She remembers their first meeting at a college fraternity party; he was from another town, then moved and took rooms in her town. They continued to go to dances, and she fell in love, another case of "moon madness." And now, abandoned by her lover, she is left to deal with "that half-feared, half-unbelieved thing that had haunted them both." She knows her mother will help her, but does not want to hurt her. She has just had a birthday, and decides she can go a long way on the gift of twenty-five dollars. She packs her clothes, tells her mother she is going to mail a letter, and leaves home.[101]

The bleakness of working-class life among immigrant families is vividly presented by Adriana Spadoni in "A Rift of Silence" (February 1913). Michael Pavlov, a young stockyard worker, who is the eldest son in a family of Russian immigrants, shares his bed with two younger brothers and cannot sleep at night because of the sounds of the other sleepers' breathing. The most he can hope for is to marry soon and live as his parents have. His father anticipates that an aging co-worker's declining job performance will lead to his firing and a vacancy Michael can fill. Meanwhile, Michael's favorite brother dies; he grieves, but also recognizes the benefit to himself, for his brother's death leaves "a rift of silence."[102]

The plucky Polish wife of a tailor who takes over her husband's business while he recovers from tuberculosis in Colorado is the hero of Phyllis Wyatt's "The Checked Trousers" (June 1917). The story is presented from the point of view of a schoolteacher, Miss Reely, who feels kinship with the tailor's wife, Mrs. Joblanska, because she is also a breadwinner and ends with the wife's triumphant report that her husband's health has improved so much that the checked trousers he made before he left must be widened. Through the sympathetic relationship between the American-born schoolteacher and the immigrant businesswoman, Wyatt makes the point that identity as a worker transcends consciousness of nationality.[103]

Struggle does not end with success in Helen Forbes's "The Hunky Woman" (May 1916), in which a housewife, Mrs. Atwood, pities her maid, Annie, despite her husband's disparaging remarks about "Hunkies." When Annie goes home from work, she is arrested because her husband is a bigamist. Annie is released after her husband is arrested and convicted, but when she returns home, she finds that her landlady has not cared for her children in her absence, and, as a result, her baby has died and her older daughter has been taken to a children's shelter. She returns to work, but lacks enough English to make her case plain to Mrs. Atwood, who responds with shock at her maid's having been in jail and, through a misunderstanding, believes briefly that she has killed her child. Mrs. Atwood turns the inarticulate, despairing Annie away; later her husband says that Hunkies are just animals, and she replies that she guesses he is right.[104]

While unusually pessimistic, the Forbes story represents another example of the distance between middle-class writers and their working-class protagonists. Annie does not have an author's surrogate to root for her, as Miss Reely roots for Mrs. Joblanska in Wyatt's story. Mrs. Atwood is mocked in Forbes's story for her prejudice and insensitivity, but in allowing her to yield to her husband's bigotry, Forbes does not allow her central character to evolve, and she remains the embodiment of the post-suffrage woman who votes as her husband does. The fiction writers were less successful than the poets in getting inside a working-class protagonist's skin and allowing her to win. The writers are sympathetic to their protagonists, but their implicit aim is to awaken or secure the sympathy of *The Masses's* middle-class readers.

The employer-maid relationship provides the framework for three stories by Helen Hull. The maid represents maternal warmth In "Mothers Still" (October 1914), a story told from the point of view of a child who is lonely because her mother, distracted by an unwelcome pregnancy and her husband's frequent absences, is unloving toward her. The child turns for affection to the maid and to a cat who has just had kittens. When the unmarried maid becomes pregnant, the mother fires her—that the baby's father is her husband is intimated—and the child then is left with only the cat as a source of maternal affection.[105] Hull's "Unclaimed" (May 1916) is about a widow who assumes responsibility for her maid's out-of-wedlock child. The family doctor informs the widow that the baby's webbed toe is an inherited trait; since such a trait ran in her late husband's family, the woman realizes that he was the child's father.[106] "Usury" (September 1916), also by Hull, is about a woman's benevolent intervention into the personal life of her black maid to make certain that the young woman is marrying the right man.[107] Class and gender interact in these three stories; the maid, the archetypal representative of female vulnerability to masculine entitlements, is dependent for survival on a woman, less vulnerable because of class, but still disadvantaged because of gender.

The theme of working-class women's patient passivity is present In Dorothy Weil's maid story, "A New Woman" (January 1916). Mrs. Bullock's diligent servant, Mrs. Knox, who also cleans offices at night, is temporarily unable to work when she goes into the hospital to have a baby—the result of a brief stop at home by the wandering man Mrs. Bullock describes as Mrs. Knox's "no-good husband." Jennie, a new maid, comes to clean in Mrs. Knox's place; the following week, both women show up, and Mrs. Bullock sets them both to work. Later, Mrs. Knox comes to Mrs. Bullock complaining that as a respectable married woman she cannot work with a woman who has an out-of-wedlock child. Then Jennie tells her story. The poor oldest daughter in a motherless family, she had no joy in life until she met Jim, fell in love, and became pregnant. Jim wanted to marry her, but because she has a serious illness, Jennie refused his proposal. He has "gone West" and done well, and he has married another woman as she had urged him to do. Jennie has had a hard time supporting her baby, but remains confident that Jim will assume responsibility for it when she dies. Mrs. Bullock tells Jennie she cannot employ her, but Mrs. Knox becomes "a new woman" by recognizing Jennie as another sharer in the common lot of women and promises to find her a job in the office building she cleans.[108]

Mary Heaton Vorse's short story contributions to *The Masses* during the Eastman years reflect the ambivalence about women that marked much of her fiction. "The Two-Faced Goddess" is a yachting story, probably based on Vorse's experiences as a one-fourth owner, together with her neighbors in her Provincetown home, Wilbur Steele, Arthur Hutchins, and Tony Avella, of a slow and leaky cabin sloop, a "tub-like craft" that her owners nevertheless thought beautiful.[109] The title of this somewhat misogynist story refers to the two faces of the goddess of domesticity: a smiling face that represents the benevolent protector of the hearthside and the angry face that demands as the price for domestic tranquility that husbands sacrifice their honor by offering up "propitiatory lies." The story is told from Vorse's frequently invoked persona, "a lone male," who, while at a summer resort, joins with three adventure-seeking married men in the purchase of a boat.

Two of the husbands are long married, but the more recently married
Stetson habitually is cowed by the tearful complaints of his wife,
Birdie. The wives, Birdie especially, resent the boat and blame the
narrator for breaking up their homes. After their purchase, the men
discover the boat leaks and requires constant repairs or new parts.
Finally, when they decide not to pay any more attention to the boat, it
stops leaking and they have smooth sailing. Concluding that "women
and boats aren't unlike," Stetson decides to stop "pumping" and ignore
his wife's tears; Birdie is humbled and Stetson is master of his
matrimonial ship.[110]

"The Two-Faced Goddess" resembles the "marketable" stories
Vorse wrote for magazines like *Good Housekeeping* and *Woman's Home
Companion*—light, quickly done domestic vignettes, the "lollipops," as
she termed them, that paid for shelter, food, clothing, household help,
and her children's schooling. But these short stories were not the work
Vorse was proud of herself for doing. In the daily notes and annual self
evaluations Vorse began maintaining from 1918 through the rest of her
life, her self-satisfaction was reflected in reports of having devoted
time to or having successfully completed "experimental" work, the
kind of writing that more accurately reflected her personality and
values and that enlarged her powers as a writer. The marketable and
the experimental work were in conflict; "the two have got to be
combined," she wrote in 1923. Her "labor things" were yet another
commitment that included writing and something more, a personal
mission; Vorse was especially pleased when she was able to correlate
"experimental writing and my activities."[111]

In "Tolerance" (February 1914) Vorse used humor and romance,
the staples of her commercial writing, in a story about people who would
not have been found in women's magazine fiction: working-class immigrants. However, her tale of the Schultzes and the Grogans has more
complexity than that description indicates, for the characters reflect
conflict on several levels: between European and American and between
conservative and radical political ideologies; between politics and religion; between early and later immigrant groups; between craft and
industrial workers; and, inevitably, between parents and children. Moreover, "Tolerance" concludes on a quasi-feminist note, when two self-
proclaimed anti-feminist women take leadership in resolving conflict.

"Tolerance" tells of two families of newly prosperous craft workers, who had left their factory town when "the Slavs, Polacks, Lithuanians, Ginnies, French Canadians and what not had poured in" and have lived harmoniously for years in adjoining suburban houses. Schultz·and Grogan fish together. The Grogan son, Lonnie, is in love with the Schultz daughter, Elizabeth, who has been brought up by her Socialist father to think for herself. The romance makes Mrs. Grogan uneasy: "'Tis none of these new women I want for a daughter-in-law; no votes for women in my house, sez, I." Grogan tells his wife she has to be tolerant, for "everybody can't be Catholic." Mrs. Schultz, as unemancipated as Mrs. Grogan, also is uneasy about the courtship; Lonnie buys Elizabeth expensive candy and flowers with money that could be spent on linen or furniture. Mr. Schultz urges her to "haf some tolerance." He and Grogan don't fight; even though Grogan's a Democrat and a papist and Schultz is a Socialist and a free thinker, "ve let it go at that." Elizabeth asks her father what his reaction would be if she did not believe as he does. He replies that he'd respect her thought as he respects his wife's non-thought when she goes to church. However, when Elizabeth tells him she wants to go to church with her teacher, he is not pleased, although her mother is. Political and religious differences come between the couple; Lonnie calls Elizabeth a narrow-minded Socialist; she calls him an idol-worshipping papist, and from there they descend to "Dutchman" and "Paddy."

The tolerance between the two families is tested further when the unskilled workers in the mill go on strike. Mr. Grogan, who supports strikes called in due time after deliberation by proper labor leaders, is unsympathetic to the walk-out by "a disorderly mob of the inferior nations." Revealing himself as an IWW sympathizer, Lonnie denounces his father's lack of sympathy for "Labor" and his "little trade union spirit." Grogan tells Lonnie to hold his peace or "I'll eye-double-double you." When Lonnie works with the strikers, his father tells him to leave the house; he turns for consolation to Schultz, who has his own disappointment: Elizabeth has become a Methodist. Grogan's ready agreement that becoming a Methodist is indeed terrible sparks a resentful reply from Schultz that he would not have a subversive syndicalist in his family.

While the two fathers destroy a friendship of years, the young couple meanwhile have overcome their differences and married. Elizabeth confidently tells her mother that Lonnie will get over his ideas about labor unions when she explains what the church means; Lonnie assures his mother that when Elizabeth understands that the class struggle is the only serious thing in life, she'll cut out all the nonsense. Mrs. Grogan and Mrs. Schultz are left with the realization that they have years of peacemaking ahead of them; Mrs. Schultz tells Mrs. Grogan that while young people get over things, old men like Schultz and Grogan "gets ofer nuddings" and they will have to convince them to get over everything.[112]

Another example of Vorse's experimental writing is represented by the narrator of her two other works of short fiction in *The Masses:* "The Story of Michael O'Shea" (November 1913) and "The Happy Woman" (April 1915). In these stories, Vorse created a memorable, authentic-voiced female character named Mrs. Phelan, a pawnbroker who spins narratives in gossip with Lester Robinson, "cub reporter," a figure who was Vorse's frequent stand-in. Mrs. Phelan tells the story of Michael O'Shea, a boarding-house resident who marries a woman he has rescued from a brutal lover. She deserts him to rejoin her lover. He follows the couple to Cheyenne; there he realizes the woman is worthless and the man is a coward. Returning to New York, he discovers that Mamie, the daughter of the boarding-house owner, is the woman of his dreams. They marry, and to Mrs. Phelan's disgust, Mamie makes her husband dependent upon her by making him too comfortable; after so much suffering the couple have become ordinary. To Lester she complains,

> "Seems queer to me now to think o' Black Michael O'Shea goin' around hitched to a cook stove an' thinkin of whether this otta be flavored a little more or otta be served hotter. . . . Real Irishmen are too full 'o fight or love or politics or sport—too full to know what they're eatin', so's there's a big dish of it."[113]

Mrs. Phelan speaks directly to "Mr. Rob'ns'n" and the reader—there is not a word of exposition—in Vorse's "The Happy Woman." Years ago, when she was "young enough and fool enough to do anything that

Phelan tol' me ta," Mrs. Phelan was in a small Canadian town waiting for her husband return from deer hunting. To amuse herself, she goes to a circus and sees the Tooseys, a prosperous couple she had known in the days when she was "Lily Regan that was." She greets them, but they run away in fear. Later she receives a note inviting her to their boarding house. She is asked if she has heard of Mr. Toosey's death, and replies she has not.

Mrs. Toosey tells her that years ago, the board of directors of her husband's company had the "bad judgment" to have a meeting two weeks before he could make good on a "loan." Having provided for his wife, Mr. Toosey planned to kill himself to avoid going to prison. Mrs. Toosey proposed instead that they both should live on the money he had embezzled. Mr. Toosey wrote a suicide note and left the country; Mrs. Toosey identified a fortuitously discovered body as that of her husband, but lonely for him, she faked her own suicide and joined him in Canada. Disregarding the couple's criminal actions, Mrs. Phelan declares that Mrs. Toosey is a happy woman because she kept her husband's love and her respect for him; most women like their husbands but they feel sorry for them "on account men's bein' the poor feeble things they is," but "Frank had always seemed like a hero in a romance" to Mollie Toosey. [114]

Vorse was exceptional in her skillful use of humor in fiction, for most of the women's stories were somber, especially those that dealt with actual events. The "Women's Citizenship" issue of October–November 1915 contained one of the magazine's most memorable stories, "The White Brute," by Mary White Ovington, a New York–born white social worker who in early life had become sympathetically involved with "the Negro and his problems" and later became one of the founders of the National Association for the Advancement of Colored People.[115] The story, based on an account Ovington overheard while traveling through the South, tells of a newly married black couple who are journeying by train through Mississippi on their way to the home the husband has lovingly, painstakingly prepared for his wife. They are obliged to change trains, and they wait on the station platform in the depot of a dreary town where twenty years earlier a black man was lynched and where, not far from the station, two white men, one of them armed, lounge ominously. Sam expresses his wonder to his bride, Melinda, that she, a woman with two years of school who had worked for white folks and learned their dainty ways, should have chosen him, an uncouth, barely literate man over his rival, a well-educated preacher. Melinda tells Sam that his strength attracted her to him; he makes her feel safe. They have left their bags in the waiting room; when Sam returns from retrieving them, he finds Melinda surrounded by the two white men, who make clear their intention to take her with them. Sam tries to appease them, but the men make clear they are not joking. "Give us this girl right quick," one commands him, "or we'll hang you from the nearest pole and shoot at you till you're thicker'n holes than a rotten tree full of woodpeckers." Sam knows he can kill the two men, but he also knows what the consequence will be, for when he was a child, his father had brought him to the town to witness the burned body of the man who had been lynched. He pleads once more, but the man with the gun knocks him down. Promising to bring Melinda back in time to meet their train, they drag her away to one of the shanties across the track. Another black man who has been sleeping on a truck tells Sam mockingly, "They got your girl," and Sam beats him until he cries for mercy.

At this point, a white man emerges from the waiting room and tells Sam he is sorry for what has happened, but the armed man is the sheriff's son and the two bullies already have killed two white men in addition to untold numbers of black men. The man assures Sam he has done the only thing he could have done. Sam waits in anguish until, just before train time, the men bring Melinda back. In late afternoon the couple arrive at their home, where, all winter, Sam had worked for Melinda fashioning a table for her use, placing a stool there, saving the brightest pictures from the papers to pin against the wall. The dresser is filled with blue and white china bought with money that he had taken from his own needs. Many a time he had gone hungry that they might have something beautiful on which to serve their first meal together.

Sam cooks supper, but Melinda, unable to eat, goes into the bedroom and cries. Sam tries to comfort her. He tells Melinda that he could have killed the two men, but he would have been killed himself and she would have suffered anyway and been left alone. Pleading for understanding, he tells her

you ain't alone now, Melindy, honey-lamb, you's got me, and I'll toil
fur you while I lives. I'll help you to forget. I'll love you and I'll tend
you if you's sick lak's if you was my baby chil'. There ain't nothing I
kin do fur you as I'll leave undid. Oh, Melindy, I'm here alive. You
wouldn't rather have a dead man than a live one, would you?

After a long while, Melinda replies that she does not know, that she is
afraid. Sam puts his arm around her, but because the strength she had
counted on has failed her, she shrinks from him. The longed-for
wedding night, perhaps the marriage, is marred. Humiliated and in
despair, Sam turns his face into his pillow and sobs.[116]

Ovington's story challenged *Masses* readers; perhaps because the
dialect was rendered without condescension and its anguished central
character was so sensitively drawn, they resisted believing its central
event could be accurate. Ovington replied to the questioning letters in
the January issue, assuring readers that the story was based on an
actual event. Why should readers doubt its truth, Ovington asked,
when only the previous year, there had been a lynching in Mississippi
and people had made a holiday of it? Could they think, furthermore,
that rape was a peril only white women faced? She knew the South
well, she assured her readers, and claimed she also knew conditions in
the Negro community of New York better than her readers did, for she
had given most of her time since 1904 to the study of Negro conditions
in the United States.[117] Ovington's commitment to "Negro betterment"
was the basis for her major writings. Having previously written *Half a
Man: The Status of the Negro in New York* (1911), she went on to write
short biographies of black leaders, *Portraits in Color* (1927), and a
history of the founding of the NAACP, *The Walls Came Tumbling Down*
(1947).

Lynching—specifically the lynching of Leo Frank—is the basis of
another remarkable story, Elizabeth Hines Hanley's "Chivalry" (June
1916), in which a man, still braced with "Red Eye," returns to his wife
the morning after a lynching; he resembles a member of the mob
described in the New York Times account of the hanging as a "closely
packed mass of men all but mad with excitement and hate." His long-
intimidated wife bursts out with thoughts that have been seething for
years. Everyone knew the man was innocent, she protests, except

those who did not want to believe he was innocent. Why, she asks, didn't the killers do something for the victim while she was still living? The wife has a daughter, too, and she does not want men murdering for her when she is dead instead of keeping her sheltered and happy while she is living.

The husband expresses shock that a southern woman can talk that way, having been bred in a land where chivalry is a household word. A word is all it is, the wife counters, except when it can be used as an excuse for violence, which no woman wants to cause. Chivalry never takes the form of real help to women. The husband lets his wife understand that if it were not for the chivalry she despises, he might hurt her. The woman thinks of her children, her daughter especially, who need her, and letting her spirit go out like a "snuffed candle," gets her husband his breakfast.[118] Hanley's story is an economic, somber, and intuitive exploration of the southern woman's captivity on a pedestal. Moreover, her central character, unlike the middle class housewives in the maid stories, recognizes her entrapment within a patriarchal culture. However, the story was not a sign of the direction Hanley's career would take, for her later work was principally juvenile drama.

Helen R. Hull moved away from maid stories in "Till Death—" (January 1917), in which, through a working-class protagonist, she depicts the desperation that fueled the campaign for birth control. Against the objections of her husband, a woman works in a department store. She denies him sex because she has not been feeling well and fears another pregnancy. "There's plenty others'd be glad," her husband says. "They wouldn't be glad for long," she responds, angry that he would pay money for prostitutes but not for food for his children. When she stops working, he tells her, he will support the family again. If they need money then, their older daughter can work. But the wife has been working to keep her daughter in school. At the department store, the woman, who usually enjoys her job selling ribbons, feels sick, and is relieved when the store doctor—whom Hull, with a surprising shift to the pronoun "she," lets us know is also a woman—asks her to come to her office during the noon hour so she can examine her. The woman confides to the doctor that she is working to save enough to leave her husband, open a store, and keep her children in school. The doctor asks if the woman's husband would support her if she did not work. The woman replies that he would, and the doctor tells her what the reader has guessed: that she is pregnant and will have to quit her job to stay with her husband "for the sake of the children."[119]

Hull's *Masses* stories formed a prelude to a long writing career that included twenty novels—the last two of them mysteries, *A Tapping on the Wall* (1960) and *Close Her Pale Eyes* (1963)—and two collections of stories and novelettes. Hull, who graduated from the University of Michigan and did graduate work at the University of Chicago, combined her writing career with an equally long academic career. She taught at Wellesley from 1912 to 1915, was a lecturer in English at Barnard in 1915, and beginning in 1916, taught for over forty years at Columbia University.[120]

One of Hull's notable novels, *Islanders* (1927), has as its central character Ellen Dacey, who assumes responsibility for the family farm when her father leaves his midwestern family to seek his fortune in the California Gold Rush; she loses her claim to the land or any reward for her labor when her father returns after twenty-five years to sell the land from under her and the brother she has worked to raise and educate cheats her out of the inheritance left her by the long-departed sweetheart who did strike it rich in California. When her brother, in whose house she has lived as an unpaid servant, loses his money in bad investments, Ellen finds herself in her old age in the Long Island home of the nephew whose success in business she has made possible by forcing her brother to educate his son or face being exposed as an embezzler of her money.

Ellen hopes to redeem a lifetime of loss by living to see her grandniece, Anne, get off the island. Anne's father owns a factory where men make "tools for folks to use" and Ellen wants Anne to be part of the world outside as men are. After struggling at several jobs, Anne becomes the secretary at a suffrage organization, and through a stroke of luck, is able to do public relations. However, Anne's liberation from the island—which Ellen lives just long enough to know is about to happen—comes not through her own efforts, but through the conventional escape route, marriage; her only defiance is that she rejects a rich suitor in favor of the poor young reporter who is on his way to Europe as a correspondent in the First World War.[121]

This patient, unrebellious acceptance of limitations—even victim-ization—in a woman's life marks other of Hull's novels. It may, in part, be connected to the fact that Hull, who died in 1971, was in a long-term lesbian relationship with Mabel Louise Robinson; the resulting inability, in this assertively heterosexual culture, to express the truth of her own life may have hampered her ability to create completely self-actualizing women characters.[122]

Under her own name, Mabel Dodge published "The Eye of the Beholder" (October 1917), a story that emerges from a conversation between two men about a once-famous actress who has left the stage and disappeared after the man who wrote plays for her betrayed her.[123] More interesting for their autobiographical content are two stories Dodge wrote anonymously.[124] In the first story, "A Quarrel" (Septem-ber 1916), a woman eagerly awaits the return of her husband, an artist. Feeling crushed by her sense of "unaccomplishment," she looks to him "to animate her sense of living and to enliven her inert fire." At the same time she hates him for being the only one who can "work this magic" for her. She also hates the struggle she must make, for it is the struggle that vivifies her, although it means "grappling with him for her life at his cost."

The husband returns from his sitting and, fearing her reaction, tells her an invitation to a party will take him away from her the following day. She seems to take the news well, and feeling he has been unjust, the husband confides his fear that she would object. His confidence and well-being offend her; feeling "charged with malice," the wife replies that he might be living away from her for all she sees of him. Knowing the cause is trivial, but the struggle itself will not be trivial, the husband tries to stop the quarrel by reasonably explaining that after refusing so many invitations, he could not get out of accepting this one. Yet he knows he cannot "fend off the obscure burden she wanted to foist upon him," and indeed, the wife, "feeling vital at last in her moment of unrighteousness," woundingly proposes they go their separate ways; he must go to the garden party while she looks elsewhere for pleasure and occupation.

After an evening spent reading, they go to bed; the husband sleeps while the wife remains awake, hating the "immunity his work gave him, both sleeping and waking, and she coveted it." She stirs restlessly, and he awakens and moves into the adjoining room. The next morning, he finds her at his bedside. She reasonably explains that she must find something to do besides loving him. He has his work; she must find hers. The husband hates her reasonableness, for although he is worn out from her struggle against him, he loves her and fears the implied threat in her proposed solution.[125]

"The Parting," in the October issue, is a continuation of this complex struggle. The wife is frightened by her destructive and self-destructive dependence upon her husband; the intellectualized longing of her heart to know him and possess him and be saved by him has turned into a flood of hatred that flows into every nerve and muscle, galvanizing her into a passionate effort to be saved from him. Yet when she proposes a separation, she is perplexed by his cheerful agreement to go away and work—and in his absence, she is miserable. She wants him to suffer as she does; she longs for death. At the end of a day apart, the wife realizes that she is responsible for their difficulties and summons him back. He returns and while stroking her hand and hair, cheerfully tells her what he has been doing since they were apart. He has not suffered as she has, and his soothing fingers provide only a temporary release from her "craving for certainty, perfection, and knowledge." She feels lost once more and sees that the next day will only bring back the same lack of fulfillment.[126]

The stories, dealing with Dodge's relationship with the artist Maurice Sterne, who succeeded John Reed in her affections and whom she married in 1916,[127] reveal insight into Dodge's own contradictory impulses—but they are more interesting, perhaps, for the withering impact of those impulses on the psyche of her lover. Dodge was in many ways the emblem of her era; she was at the center of and often the moving force behind some of its memorable cultural phenomena: the Armory Show, her salon on lower Fifth Avenue, the Paterson Pageant. She underwent Freudian analysis.[128] She had credibility as a leader and thinker; Max Eastman invited her to join his editorial board in 1913,[129] and in 1917, she became an advice columnist for the Hearst chain. Yet, as *The Masses* stories reveal, Dodge, far from arriving at a harmonizing ideal, or reaching personal liberation, was filled with inner conflict, torn between a desire to fill "the time-honored female role" of nurturer to male egos and the need to achieve success as men measured it.

The short fiction contributions by women often were given prominence through an announcement of the cover—"A Story by Adriana Spadoni"—or, like Hanley's "Chivalry" or Ovington's "The White Brute," a position at the front of the issue. However, in the area representing the magazine's intellectual identity, nonfiction prose, women were not well represented. As reporters or essayists, women never appeared issue after issue with the consistency of the "regulars," who, after Eastman, Dell, and Reed, included Horatio Winslow, Horace Brubaker, William English Walling, Charles Edward Wood, and later Arturo Giovanitti and Frank Bohn. *The Masses* published nonfiction prose contributions from approximately twenty-five women during its five years under Eastman, and, as in the case of the poetry and fiction, most of them were one-time contributions of singular, slight pieces like Isabel R. Mayer's "Culture and Crochet," an account of John Cowper Powys's lecture on August Strindberg's *The Father* to an audience of teachers, two of whom diligently crocheted while Powys spoke.[130] Articles like this one, probably unsolicited and perhaps published because they usefully filled up a page, were inconsequential when placed in context with Eastman's jeremiads, Dell's deft analyses, and Reed's reports of late-breaking events in distant cities or frontiers. Moreover, an issue that included one or even three nonfiction prose articles by women, typically would have five, eight, or even a dozen essays by men—Eastman, Dell, or Reed often accounting for several each.

Of the relative handful of women whose prose pieces were published, a number no doubt were chosen because of their authority, or even celebrity, in other fields. Expertise was not necessarily incompatible with lively writing. For example, the Socialist Party leader Kate Richards O'Hare's April 1915 essay, "Booze and Revolution," made the claim that legislation sponsored by the ruling class to control liquor consumption actually would speed the revolution, because a more sober and thus more efficient and clear-headed working class no longer would be satisfied with "a slave's hut, a serf's cot or a modern city slum."[131]

O'Hare's essay, although brief, provides evidence of the quality that made O'Hare a formidable Socialist organizer like Eugene Debs.

She toured the country tirelessly from 1902 until 1918, taking time out to give birth to four children, including twins, Eugene and Victor. She was a Socialist Party candidate for Congress in Kansas in 1910, and, in 1916, she ran for the United States Senate in Missouri. Her anti-war speeches and writings resulted in government prosecution. She was indicted and convicted under the Espionage Act in 1917, and, after appeals failed, she entered the Missouri State Penitentiary in April 1919. O'Hare's prison experiences, especially as a pieceworking seamstress under a system of contract labor, led to a career as a prison reformer following her release in 1921.[132]

A connection to a *Masses* man also could result in an appearance in its pages. Traveling in Europe with John Reed during the summer of 1914, Mabel Dodge sent back her debut article, "The Secret of War," an account of the excitement she found everywhere about the approaching conflict. With the Germans only a few miles away, Dodge compared Paris in the sunshine to "a great lady going to the guillotine in grande toilette." Machinery was transforming war, a wounded soldier informed her; in hand-to-hand combat, men could not keep mowing each other down, but with the machine gun, "you just go on turning the handle." The war machine also was turning out propaganda inciting people with images of the brave boy at the front. Few people saw that behind the war machinery to which they were sacrificing their sons was a power struggle between competing ruling classes. Only women questioned the reasons for the war. The "secret" Dodge had discovered was that men were aroused by the noise and pageantry of combat; the only hope for permanent peace, in Dodge's view, lay "in a women's war against war."[133]

After leaving her Portland, Oregon dentist husband to join John Reed in New York, Louise Bryant became a *Masses* contributor. Her essay of April 1916, "Two Judges," paid tribute to two judges in her home state, one who refused to sentence unemployed men to the rock pile and another who dismissed charges brought against Emma Goldman because "everyone knows we are all shocked by things publicly stated that we know privately ourselves."[134] Bryant accompanied John Reed to France in 1917 to report on the war, and was listed as co-author with him of "News from France," an article dealing with the wartime experiences of common soldiers.[135]

One of the magazine's literary editors, Mary Heaton Vorse, wrote only one article for *The Masses*: "Accessories before the Fact," an account in the November 1916 issue of the strike by ironworkers at the Mesabi Range in Minnesota. Vorse's trip to the iron range had been costly in personal terms; recently widowed for the second time, she was responsible for the care of three children, the youngest her two-and-a-half-year-old son by Joe O'Brien. Only a pressing letter from Elizabeth Gurley Flynn, following on a telegraph from Bill Haywood, persuaded her to leave her children with her mother-in-law and go to the midwest.[136]

In her *Masses* account, Vorse wrote of the imprisonment of a young miner, his wife, and three miners boarding in their home under a charge of having murdered one of the deputies who had come to their home because the husband was "wanted" for an unspecified crime. When two deputies had entered the home and assaulted the couple with clubs, the three boarders had come to their defense; during the ensuing brawl, the deputies had drawn their guns, a shot had been fired, and a deputy had been killed. Wholesale arrests followed the deputy's death, along with mass entry into and searches of the striking miners' homes. Also arrested were Carlo Tresca, Joe Schmidt, Sam Scarlett, and two other IWW organizers (Vorse did not identify the strike leaders as Wobblies in her article) on a charge of accessory before the fact, which, Vorse claimed, often was used in labor disturbances in order to attribute any resulting violence to the incendiary talk of organizers.

Another familiar feature of labor conflict, Vorse informed her readers, is the army of gunmen who enter a community after the company owners, aided by a cooperative press, have stirred up public opinion against the strikers and the "outside agitators" who lead them. Then the gang of "crooks and disorderly characters" are imported, and "it's a pretty poor crowd that can't start something so that we presently find the strike leaders in jail charged with murder as accessories before the fact." The mayors and businessmen of the communities affected by the strike were pressing United States Steel to settle the strike, but the company had refused to deal with the strikers "and with its limitless power it will try to crush all attempts at organizing among its workers." [137]

Another significant *Masses* contributor, Elsie Clews Parsons, wrote essays that were subtly subversive of patriarchal mores confining women's sexuality. In "Marriage: A New Life" (September 1916), Parsons examined the ways in which brides in many societies traditionally had been expected to change their homes, religions, clothing, and ornamentation after marriage. Although women now were expected to make fewer such changes, marriage still was regarded as the moment of supreme importance in a woman's life. By making marriage a novel and rare occasion, society concentrates sexual relationships within marriage. Once a woman marries, Parsons observed, her sexuality "must stay put."[138]

Parsons continued this theme in "Engagements" (November 1916), arguing that the betrothal ritual enables outsiders rather than the couple themselves to adjust to an impending marriage, for a betrothal period seldom was a time for a couple to become acquainted. Parsons cited the avoidance taboos of a number of societies arising from apprehension of "an untimely anticipation of conjugal rights." Alternative to the separation of the couple in order to relieve the anxiety of onlookers, the couple could be obliged to undergo "compulsory association," requiring them to be circumspect before others while being conspicuously devoted to each other. However, onlookers found engagements far less satisfactory than marriage, and once a couple announced their intention to wed, they were expected to wed; they were expected to marry promptly, and they certainly were not to consider their own preferences with respect to marriage.[139]

Although Inez Haynes Irwin was less involved in *The Masses* during the Eastman years than she had been during the Vlag years, she contributed several insightful essays. In "Stray Thoughts on Chivalry" (October-November 1915), she analyzed the lynching of Leo Frank in terms of the hypocrisy of the southern code of chivalry that had provided the rationale for the murder, pointing out that if child labor laws had been in effect in Georgia, the thirteen-year-old victim, Mary Phagan, still might be alive. Echoing the point Elizabeth Hines Hanley had made in her short story, "Chivalry," Irwin asserted that if the state of Georgia truly were interested in protecting its womenfolk, it would not have a factory system based primarily on the labor of white female minors.[140]

During the Vlag years, Irwin had written cheerful stories about young women's romances with Harvard students and sentimental stories about unhappy children. The change in the tone and substance of her articles for *The Masses* can be accounted for by her experiences in San Francisco, where she went in 1913 in order to establish residence before divorcing her first husband, Rufus Hamilton Gillmore. Through a friendship with Maud Younger, a woman from a wealthy family who had become a waitress and then a union activist, Irwin met people in the labor movement. She became involved in a strike of California hop pickers organized by the IWW. Her activities on behalf of the Wobbly-led strikers produced a consequence Irwin probably had not anticipated: a reputation as a radical that followed her back to New York.[141]

The California hop pickers' strike transformed Irwin as the Lowell textile workers' strike transformed Mary Heaton Vorse. In 1915, Irwin attended sessions of an investigation into industrial conflict conducted by the Federal Commission of Industrial Relations under the leadership of a Wilson appointee, Frank W. P. Walsh. Irwin wrote for the March 1915 issue of *The Masses* about these hearings, which, in New York, were held in the elegant Board of Estimate Room of City Hall; there, before an emotionally charged audience that included "single-taxers, socialists, anarchists, members of the AF of L, the IWW, poets, novelists, dramatists, investigators of all kinds, reformers and revolutionists of every description," an equally diverse group of witnesses gave testimony. A mother told of the deaths of her three children when the militia attacked the tent colony at Ludlow, Colorado occupied by workers striking against a Rockefeller subsidiary, the Colorado Fuel and Iron Company. A pick-and-shovel operator for the American Agricultural Chemical Company in Roosevelt, New Jersey spoke of the conditions that finally had led to a strike during which striking workers had been shot.

But a large group of leaders of the industries in which these violent events had occurred also testified and Irwin's writing about them is especially vivid. She qualified their testimony by dividing them into four classes: those who claimed not to know or be interested in the conditions of workers, such as J. P. Morgan; those who knew about the conditions, but, with their backs to the wall, were fighting labor, like the Rockefellers; those who knew the conditions and were willing to give way but not enough to cut profits, like Guggenheim; and those who thought a paternalistic system would resolve conflict, like Ford.

Irwin went on to describe individual capitalists: Morgan seemed like "a delightful dinner guest, and ideal weekend visitor"; Andrew Carnegie's impaired mentality was compensated for by the warm personality of a "little Santa Claus"; John D. Rockefeller, Jr. was "gentle, Christianish, but cold as steel and as unmalleable as stone"; and John D. Rockefeller, Sr., if given the clothes of the period, could have emerged "from the portrait of some medieval monarch." Irwin admitted that she had gone to the hearings apprehensive that she might discover these "Napoleons of Finance" unfairly endowed by nature with a commanding genius that labor should not even attempt to oppose, but when she compared their "fox-like evasions and downright mendacity" with the "passionate conviction and forthright expression" of the leaders of labor, they seemed "to belong not only to another generation, but to another century, to another world . . . .members of an order that is passing."[142]

Irwin attended the Washington sessions of the Commission hearings and sent back an account, "Shadows of Revolt," to the June 1915 issue of *The Masses* which was dominated by one personality, the arch-antagonist of capitalism, Mother Jones. Irwin described the venerable organizer as a "little, trim, tight-waisted old lady with . . . soft white hair and kind blue eyes," a woman one would think of as a gentle grandmother until one studied the adamant, close-set lips, and the "eternal anger" in the eyes and saw the "warrior spirit" in the face. In one of the excerpts from Jones's testimony Irwin included, the organizer told of a night in Ludlow when all the women were arrested and put in jail with their babies, and she said to them, "'You sing all night.' And the women sang all night and the men in the jail told them to shut up and the women wouldn't shut up and the children wouldn't shut up and the babies wouldn't shut up and nobody wouldn't shut up and so the next morning they let them out."

Irwin wrote that the commission had performed a service for labor by allowing it to tell its story for the first time, in its own way, at its own length—with an entire country for its audience. Irwin confided that as she tried to piece together the parts of the labor story she had heard from California labor men and other witnesses in the cities where hearings had been held, she concluded that in the struggle "to the death" with capital, "labor shall go on and on and on."[143]

Irwin's romantic view of the American labor movement strongly flavored her account of the AFL Convention in San Francisco (February 1916), which she reported in the context of other events she had witnessed: Henry Cabot Lodge making a brilliant speech in Boston; Russian revolutionaries gathering in France to throw flowers at their comrade, Vera Figner, released after twenty years in a Russian prison; strikers in Paterson roaring when Elizabeth Gurley Flynn suddenly came out on the speakers' balcony. These had all been wonderful moments, Irwin wrote, but nothing had been as thrilling as the convention. Never, she wrote, had she seen men of such size, weight, and girth; watching the delegates file into the hall was like seeing "lions leaping into the arena for their act." Irwin recorded the dazzling sexual attraction of the delegates' "extraordinary physique":

> High-standing, erect, incredibly broad-shouldered and deep-chested, arms and legs like young tree-trunks; torsos muscle-packed to a heroic brawn and bulk; bodies of a granite hardness, yet lightly-handled, perfectly poised; faces burned by the weather to a permanent deep red; straight-gazing eyes, clear as mountain lakes; jaws that set themselves in the lines of adamant; faces, in quiet, of a calm, clear keenness; watchful, patient, appraising, humorous; in anger, iron masks that poured fire from eye-sockets and thunder from mouth-orifices; voices that roared and rumbled, tore and thrilled; those voices echoed through my consciousness long after I had gone to sleep at night.

Irwin spent four and a half days at the convention, studying the men of many nationalities who somehow had blended into what she viewed as the ideal type of American to emerge from the democratic experiment. At the end of her mission to educate herself on American labor, she came away with an appreciation of how much the men knew about living conditions and the economic laws behind them, about world movements and the economic laws behind those. As Mary Heaton Vorse had concluded after her experience in Lowell that the strike was a college for workers, Irwin concluded that the trade union was "the only institution in this country that offers a training in citizenship."[144]

This was the last account Irwin would write for *The Masses.* In the same month her AFL article appeared, she married Will Irwin, a correspondent for the *Saturday Evening Post,* and accompanied him to Europe where he reported on the war for his magazine and Inez wrote for other publications, including *The Liberator,* which Eastman established after the government suppressed *The Masses.*[145]

Irwin's work includes her 1914 novel, *Angel Island,* a book with a feminist theme about marriages between five men shipwrecked on a tropical island and the five winged women they find there and capture. Having clipped their wives' wings, the men settle with their angelic partners into a domestic routine that eventually leaves them all discontented. No longer able to fly and unable to walk, the women are bored with the domestic routines of husband-tending and child-rearing and are resentful that their husbands, for whom they were once new toys with a secret spring, no longer find them enchanting and prefer work to sex. Finding their immobile wives burdensome, the men complain of the limitations they have imposed on the women. Having secretly taught themselves to walk, the women rebel and leave the community. Eventually the couples are reconciled when the men understand and agree that the women must have mobility and purposeful work.[146]

The first article by Helen Marot, who was the only woman essayist to appear consistently for a period of time in *The Masses,* had more sophistication about the labor movement because Marot, being a longtime labor activist, had none of Irwin's romantic idealism. In "Revolutionary Spirit at Seattle" (January 1914), Marot supported the opposition mounted at the AFL convention by a group of California trade unionists to the leadership of Samuel Gompers on the grounds that when they had struck against the Pacific Gas and Electric Company, the federation had offered to supply electrical workers to the company, thus engaging in strike breaking.[147]

Marot's articles began appearing more regularly after *The Masses* merged in April 1916 with *The New Review,* which Eastman had set up in 1913 as "a journal of American Marxism."[148] Thereafter, articles by Marot, each on some aspect of American trade unionism and each

initialed "H.M."—as was the practice among the regular writers—
appeared monthly, sometimes several in a single issue. In "Actors and
Teachers" (June 1916), Marot reported on efforts within each profession to affiliate with the trade union movement; only by surrendering
the illusion of their independence as artists and professionals and
recognizing their identity as workers, Marot argued, could actors and
teachers achieve any real power. Moreover, any success they achieved
would only make people aware of "trade unionism's revolutionary
significance," inspire a new desire for power within the labor movement, and bring about an era of real industrial democracy.[149]

In "Revolution and the Garment Trade" (August 1916), Marot
attacked the undemocratic practices of the Jewish leaders of the
garment trade that had caused, it will be remembered, a rift with Rose
Schneiderman. From the perspective of a trade union insider, Marot
claimed that the rise of Russian Jews to leadership in the garment
unions had resulted in successful organization at the sacrifice of
democracy, a loss resented by Italian garment workers, whose concepts of revolution and democracy were like those of Americans.[150]

In "Educating the Teachers" (August 1916), "H.M." predicted that
the non-rehiring of eighteen Chicago teachers who had belonged to a
union would give momentum to the trade union movement among
teachers. She also added, uncharitably, that the eighteen fired teachers
would have an opportunity to come down from their pedestals "to my
level and into the common experience of wage earners."[151]

"Railroads and Revolution," the featured article of the November
1916 issue, demonstrated Marot's skill in making complex issues
accessible to readers. For over thirty years, Marot explained, the
leaders of the railroad brotherhoods had tried to gain better wages and
working conditions without striking. In Marot's analysis, an idealism
"that might have emanated from Brook Farm" made the leaders certain
that when managers recognized that trainmen were adamant, they
would concede. But when the railroads had experienced a great
expansion of business yet still refused to yield to the trainmen's
demands, on the grounds they wanted to reserve surplus profits for
capitalization in order to get still more business, A. B. Garretson, their
leader, at last called a strike and even rejected President Wilson's
appeal to postpone it. His position had caused Congress to legislate

wage concessions to all railroad workers, including those not eligible for membership in the brotherhoods, thereby accomplishing what the brotherhoods in thirty years had been unable or unwilling to do: extend economic gains among all workers in the railroad industry.

However, there was a drawback, Marot explained. Unless the Supreme Court declared Congress's action unconstitutional, the fixing of wage conditions was shifted from collective bargaining to Congress, and workers therefore were under government ownership, bound by obligations the corporations could evade by forcing concessions from Congress. The brotherhoods had not wanted settlement through legislation, but had accepted it rather than involving the nation in a strike. However, Marot alerted her readers, railroad directors already were challenging Congress's action, or flouting it out of certainty that the Supreme Court would reverse the decision. If the court so acted, Marot warned, the country would sell out the trainmen, and "may have to face the wrath of good men." [152]

Marot's articles consistently balanced advocacy of trade unionism and opposition to anti-labor actions with criticism of elitism within the labor movement. In "The Railroad Question" (April 1917), the last article Marot wrote for the magazine before it stopped publishing, she again turned to the railroad dispute. A bill had been introduced in Congress that granted the president power to take over the railroads whenever it was necessary to overcome obstruction in mail transportation. But even with this anti-strike action, Marot explained, the railroad brotherhoods were at an impasse, for the hope of promotion from one class of service to another that had made men support conservative policies was gone because of the innovation of the big locomotive. Demotion and unemployment had followed the improvement of engines; since craft union distinctions had disappeared with advanced technology, Marot therefore urged the industrial organization of all workers connected with railroad transportation. [153]

Marot's dominating presence in *The Masses* may have been a reason why, except for Rose Pastor Stokes, Socialist Jewish women associated with the labor movement were not among the magazine's contributors. Theresa Malkiel wrote regularly for the *Call,* and she and Pauline Newman also wrote on labor issues for *Socialist Woman/ Progressive Woman.* Malkiel also contributed critical essays, including one on *Hedda Gabbler,* reflecting that if Hedda had had "free access to the general sphere of life; if she had been taught the means of guiding her own destiny . . . she would have, in all probability, never married Tesman, thus saving herself from destruction and society the loss of two human lives."[154]

This kind of analysis, which would have been appropriate in *The Masses,* was representative of the wide-ranging writing that the editor-publisher, Josephine Conger-Kaneko, included in each issue. Unfortunately for the magazine's talented contributors, Conger-Kaneko was too independent to follow the Socialist Party line, and her recruitment of non-Socialist subscribers brought a charge that *Progressive Woman* was not a Socialist women's magazine.[155] Seeking to build on the popularity of an earlier Socialist journal of the 1890s, she changed the name to *Coming Nation,* but despite a valiant struggle to keep her publication alive, opposition from women party leaders left her politically isolated and without funds. Her magazine folded in 1914.[156] Ironically, Conger-Kaneko's best hope for saving her magazine may have been to merge with Piet Vlag's *Masses,* a plan that failed when the magazine's collective chose Max Eastman to be editor.

After *The Masses* stopped publishing, Marot became an editor at *The Dial,* bringing to that publication the political perspective she had been able to sharpen through her experience at *The Masses.* The events that forced Marot and the other contributors to move on from their *Masses* base were unremarkable. In early summer 1917, when the magazine collective's principal leaders were occupied with projects closer to their individual hearts, the responsibility for putting out the August issue was left to a recently hired twenty-year-old assistant editor, Dorothy Day, whose editorial decisions resulted in the arrest and trial of her absent colleagues for the crime of treason.[157]

CHAPTER 10

Aftermath

THE MOOD OF THE NATION darkened ominously after the United States entered World War I in April 1917. What formerly had been patriotic hysteria during the "preparedness" era preceding America's entry into the conflict—when meetings of the New York Woman's Peace Party had been broken up by violent patriots[1]—burst into full-blown repression after the declaration of war in April. The Espionage Act, passed by Congress in June 1917, made—for the first time since the eighteenth century—words as well as deeds liable to be treated as treasonable. When the August issue of *The Masses* was declared "unmailable" by the New York postmaster, three more issues were distributed on newsstands before the magazine was forced to go out of business.[2] Eastman, Dell, Reed, Art Young, and Merrill Rogers, the business manager, were indicted under the Espionage Act; their nine-day trial in April 1918 ended in a hung jury. A second five-day trial in October also ended in a hung jury, and the government dropped its case against *The Masses*.[3]

Eastman recruited his sister Crystal to join him as "co-editor and manager and money-raiser" of a successor publication, *The Liberator.* This arrangement with his "brilliantly executive sister" enabled Eastman to preserve the glamorous institution that had, he claimed, grown up in his hands of its own spontaneous will, while at the same time leaving him free to live his "creative life." However, the new magazine was to differ in three important respects from *The Masses*. It was to be less "rambunctious"; Floyd Dell and Crystal Eastman were to share responsibility for the magazine, allowing Eastman to enjoy his creative "truancy," and all pretense that the magazine was collectively run was to be abandoned.[4]

The Liberator's circulation in its first month doubled that of The Masses and rose to 60,000 at its peak. It published some remarkable documents: V. I. Lenin's "Letter to American Workingmen"; articles by Bill Haywood, William Z. Foster, the leader of the 1919 steel strike, and the Hungarian Communist leader, Bela Kun; and contributions from Edna St. Vincent Millay, William Carlos Williams, S. N. Behrmann, e. e. cummings, John Dos Passos, Louise Bogan, Edmund Wilson, and Sherwood Anderson.[5] But the war and its repressive aftermath had an impact on the magazine that made its tone, style, and content markedly different from those of its predecessor. During the war, poems and essays from imprisoned "Wobblies" and conscientious objectors appeared regularly; afterward, articles about labor struggles in the United States, class conflict in Europe, the consolidation of the Bolshevik revolution in the Soviet Union, the deportation of foreign-born dissenters,and racism throughout the nation and terrorism in the South produced an increasingly serious and ideological magazine.

Eventually, all connections were severed with the Socialist Party, or what remained of it after the party conference of 1919 split the Socialists into three factions: the old right wing and two communist parties, one led by Russian immigrants, one an American party of which John Reed was the principal organizer and leader. After quickly being driven underground, the two communist parties reemerged in 1921, joining forces in an effort to establish a legal entity, the Workers Party. The editorial group that eventually took over The Liberator were militant members of this party.[6] The old Masses triumvirate passed from the scene. John Reed returned to Russia, traveling as a stoker on a Scandinavian liner, to attend the Second Congress of the Communist International where he was elected to the Party Executive Committee. He later was stricken with typhus and in October 1920, was "dead at his Revolutionary post."[7] Max Eastman, who had always intended to "loose the chains" that bound him to The Liberator in order to be free to write poetry and criticism, resigned as co-editor in January 1921.[8] Although Floyd Dell remained involved in the magazine, his connection waned after he became happily married and absorbed in family life and novel-writing in Croton, New York.[9]

Crystal Eastman, who had been left in charge after her brother resigned, became ill and withdrew from the magazine in March 1921.[10] However, she insured the magazine's continued life by installing as successor another competent woman—the business manager, Margaret Lowe, who afterward was succeeded by yet another competent woman, Lena Borovitz.[11]

The Liberator underwent several subsequent regimes; in its final stage before being absorbed into the Workers Party in October 1924, the editorial staff was listed under two columns, one titled "Political," the other titled "Art." The principal successors were, at various times, Michael Gold, who as "Irwin Granich" had contributed to *The Masses* in his teens; Joseph Freeman, the son of prosperous immigrants; Claude McKay, a Jamaican-born poet; and Robert Minor, a cartoonist who had renounced his art for politics.[12] Together with a secondary band of Workers Party militants such as Jay Lovestone and Carl Haesden, this group—in the final stages whittled down to Robert Minor—led *The Liberator* away from *The Masses's* irreverence to grim dogmatism, culminating in the pledge published in the final October 1924 issue that when it reemerged as *The Workers Monthly,* the political struggle of the working class against the complacent dictatorship of the United States and the world would be summarized and interpreted in the light of Marx and Lenin.[13]

After Eastman's departure as executive editor, little of the magazine he had brought to life remained. The artwork that had emblazoned and often dominated *The Masses* became more illustrative. Floyd Dell continued to write essays celebrating family life and literature and analyzing relations between the sexes; these topics were of little interest to the Young Turks with whom he debated in the family atmosphere of *The Liberator* office and to whom he often served as father-confessor during weekends when they were guests in his Croton home.[14] However, the affection in which Dell was held by the young men eager to break from society and enter the worldwide revolutionary movement did not prevent them from being contemptuous of the era he symbolized to them: the irrelevant, trivial bohemia of prewar Greenwich Village.

In a flash of old *Masses* wit, Dell retaliated against their dogmatism in "Explanations and Apologies," an essay in the June 1922 issue.

Acknowledging that he had called Michael Gold—"off attending conventions and reporting strikes"—middle-class, a charge that had dismayed the staff, Dell insisted that not only was Comrade Mike middle-class, but so was Comrade Max, and "all the rest of them; and so, of course, am I." The difference was that Dell knew he was middle-class and they did not. Moreover, Dell felt no reason to be ashamed of being middle-class; he did not want to join the proletariat. He wanted to assist them to become aesthetes. Comrade Mike, by contrast, idealized the strength involved in labor; he "falls down in prayerful awe before Steam and Steel and Mother Earth, and Mud and Heat, and such things." That attitude, in Dell's opinion, confirmed Gold's middle-class status, for the man who must work at such things puts up with them because he must and afterward tries to forget them.[15]

Another principal difference between the men of *The Masses* and the men of *The Liberator* was their attitude toward women. Eastman, Reed, and Dell, if not egalitarian in their relationships with women, nevertheless were interested in them. As far as their successors were concerned, women were irrelevant. Eastman had maintained in *The Liberator* his fervent support for suffrage, in the first issue characteristically hailing Women's Party leader Alice Paul and "her young army of militants" as one of the powers "that may sweep the country clean for liberty."[16] However, after the departure first of Max and then of Crystal Eastman, feminist issues were almost never raised, either by the men who were in charge of the magazine, or the few women who continued to contribute to it. Poetry was included in *The Liberator,* for it easily filled empty spaces. Hortense Flexner, Babette Deutsch, Lydia Gibson, Rose Pastor Stokes, Jean Starr Untermeyer, and other women who had contributed poems to *The Masses* were *Liberator* contributors, along with newcomers such as Genevieve Taggard, who collected the poetry of *The Masses* and *The Liberator* into an anthology, *May Days.* However, the joyful eroticism of many women's poems in *The Masses* was gone, and a poem about menstruation would have been rejected with disgust by Eastman's successors.

Short stories by women were fewer than they had been in *The Masses,* but so were short stories by men, since *The Liberator* became dominated by accounts of labor conflict and political repression in the United States, the spread of fascism abroad, and accounts of pilgrimages to the Soviet Union by Max Eastman, Robert Minor, Claude McKay, Rose Pastor Stokes, and others. Mary Heaton Vorse was often in Washington after *The Liberator* was launched, writing articles on labor under wartime conditions and propaganda pamphlets for the government on the struggles of the small captive nations—Poland, Czechoslovakia, and Yugoslavia—to free themselves from "the Hapsburg yoke." Later she went to Europe, employed by the American Red Cross to publicize its campaign to aid war victims and under assignment to write articles for *McCall's* and *Harper's* magazines.[17]

When she returned to the United States, Vorse got assignments to write on the industry-wide steel strike of 1919. A report on the strike was Vorse's first contribution to *The Liberator*.[18] The strike provided the background of several stories she wrote for *The Liberator*, all of them expressing the bleak mood of the postwar era. In "The Hopper," for example, a working-class Canadian veteran returns home to his wife and three children. During the war, the couple had "imagined a marriage that had never been," and finding in each other "no resemblance to the sweethearts they had each dreamed," they both feel cheated and injured. The man works as a packer; he loses the job and gets drunk. He dreams of feeding his own limbs into a huge hopper; awake and sober, he tries to run away, but knows he must return home. As a soldier he never had deserted, had done things he had not known himself capable of doing, and now he must be a husband and father, a task "harder to face than death."[19] This and other stories Vorse wrote for *The Liberator* reflect the pessimism of the times and have none of the wit and humor that marked "Tolerance" or the Mrs. Phelan stories she wrote for *The Masses*.

With respect to journalism contributions, Vorse wrote, in addition to her report on the steel strike, articles about conditions in the coal industry and the activities of Alexander Howat, an organizer and dissenter in the United Mine Workers of America, led by John L. Lewis.[20] Mary White Ovington reported on the efforts of black and white lumber workers in Louisiana to integrate their union, and on the terrorist campaign against the workers led by the Great Southern Lumber Company, which resulted in the lynching of a black worker and a fatal assault on three white workers.[21]

The *Masses/Liberator* women also recorded the turbulent conditions in Europe. These contributions include Inez Haynes Irwin's remarkable account of the war in Italy, "Just Before the Drive," in the May 1918 issue. Traveling with her husband to the front lines, Irwin wrote of seeing so many wounded Italian soldiers returning from the front, "that if I had been told I had seen a hundred thousand, I would have believed it." She reported passing hospitals, motorized military transports, and farm animals bearing the household goods of fleeing civilians. At rest stations Irwin saw groups of men washing, "beating the soiled clothes with stones, and every bush, every wall, every door, every window, every roof held drying masculine garments of some sort."[22]

Traveling in Europe after the armistice, Crystal Eastman sent back reports, including interviews with the Hungarian Communist leader Bela Kun—one when his government was in power and a second when he was interned in Austria after the fall of his government.[23] Louise Bryant, traveling on assignment from the International News Service, had journeyed to the Soviet Union to be reunited with John Reed. On the morning of September 15 1920, he ran shouting with joy to greet her in her Moscow hotel room; a month later, weakened by solitary confinement and a diet of raw fish during his imprisonment in Finland, further weakened by twenty-hour workdays offered in service to the revolution, Reed fell ill of typhus and died. Bryant sent back to *The Liberator* an account of Reed's last days:

> He was never delirious in the hideous way most typhus patients are. He always knew me and his mind was full of poems and stories and beautiful thoughts. He would say, "You know how it is when you go to Venice. You ask people—is this Venice?—just for the pleasure of hearing the reply." He would tell me that the water he drank was full of little songs. And he related, like a child, wonderful experiences we had together in which we were very brave.
>
> Five days before he died his right side was paralyzed. After that he could not speak. And so we watched through days and nights hoping against hope. Even when he died I did not believe it. I must have been there hours afterward still talking to him and holding his hands.

During Reed's funeral in Red Square, Bryant collapsed, and she awoke later in her own bed with Emma Goldman, Alexander Berkman, two doctors, and a young Red Army officer in attendance. She was suffering from what was diagnosed as a "very severe heart attack," but her recuperative powers were stronger than the doctors believed, Bryant claimed, and she vowed to return home to keep her promise to Reed that, in the event of his death, she would put his works in order.[24]

However, after recovering, Bryant did not return home, but went, with Lenin's permission, to report on conditions in Turkey, Afghanistan, and Bokhara.[25] She produced a series of articles on the revolution in its "gray days," when it had settled down into the monotonous task of reconstruction; this series included one notable article on Emma Goldman's unhappy shared exile with Alexander Berkman.[26]

Meanwhile, the triumphant end in 1917 of the long struggle to achieve suffrage in New York immediately was challenged by mean-spirited editorials in the *New York Times*. On November 8, the day after the suffragists won the franchise, the editors played to the xenophobia of the citizenry by reminding them that many more than a third of the city's population were foreign-born, and that Tammany would be "indefatigable" in getting naturalized every foreign-born woman on whose vote it could count.[27] The next day, the *Times* editors delivered another attack by observing that the suffragists' Cooper Union celebration was "naturally given to rejoicing and rose-wreathed anticipation after the New York victory, by whatever pacifist and pro-German aid attained."

The editorial challenged the suffragists, because of the many Socialists and pacifists among them who were solidly against the war, to "declare their patriotism."[28] The soundly trounced anti-suffrage organization immediately disbanded and challenged suffragists to join them in a campaign to "get behind the war."[29] Some anti-suffragists went so far as to attack suffragists for being pro-German.[30] The journal of the National Association Opposed to Woman Suffrage, the *Woman's Protest*, lumped suffragists, feminists, pacifists, and socialists together as a "movement which weakens government, corrupts society, and threatens the very existence of our great experiment in democracy."[31]

The indefatigable *New York Times* continued its campaign against disloyalty, with an emphasis on public schools. Days after questioning the patriotism of suffragists, it railed that the

teacher's desk has been made a soap-box platform. Pacifism, opposition to the war, attacks upon the Government have prevailed. There
has been a deliberate campaign of disorder; and the mutinous and
violent demonstrations of so many public school pupils in the
municipal were only one crop of the seeds of treason sedulously
scattered by teachers.[32]

The *Times* went on to decry the "education of traitors" and the
transformation of schools into "annexes" of the German empire, and
insisted upon "the thorough Americanization of the schools." The
Times demanded that a number of teachers accused of disloyalty be
transferred or suspended, actions that were supported by the faculties
of many schools, most supervisors, Board of Education members, and
the Vigilance Corps of the American Defense Society. In such a climate,
opposing the practice of suspension without trial, as did the Teachers
Union and individuals such as Clara C. Cortland, a junior high school
principal, required courage indeed.[33]

     Never one to lack courage, Emma Goldman organized anti-
conscription rallies, even when the police ordered managers of assembly halls not to rent their premises for the meetings. Her anti-war
activities led to her arrest, and despite a spirited defense by Goldman
and Alexander Berkman that included testimony from a number of
witnesses to the effect that the defendants never had urged anyone not
to register for the draft, the prosecution played upon the prejudices of
the jury, who, after deliberating for thirty-nine minutes, convicted
them of conspiracy against the draft. Goldman served two years in the
Missouri State Penitentiary in Jefferson, Missouri, where her neighbor
in the cell on the right was Kate Richards O'Hare, convicted on an
espionage charge. "Red Emma" and "Red Kate," who, Goldman
acknowledged, might have remained strangers on the outside, became
fast friends in prison, and O'Hare began in Jefferson the improvements
in the conditions for women prisoners that evolved into a career as a
prison reformer following her release.[34]

     The war had caused deep rifts within the suffrage movement and
among feminists, but Heterodoxy survived a crisis when "super
patriots" were shocked at the anti-war sentiments freely expressed at
meetings and demanded the expulsion of Rose Pastor Stokes and

Elizabeth Gurley Flynn. When the club refused, they resigned. But the Russian Revolution caused an even deeper shift in loyalties. Stokes became a charter member of the American Communist Party. Flynn, who still considered herself an IWW in her convictions, was finding her views considerably modified by her association with suffragists and Communists and was busy, as an employee of the Workers Defense Union—which later merged with the American Civil Liberties Union—trying to bridge differences between and within political groups in order to maintain a united front for political prisoners.[35]

Despite the curtailment of civil liberties 1919 began with optimism: the Senate had passed the suffrage amendment and ratification was achieved in the following year. During the war, women had taken jobs in steel and lumber mills, the aircraft industry, and electrical and chemical plants. Almost one fifth of employed women belonged to trade unions, and, under pressure from the Women's Trade Union League, the National War Board moved to equalize women's pay.

But the end of the war resulted in women being forced out of the "men's" jobs they had entered during the war. The year the Nineteenth Amendment was ratified,1920, was also the year the Eighteenth Amendment—Prohibition—went into effect. Having originated in the desire of women to prevent their husbands from spending on alcohol the earnings that were needed for a family's food, clothing, and shelter, the law had the ironic result of elevating liquor to a glamorous forbidden status. The flapper replaced the feminist and "speakeasies" replaced suffrage gatherings. To the women of the 1920s, rebellion meant "smoking, dancing like Voodoo devotees, dressing decollete, 'petting' and drinking." The modern college woman, "armed with sexual knowledge," "kisses the boys, dances with them, drinks with them," all in a spirit of comradeship "running rampant." But in claiming the heterosexual pleasures, these young women did not acknowledge the debt they owed to the feminists of the previous decade, whom they viewed somewhat disdainfully across a generational divide, and they would not for the world have recognized themselves as members of the same breed. "Sex consciousness," one of the younger generation declared, "was one of the first things which had to be left behind." According to one suffrage veteran, "Oh, do have done with this eternal talk about women!" was the typical response of the young.[36] Charlotte Perkins Gilman expressed gratification that full suffrage for women had been attained, but complained that she had expected better things of women: "They remain, for instance, as much the slaves of fashion as before, lifting their skirts, baring their backs, exhibiting their legs, powdering their noses, behaving just as foolishly as ever, if not more so." Gilman remained hopeful, however, that "this backwash of primitive femininity" would be gradually overcome and real progress in woman's social development would occur.[37]

But the progress that might have been predicted by the great surge of the women's movements in the teens did not occur in the next decades, either because women were absorbed into the two-party system where a rise to political office was beyond the reach of a woman, or because the women divided in the postwar years, when anti-German sentiment turned to anti-Bolshevism. The blending of feminist and socialist politics that characterized women's organiza- tions in the prewar years broke down as the lines between feminism and socialism hardened—feminists adhering to the National Women's Party, radical women taking the Communist line, scorning women's rights as "reformist" and taking a stand in favor of revolutionary class consciousness.[38]

Charlotte Perkins Gilman, who had left Heterodoxy when "the heresies seemed to center on sex psychology and pacifism," regretted the replacement of native-born Americans by Jews, Italians, Germans, and others and denounced the obliteration in the public mind of Socialism by "the Jewish-Russian nightmare, Bolshevism."[39]

Gilman's disciple, Rheta Childe Dorr, who had written of exploited women wage earners in the first decade of the century, later wrote for The Masses, and had joined the Socialist Party and Heterodoxy early in the teens, changed course in the middle of World War I to support the entry of the United States. She made an even sharper swing to the right after the Bolshevik Revolution, when she scorned her former allies as "Reds" and deviants. By contrast, Rose Pastor Stokes, who had also been a Heterodite, birth control activist, and socialist suffragist, was trans- formed after helping to found the Communist Party into denying the existence of any "separate woman's problem."[40]

One way for the formerly active women's groups to remain vital was to hew to a narrowly defined single issue. This was the strategy of Alice Paul's National Woman's Party, which focused solely on women's rights, and of the birth control movement under Margaret Sanger's leadership. Both of these organizations owed their continuing existence to the support of affluent women. The Women's Trade Union League lost membership when the unions, as Pauline Newman recalled, used their own people to do the work the WTUL had done for them. However, the WTUL's purpose—to raise the trade union consciousness of women industrial workers as well as to enrich their lives through association—was taken up by the formation of Industrial Clubs by the Young Women's Christian Association, which ended its requirement in the 1920s that members be Protestant Christians and organized black as well as white women into its ranks.[41]

Of course, many of the formerly active women's groups, weary of struggle, retreated from confrontational politics. The National American Woman Suffrage Association gave birth to the National League of Women Voters. Other organizations that had been active for suffrage prior to 1920 declined or ended, to be replaced by organizations working for world peace, such as the Women's International League for Peace and Freedom, or working for civic improvement, such as the Parent-Teachers Associations. All of these organizations operated on the model for appropriate womanly activity publicized in the *Times* prior to great era of suffrage activism.[42]

The ascendancy of Freudian psychology justified the claims of professionals in this field to define normal "femininity" within parameters they claimed were scientifically verifiable. The world of work was defined as a male sphere, and a man's ability to take care of his family was crucial to his self-esteem. The sociologist Ernest Groves, who understood that women also gained satisfaction from gainful employment outside the home, warned that the woman who was "coarsened or hard-boiled" by business life would "repel men." Groves further predicted, as had the race-suicide "croakers" of the first and second decades of the century, that women's opportunities for gainful employment would reduce the marriage rate—because women would become too independent and dissatisfied with the marriage partners available to them, and because men would not be attracted to these toughened women.[43]

The social science practitioners uniformly focused on feminism as a phenomenon their disciplines could explain and believed they could lead in solving the problems feminism presented, especially the problem of "what do women want?" The "scientific" conclusion of a prominent behaviorist, John Broadus Wilson, was that a militant suffragist was a woman whose sex life was not well adjusted—an analysis that women of this century's second wave of feminism no doubt have heard expressed more crudely, if with less pretension to scientific accuracy. Such analyses, accompanied by claims served up as credentials and anecdotes masked as data, strengthened the ancient bias against which Charlotte Perkins Gilman had more than thirty years earlier protested: that women's role was to serve men's needs and pleasures.[44]

The reimposition of traditional gender roles, combined with the loss of cohesion following the suffrage victory and the accompanying tense political climate after the Bolshevik Revolution, was long-lasting. Having learned again to define themselves through male approval, women saw each other as rivals. On the other hand, closeness between two women might be seen as deviant and/or immoral. The frank and passionate expression of women's love for each other, expressed, for example, in the letters of Heterodites Doris Stevens and Sara Bard Field—both of whom were deeply involved with men—became taboo.[45] These mores prevailed until the 1960s, when participation in the civil rights and anti-war struggles led women once again to claim a movement for themselves, often without knowing that they were taking up work that predecessors had begun. Until feminist scholars reclaimed women's history, activists in the early days of the second women's movement could not know, for example, that the exuberant "consciousness raising" groups of the late sixties and early seventies were linear descendants of the Heterodoxy luncheon meetings where women gathered to talk, off the record, about themselves.

By 1919, when the suffrage victory was within sight, much of the fun and gladness Inez Milholland had found in the movement had been overshadowed by the climate of violent nativism, anti-Bolshevism, labor unrest and anti-labor terrorism, the suppression of civil liberties, and lynchings. The first woman to feel the brunt of government reaction fostered in this climate was Emma Goldman.

Released from the Missouri penitentiary in late September 1919, she was seized, months later, along with 148 other radicals—including Alexander Berkman, who had been incarcerated in Atlanta—in raids organized by Attorney General A. Mitchell Palmer for deportation to Russia under the terms of the 1918 Immigration Act, which made conviction of anarchism or membership in an anarchist organization a deportable offense. On December 21, 1920, Goldman and Berkman left New York on board an old and unseaworthy vessel, the *Buford*, which docked in Finland in mid-January; from there they traveled by rail to Petrograd, where they remained before journeying to Moscow.[46]

At first glad to be in Russia, where the deportees were greeted warmly as comrades, Goldman soon became uneasy about the suppression of free speech and the widespread hunger among many while Communist Party members had good food and their children attended good schools, along with other injustices, but she resisted recognizing the Bolshevik betrayal of the revolution. She looked to John Reed to clarify her confusion, but his dismissive contempt for the shooting of 500 prisoners as of no significance within the context of world revolution alarmed her.[47] Still she searched for reasons to keep faith in the revolution, but the attack in March 1921 on the sailors of the Kronstadt naval base who had made common cause with striking Petrograd factory workers "broke the last thread" that held her to the Bolsheviks.[48]

But in the meantime, Goldman and Berkman had undertaken the "Museum Expedition" to express their support for the revolution, traveling in a renovated red-painted railroad car to display household goods from the Tsar's Winter Palace to the people of the Soviet Union.[49] They were visited by delegates to the Soviet Congress, staying nearby in the Hotel de Luxe. Bill Haywood, convicted in Chicago of "criminal syndicalism" for his IWW activity and sentenced to twenty years in Leavenworth Prison,[50] frequently had been Goldman's guest in New York and greeted her warmly after arriving in Moscow following his flight after release on bond. But after Goldman's criticisms of the Bolshevik Revolution were "translated" to him, he never returned for a promised visit. Goldman also was shunned by other former allies and friends: the labor organizer, Ella Reeve Bloor; Mary Heaton Vorse; and her partner, Robert Minor.[51]

In April 1921, Goldman went to Germany, where she completed *My Disillusionment in Russia,* but, feeling herself friendless, was unhappy there as well. And she would continue to be unhappy in her attempts to find a political home. In London, where she went in 1925, she alienated potential allies among the English Socialists by her vitriolic attacks on the Soviet Union. In 1925, she married a Welshman, James Colton, in order to have a British passport and went to Toronto. She gave a series of lectures, but again was dissatisfied with the people she met. She left Canada for France in 1928, settling in St. Tropez, not far from Berkman, who lived in Nice with the much younger woman he had met in France, Emy Eckstein.[52]

Goldman completed her well-received autobiography, *Living My Life,* in 1931, and traveled in Europe except for a period of three months in 1934 when she was readmitted to the United States on a visa that she futilely hoped would result in a permit to remain permanently. But she was granted one form of rehabilitation: by the mid-thirties, as more liberals became aware of the reality of the situation in the Soviet Union, her indictment had gained credibility.[53]

Her longtime comrade, Alexander Berkman—Sasha—suffering from prostate cancer, used a gun to end his life in 1936, although his aim was not much better than in his attempt on Henry Clay Frick so many years before, and he spent many hours in agony before his suffering ended. Goldman went to Spain to work with the Anarchists under the Republican government, but the growing power of the Communists alarmed her, and she returned to England as the Republic fell. She went once again to Canada in 1939, where she continued her work on behalf of Spanish refugees. She suffered a stroke in February 1940 and died in May. The United States government finally granted her in death what it had withheld in life, and Emma Goldman was buried in Chicago's Waldheim Cemetery, with Ben Reitman among the mourners.[54]

The harsh uprooting of deportation blighted Goldman's life, for she was ever after a stranger. She came to realize, in her long years of exile, that the United States was her true home, and New York was at the center of it. But the course of Emma Goldman's life was set when she and two comrades plotted an assassination as if it were a high school prank. One finds in her writing much self-justification and much blaming of others, but one does not find a substantial ideological basis for her early or later actions. One does not even find from Goldman a working analysis of anarchism.

Goldman's other great loss, besides her homeland, was a lasting love. During her long exile, she took lovers; the relationships were usually in the Reitman pattern—younger men looking for "mommies." In 1934, when she was sixty-five, she was met Frank Heiner, a thirty-six-year-old graduate student in sociology at the University of Chicago. He was a blind married man whose wife had to read Goldman's letters to him. Although their affair was largely by correspondence, Heiner did visit her in Toronto, and Goldman was ecstatic. She naturally hoped for more, but Heiner did not return, and at some point he sent her a letter admitting that their relationship had fit a pattern in his life, for he craved "women who were above the average weight who could give me maternal responses." Their correspondence ended in March 1936.[55]

Goldman envied Berkman; he had, without invoking criticism, established a series of relationships with much younger women, the last of whom, Emy Eckstein, was devoted to him until his final hour. Goldman did not escape criticism for her affairs, and women were often her harshest critics. Indeed, Dorothy Day wrote primly after her conversion to Catholicism that she was "revolted" by such promiscuity and could not even read Goldman's autobiography "because I was offended in my sex."[56] Emma acknowledged to Berkman that as women, no matter how modern, grew older, they began to feel "the utter emptiness of their existence, the lack of the man, whom they love, and who loves them, the comradeship and companionship that grows out of such a relationship, the home, the child."[57]

Unlike the Heterodites, who relied for support on their circle of women friends, Goldman isolated herself from the companionship of women. Berkman once reminded Goldman that she "was not a very easy person to live with."[58] And she was not. She was imperious, self-pitying, and demanding—but she also was wonderful and, as the literature about her demonstrates, utterly fascinating.

Mary Heaton Vorse became embittered by the arrest, conviction, and jailing of many of her friends following the United States's entry into World War I. The IWW was a favorite target of government repression; fifty Wobbly offices around the country were raided, and many members were subsequently jailed, including her friend Bill Haywood. When Vorse was asked to go to Europe to publicize the work of the Red Cross there, she left her two younger children in the care of an English nanny, Miss Selway—her older son, Heaton, was away at school—and sailed to Europe to take the assignment.

In Paris, she met and fell in love with Robert Minor, a Texas-born Socialist and a talented cartoonist. At thirty-five, he was ten years younger than Vorse, a difference she uncharacteristically did not reveal to him. Vorse felt herself growing young again with passion for a man who seemed supremely sure of himself and who approved of her need to escape the restrictions imposed by tradition and maternal responsibility.[59]

After returning to the United States, she reported on what would be known as the Great Steel Strike of 1919. She worked tirelessly to publicize the plight of the wretchedly paid steelworkers and their families, on whose exploitation the enormous profits of Big Steel depended. Her stories appeared in the labor press, *Outlook,* and the *Nation,* but could not balance the hostile, red-baiting national press.[60]

Following the failure of the strike, Vorse worked as an organizer for the Amalgamated Clothing Workers, supporting herself and her children through fees for "lollipops" and for articles on labor and postwar Europe from journals like *Harper's.* She produced two books of light fiction and completed her manuscript about the steel strike. She spent the summer of 1920 in Provincetown with Minor, who, like Vorse, had been critical of Bolshevism, but now was avidly studying Bolshevik theory, to which he would become a complete convert. Vorse did not share his views, but neither could she bring herself to oppose the overbearing self-righteousness of the true believer Minor had become. In 1921 Minor invited Vorse to join him at the Moscow meeting of the Third Congress of the Comintern, to which he was one of the American party's delegates. When Vorse arrived in Moscow, her passport identified her as Mary Heaton Vorse Minor, thirty-nine years of age.[61]

Like John Reed, Minor was angry with Berkman and Goldman about their concern for imprisoned anarchists, who, in his view, mattered little in the context of the "greatest revolution the world has ever seen." Goldman argued that the life of individuals was important and "should not be cheapened and degraded into mere automation."[62] She cited Vorse's failure to visit her in Moscow as evidence of "superficial political leanings"; when Vorse had been with Joe O'Brien, she was a member of the IWW, but now that she was with Minor, she was a Communist.[63]

The charge was not completely fair, and Vorse must have felt injured when she read Goldman's autobiography. Vorse was a woman of principle, and no doubt her failure to see the brutally exiled Goldman troubled her conscience. However, she probably was unwilling to risk a quarrel with Minor over Goldman at the point when their political views were growing apart—for Vorse, like Goldman, was becoming disillusioned by what she was witnessing in the Soviet Union, especially the evidence of widespread famine and the starvation of children. Nevertheless, in her own 1935 autobiography she retaliated against the charge that she got her politics "by proxy" by charging the Goldman and others exemplified Lenin's analysis of anarchists—that their ideology would lead them inevitably to fight "the revolution with the bourgeoisie."[64]

In 1922, Vorse and Minor shared an apartment in New York; Minor was working at *The Liberator* alongside the poet Lydia Gibson, whom he had met and fallen in love with in San Francisco years before. In April, at the age of forty-seven Vorse realized she was pregnant. In early summer, she moved with her children to an apartment in Highlands, New Jersey, across the bay from New York, where each day, she walked down a wooden staircase from the top of the bluff to the beach below. In mid-July, when she was four months pregnant, she stumbled and fell to the bottom of the long flight of stairs. She immediately miscarried and was treated by a local woman doctor with morphine to ease her pain. As a result of this medical treatment, Vorse became addicted to the drug.

Less than a week later, while Vorse was still in bed recovering, Gibson and Minor appeared in her bedroom, informed her that they were in love and were going to be married, and abruptly left.[65] Despite her pain, and despite her need to struggle against her addiction to morphine, Vorse refused to feel sorry for herself. Her entries in the notebooks she kept of her daily life reveal an absence of regret. "Am I really unhappy about my life—or remorseful? . . . would I give up if I could Bobby, all I saw that year—the Steel district, Russia?" she queried herself in March 1923. The response was no. "The last few years have been unhappy, unsatisfactory years I hated, but how interesting when I look at them objectively."

Vorse took satisfaction because her life had been "crowded with events from 1914 on," and although she had no time for reflection, she had continued to write stories effortlessly with her "left hand." She also was proud that, in spite of her poor clothes and neglected looks, interesting men liked her and she had "had a greater share of popularity than most women." However, her chief regret was not having taken better care of her children: "I have rounded out a very complete experience of sex and now is the time to put that definitely to one side," she vowed; now, she would devote herself to her children. "Every other thing must be secondary to them for five years," she declared.

Vorse's first priority was regaining her health, by which Vorse probably meant overcoming her addiction. Then she must establish financial security. Having gained these, she believed she could accomplish her main object, which was to give her children the best surroundings within her means. Then she would arrange her work so that her children would be barely conscious of it, and "within the frame of this limitation I will experiment in stories all I can."[66]

Vorse did not again establish a long-term relationship with a man, perhaps because of the scarring impact of Robert Minor's betrayal. "I am still close enough to RM after nearly three years," she wrote in her notebooks of 1925, "to desire his death."[67] Well beyond the five-year period she had pledged in 1923, Vorse contributed to the support of her children, and then of her grandchildren.[68] The financial burden was increased when, after 1925, the "lollipops" that had been the main source of her income began not to sell.[69] Moreover, Vorse never was able to meet her aspirations for herself as a writer. Her ability to produce marketable work quickly had rendered her unable to concentrate in order to produce the "experimental" work she valued.

Perhaps the larger obstacle to becoming the kind of writer she admired was her refusal to deal with the events of her life. Commenting on her work in her notes of 1925, Vorse acknowledged, "how

unrelated this fiction is to my life. My earlier stuff is about babies and
boats and old ladies and death and the day of judgment . . . only
surface observation but for the tears and laughter."[70]

Vorse returned to labor journalism in 1926, serving as publicity
director of the Passaic, New Jersey textile strike. She went to Gastonia,
North Carolina in 1929 and to Harlan County, Kentucky in 1931 to
report on strikes by textile workers. Vorse reported on the farmers'
strikes in the midwest, the unemployed marches, the trial of nine
young black males—known as the Scottsboro Boys—falsely accused of
rape in Alabama, the automobile workers' strike in Flint, Michigan,
and the subsequent struggle of the Congress of Industrial Organizations (CIO) in 1937. She also recorded the rise of Adolph Hitler and
the events of the Soviet Union under Joseph Stalin.

In the 1940s Vorse again went to Europe under the coveted
designation, "War Correspondent."[71] After the war, she traveled
widely throughout the United States, sitting up all night in trains
without Pullmans; she spent six months in Mexico and returned to
report on the steel strike of 1949, traveling through thirty steel
centers.[72] In semi-retirement in Provincetown, she continued to write
about corruption in the waterfront unions, migrant farm workers, and
civil rights in the South. Her last big story was on crime in the
International Longshoreman's Union in *Harper's* in 1952.[73]

Vorse's first major effort to translate a labor conflict, the Gastonia
textile workers' strike of 1929, into a serious work of fiction was not
very successful. The notebooks she kept while writing *Strike!* reveal
her ambivalence about the strike, as well as her disappointment in the
young organizers who became the central characters in her novel, and
in her own performance as a labor advocate, labor reporter, and
novelist. As she completed the novel, Vorse wrote of her work, "I tell
of important and striking events without significance."[74]

Her solid achievements are *Men and Steel*, a study of the great steel
strike of 1919; *A Footnote to Folly*, her careful, elliptical autobiography
covering the years from 1912 to 1935; and *Labor's New Millions*, her
study of the organization of the CIO. Vorse characteristically blamed
herself for shortcomings, defeats, and failures, seldom considering the
limitations a male-dominated society imposed upon a woman who
attempted as much as she did. Only occasionally in her private writings

did she take credit for what she did accomplish: bringing up and supporting three children, contributing to the support of grandchildren, reporting many of the major events in the United States and in Europe during the first half of the twentieth century, and keeping faith through her long life—Vorse was ninety-two when she died in 1966—with the vow she had made over a half-century earlier to write about the struggles of working people always. She had, in her own way and despite obstacles, achieved the feminist goal of "having it all"—and achieving it with gallantry. In 1940, Vorse wrote in her notes, "everything good comes from loving people and meeting life with courage."[75]

The principal forerunner of the first twentieth-century women's movement, Charlotte Perkins Gilman, moved with her husband to Norwich, Connecticut in 1922. In the following years, Gilman completed an autobiography, revised her earlier book, *Social Ethics,* and wrote a "species of detective story," but none of these were accepted by publishers. She tried unsuccessfully to get lecturing engagements; the rejection was painful for a woman of international reputation who had worked so many years for the advancement of women, "with so much that was new and strong to say to the coming generation." When she found in January 1932, that she had inoperable breast cancer, her greatest distress was for her husband, who, when she told him, urged her to try radiation therapy, which brought her relief. Houghton's sudden death in May 1934 ended his pain over her illness that Gilman correctly had predicted would be greater than hers.

In the autumn of that year, she went to California, where she shared a home with her lifelong friend, Grace Channing, quite near the home of her daughter, son-in-law, and grandchildren. Gilman completed her final revision of *Social Ethics* and prepared her autobiography for publication. In August 1935, she acted on her belief that "when all usefulness is over, when one is assured of unavoidable and imminent death, it is the simplest of human rights to choose a quick and easy death in place of a slow and horrible one." Gilman administered to herself the drug she had bought years before to end her life, with the declaration, "I have preferred chloroform to cancer."[76]

Hardship in the postwar years befell the younger, most militant activists in the great women's movements of the teens. Rose Pastor Stokes had supported, then opposed the entry of the United States into the First World War. An anti-war speech in Kansas City and a letter published in one of that city's newspapers led to her arrest and trial in 1918 for violating the Espionage Act. Her conviction was overturned in 1919, the same year in which, at the fractious Socialist Conference in Chicago, she became one of the founders of the American Communist Party. Her increasingly radical politics led to an estrangement from her husband, who divorced her in 1925. In 1927, she married Victor J. Jerome, a translator and party member. But illness—and undoubtedly her much reduced circumstances—led to a decline in her political activity and influence. She died of cancer in 1933.

In her writing, Stokes, who claimed she never had felt comfortable in the wealthy environment to which her marriage had brought her, kept faith with her working-class background. She translated, with Helena Frank, Morris Rosenfeld's Yiddish poems about working-class life (1914). She wrote plays about the struggles of working-class people, notably a full-length drama, *The Woman Who Wouldn't* (1916).[77] The play's hero is Mary, a daughter of a Pennsylvania mill family who makes flowers for a living and is engaged to Joe, a young mill worker. She becomes pregnant, but when she discovers Joe has fallen in love with another woman, she refuses to let him know about the impending baby, telling her mother she won't live like their neighbor, "who made Parker marry her and a dog's life she's had since."

Mary leaves home, but eight years later, she returns in her new identity as Mother Mary, a renowned labor organizer. Her mother is dead; her younger sister has left home; her father, once militant but now broken in spirit, shares his home with Mary's older sister and her husband. Mary introduces her daughter to her family and tells them of her struggles in the intervening years. Although she initially had received help from a union organizer and his wife, she soon supported herself, first as a scrubwoman, then as a wet nurse after her baby was born, and later as a waitress. She read books about the labor movement that led her to understand there was no chance for her baby, legitimate or not, "unless there were chances for all babies." She joined the union, and her career as a labor organizer was launched when she became involved in a strike.

Her family tell Mary that the woman Joe had married died in childbirth. He visits their home, and Mary introduces him to their daughter. Mary is pleased that Joe, who formerly resisted the union, has become an active member at the mill. He pleads with her to marry him, but she refuses. She no longer loves him, and believes a child cannot be happy in a home where love has died. Mary wants her daughter to respect her, for "when a girl has a big, live faith in her mother, she's never homeless." The play ends with the family at dinner; everyone is enchanted with Mary's daughter, and Joe understands that he and Mary never will be more than comrades.[78] It is plausible to read *The Woman Who Wouldn't* as the vision Stokes—who never had children—held of an alternate life for herself as a self-sufficient worker in struggle within a mass movement, accepting help only from other members of the working class; as a mother; and as an inspiring heroic leader like Mother Jones. This identity is proclaimed in the title of Stokes's autobiography, *I Belong to the Working Class.*

After Crystal Eastman and her brother launched *The Liberator* in March 1918, Crystal contributed articles expressing her radicalization by her wartime experiences. She had seen many of her friends abused and imprisoned because they, like her, had lobbied against preparedness and conscription. The Espionage and Sedition Act of 1918 had rendered illegal all Crystal Eastman's wartime activity and had purged all radical publications from the mails, including *The Masses* and *Four Lights.* But *The Liberator* would take up where *The Masses* had been forced to stop. *The Liberator* was the only monthly magazine to publish information about socialist movements around the world. In addition to reports by John Reed and Louise Bryant from Russia, it published contributions by Helen Keller, Norman Thomas, Roger Baldwin, Lenin, and Dorothy Day. The men of *The Masses* always had written sympathetically of black people, but at *The Liberator,* Crystal Eastman actually broke the color line. After reading the poetry of Claude McKay, which *The Masses* editors consistently had rejected, she invited him to call on her at *The Liberator,* and soon afterward, McKay's career with that magazine began.[79]

Crystal Eastman served as manager, fund-raiser, and investigative reporter for *The Liberator* while caring for her two young children. In addition, she had worked ceaselessly for peace before and during the war and had undertaken such political projects afterward as organizing the First Feminist Congress in March, 1919. In 1921, her health was severely impaired by dangerously high blood pressure, a bad heart, and nephritis, a painful and then little-understood disease. Doctors insisted she resign as editor of *The Liberator*. She became a contributing editor to the magazine, but the loss of her full-time salary drastically affected her family's circumstances—for her husband, Walter Fuller, earned very little as the editor of *The Freeman*, a socialist paper. In the spring of 1922, he returned to England to try to get a better job. Left alone to support her children, ill, and lonely for her husband, she found herself unable to get work; her militant feminism and anti-militarism had caused Crystal Eastman—attorney, social investigator, and writer—to be blacklisted.[80]

In the postwar years, Eastman differed with social reformers, such as Jane Addams and Florence Kelley, who supported the protective legislation for women workers that was used to dislodge them from industries and professions from which they had been barred before the war but had entered in great numbers during it. The debate over protectionism versus equal rights split the women's movement in the twenties as the choice between peace and suffrage had divided it in the teens. Eastman recognized that the "family welfare" protective legislation was a device to deprive women of jobs men wanted to keep for themselves.[81]

Barred from meaningful work and isolated politically, Eastman went to England where she found employment on the feminist weekly *Time and Tide*, published by the wealthy coal mine owner, Margaret Thomas, the Lady Rhondda. However, Eastman disliked England, for she felt politically isolated there as well, and she decided to return to the United States. She got a temporary job at the *Nation*, with the plan that her husband would join her when she found more permanent work. However, he died of a stroke in September 1927, and Crystal Eastman, ravaged by nephritis, died ten months later at the age of forty-six. Her children were adopted by her friends Agnes Brown Leach and Henry Goddard Leach.[82]

Louise Bryant had gone with John Reed to Russia to witness the consolidation of the Bolshevik ascendance; after her return, she published an account of her experiences, *Six Red Months in Russia*, and went on a nationwide speaking tour. She then went to Washington to testify about the revolution before a subcommittee of the Senate

Judiciary Committee, also using the time there to join the National Woman's Party's demonstration before the White House. There, along with other suffragists, she was arrested and imprisoned. After recovering from her illness following John Reed's death, she became a prominent correspondent for the Hearst papers, for which she wrote articles on Lenin and interviewed Benito Mussolini.[83]

Bryant's second book on the revolution, *Mirrors of Moscow*, published in 1922, contains a collection of portraits of Lenin and Leon Trotsky, as well as other leaders, and reflects her continued commitment to the revolution, but is more sober in its assessment of socialism and suffrage in a nation struggling for survival. Bryant, who had been attentive to the condition of women and had written in her earlier book of notable women in the revolution such as Marie Spirodonova and Alexandra Kollantai, reported in her second book that the revolution had not succeeded in wiping out prostitution because women, limited to work as unskilled laborers, earned less than men. Women had received suffrage before they had received political education; therefore they were politically backward. Before the revolution, women had been politically active, but when the revolution came, women sank mysteriously into the background.

Symbolic of this decline was the fall from power of Alexandra Kollantai, the Commissar of Social Welfare and the only woman cabinet member after the Bolshevik ascendance; she had "allowed her love for her husband to interfere with her political judgment." Kollantai's husband, a leader of the Kronstadt sailors, was arrested for having entrusted ships under his command to officers of the old regime. Kollantai had publicly defended her husband, and she was removed from her post by party leaders. She nevertheless had remained a committed feminist, urging Soviet women, as Charlotte Perkins Gilman had urged American women, to free themselves from domestic drudgery by establishing community restaurants, kitchens, and laundries.[84]

In December 1923, when Bryant's career as a journalist was flourishing, she married William Bullitt, who came from a Philadelphia Main Line family and was a writer, a diplomat, and—although he was an essentially conservative man—a professed admirer of the Bolshevik Revolution. Bryant became absorbed in her marriage and in the elegant life Bullitt provided her in Paris. She gave birth to a daughter, Anne, but continued her writing. However, in 1925, after she had given up her career as a Hearst journalist, her independent income, and her identity as the heroic partner of John Reed, she was stricken with Dercum's disease, or *adiposa dolorosa,* an incurable but not fatal disease marked by painful subcutaneous tumors, obesity (although Louise was not obese), weakness, and depression. Her relationship with Bullitt declined, but her illness prevented her from returning to work and independence.

She went to Baden Baden to recover, planning to leave Bullitt.[85] But, as she had written of Kollantai, she had forgotten "how easily wings are broken in the age of steel."[86] The couple returned to the United States for a visit, but after Bryant returned to Paris, the powerfully connected Bullitt sued her for divorce in Philadelphia, accusing her of lesbianism and excessive drinking, and was granted the divorce and custody of their daughter in 1930. Deprived of her daughter, humiliated by her husband's treatment of her, reclaimed by her illness, Louise Bryant lived unhappily and shabbily in Paris, lapsing into alcoholism and unable to work, her once glorious appearance transformed into a bloated ugliness that shocked her friends. She died of a cerebral hemorrhage in January 1936.[87]

The activist who had been involved in all of the great movements of the teens, Henrietta Rodman, directed her ardent activism during the war and in postwar years to building the Teachers' Union and leading the opposition to the suppression of civil liberties within schools. In 1914, in the midst of the mother-teacher controversy, she married Herman de Fremery—but shortened her name to de Frem "to get away entirely from the aristocratic sound"—and they adopted two children. In October 1922, she was one of twelve teachers from whom the Department of Education withheld certificates guaranteeing their loyalty. She and another teacher refused to appear before the department's Advisory Committee to answer questions about their beliefs. In late December 1922, she was stricken with a cerebral tumor and died in March 1923.[88]

Elizabeth Gurley Flynn spent the postwar years from 1918 to 1924 working for the Workers Defense Union, a branch of what became the American Civil Liberties Union, to publicize the cases, to provide funds for the defense, and to prevent the deportation of individuals arrested under the Espionage Act of 1917, the Sedition Act of 1918, and the Immigration Act of 1918. Later she organized the defense campaigning for Nicola Sacco and Bartolomeo Vanzetti. But in 1926, upset by Carlo Tresca's unfaithfulness, overworked by the pressure of speaking and organizing, and worried about the lack of time she could spend with her son, Flynn had a breakdown. She was comforted in this crisis by her best friend, Mary Heaton Vorse, undoubtedly the person most capable of understanding her pain.

Flynn's health had, of course, been affected by her situation, and she spent the next ten years recuperating at the home in Portland, Oregon, of Dr. Marie Equi, an IWW supporter, birth control advocate, and abortionist. In 1937, she returned to the East and, to the dismay of her friends and family, joined the Communist Party.[89] In 1940, her son Fred Flynn died; she suffered another blow three years later when Carlo Tresca was shot, probably by Carmine Galante, a Mafia leader acting on orders from Mussolini, whom Tresca had attacked—along with many others—in his journal, *Il Martello* (The Hammer). Tresca remained her great passion, although unlike Mary Heaton Vorse, she did not remain celibate; she was romantic all her life and had affairs with other—often younger—men[90]

In 1937, Flynn started a regular column in the *Daily* and *Sunday Worker,* called "The Feminine Ferment" and devoted it to discussing labor issues from a woman's point of view. The purpose of her writing and her speeches was to educate women about the history of class and gender struggle in the United States and in Russia. She was elected to the Communist Party National Committee in 1938, and in 1942 she ran for New York State representative-at-large on the Communist Party ticket. From 1945 to 1953 she was chair of the Women's Commission of the Communist Party, and although she was often critical of the party's failure to include women, she was unwilling to challenge the party and insist on a woman's rights program. She toed the party line.[91]

In 1945, the party claimed at least a quarter of the membership of the CIO and controlled a third of the votes on the executive board. By 1948, the party had lost its base in the labor movement: Communist leaders were jailed, and the party was outlawed. Many of the leaders went underground, as the media stirred up public hysteria against the

"Reds." Harry Truman, on the eve of the 1948 election, felt compelled to demonstrate he was not soft on Communism by ordering the arrest of twelve top Communist Party leaders under the terms of the Smith Act, passed in 1940, which outlawed the teaching and advocating the overthrow of the United States by force and violence. As Flynn's biographer Rosalyn Baxandall has observed, the political repression of the 1950s was different from the repression of the 1920s because the intimidation of McCarthyism was all-pervasive, yet more subtle and difficult to oppose, "coming from television sets rather than from police raids and guns."[92]

Flynn, a member of what was referred to as the "second string Communist leadership," was arrested on June 20 1951 under the Smith Act. She defended herself at her trial, which ended in the conviction of all defendants in January 1953. Because the case was appealed up to the Supreme Court, she did not enter prison for two years. In January 1955 she began a twenty-eight-month sentence as Prisoner 11710 in the Federal Reformatory for Women at Alderson, West Virginia; during this time she completed her autobiography, Rebel Girl (1955).[93]

When she was released from prison, Flynn put aside her plan to settle down on the West Coast to write the second part of her autobiography, The Alderson Story: My Life as a Political Prisoner (1963), and immersed herself once again in party politics, running as a candidate from the Lower East Side for the New York City Council and writing weekly columns for the Daily Worker. She traveled to Copenhagen to a conference on the fiftieth anniversary of International Women's Day; she accepted invitations to speak in Europe and went to a May Day celebration in Moscow. While in the Soviet Union, Flynn was an honored guest, staying at fine hotels, attending ballet and theater performances, and dining with dignitaries at celebrations in her honor.[94]

A month after her return, Eugene Dennis, chairman of the Communist Party, died, and Flynn was elected his successor. In countless speeches, displaying the voice and charismatic presence she had possessed since childhood, she defended the party's right to exist, opposing the McCarran Act, which required Communists to register with a Subversive Activities Control Board as agents of a foreign power. She was heartened by the stirring of the early civil rights movement, predicting that the sixties would be a landmark in progressive history. With Herbert Aptheker as her lawyer, she successfully fought to the Supreme Court the denial to her of a passport and then she traveled for a rest to the Soviet Union, where, a month after her arrival, she died on September 4 1964, at the age of seventy-four. She was given a state funeral in Red Square, with twenty-five thousand people in attendance and such heroes as Dolores Ibarruri—the Spanish Civil War's La Pasionaria—paying tribute.[95]

Of course, the pattern of glorious youth followed by the loss of love or career, illness, and early death was not the lot of every activist. Wealth and professional status preserved Elsie Clews Parson from harm. Academic position enabled Helen Hull to maintain her career as a novelist, and her long partnership with Mabel Louise Robinson sustained her emotionally as Helen Marot and Caroline Pratt and Elizabeth Irwin and Katherine Anthony had been sustained by their long relationships.

Inez Haynes Irwin enjoyed a long, happy marriage and a pleasant life in homes in Greenwich Village and Scituate, Massachusetts, but her absorption in that marriage limited her career as a writer.[96] "I am not a trained, skilled, or experienced writer. You turn out articles so often and with what seems like extraordinary facility that you cannot guess how difficult it is for me," she declared in a letter of January 1920 to Mary Heaton Vorse in which she outlined the reasons she could not accede to Vorse's request to write a sympathetic article about the IWW. Out of her two years of war experience, she had written only four articles, and only two of these had been published; out of a writing experience of eighteen years, she had published only eight articles. Moreover, she explained to Vorse, she was exhausted after having completed her history of the Woman's Party, the most difficult project she had ever attempted. Irwin described herself as a "wantwit," possessing a "vague, inchoate, unconcrete" mind that left her helpless in the face of a mass of facts.[97]

Irwin's sad appraisal that she never wrote anything important does not do her justice. She was responsible for forty books. Her account of her visit to the European fronts appeared in the magazines of three countries. After publishing sentimental novels and short stories about orphaned children and an idealized brother and sister, Irwin produced feminist articles and fiction that addressed the issues underlying the suffrage movement: *Angel Island* and the undervalued novel *The Lady of the Kingdoms* (1917), in which, through two young heroines, she examined the conventional morality that society imposes on women, as well as the unconventional moral choices some women make for themselves. She wrote two novels dealing with divorce, *Gertrude Haviland's Divorce* (1925) and *Gideon* (1927); her nonfiction works include, in addition to *The Story of the Woman's Party* (1921), a more ambitious work—a history of American women entitled *Angels and Amazons* (1933). In the latter part of her career, Irwin's creativity waned; during the 1930s and 1940s, she wrote murder mysteries about upper-class characters, returned to sentimental novels, and produced the "Maida" books, a series of moralistic children's books.[98]

The postwar Red Scare saddened and depressed Margaret Sanger, who, worried about the toll her work was taking on her health, went to Europe.[99] She returned to New York in 1920 to face the controversy surrounding the publication of *Woman and the New Race*, a book that emphasized the relationship of birth control to women's rights. She needed to reestablish herself as the foremost spokeswoman for the birth control movement—for, in her absence, other women had come forward, notably Mary Ware Dennett, who had founded the Voluntary Parenthood League in order to shift the focus from state to federal lobbying in a campaign to remove the words, "prevention of conception" from federal laws. Dennett's exhausting efforts to lobby Congress eventually failed, and Sanger was again the undisputed leader of the birth control movement.[100]

Sanger had learned the value of restraint. When police, acting at the behest of the Catholic Church, forcibly suppressed a forum on birth control at midtown Manhattan's Town Hall in November, Sanger, carrying a bouquet of long-stemmed roses, remained serene and composed as she was hauled away by the police, booked on disorderly conduct charges and then released on her own recognizance. The display of force drew a crowd of protesters and a sympathetic response from the press. The forum was rescheduled, this time with police protection. She attracted support from socially powerful women, but although she publicly embraced wealth and privilege, she discreetly maintained her support of radicals and their causes.[101] In a second book, *The Pivot of Civilization,* she confronted the class bias of eugenicists within the birth control movement, disputing their claim that the fecundity of poor women was driven by blind instinct and arguing that the great majority of women, if given the opportunity to do so, willingly would control their fertility.[102] Her two books sold well between 1920 and 1926, providing her with a sizable income for the first time in her life. Her growing prominence in the twenties, bolstered by flattering accounts in the press, established her as a popular lecturer, despite efforts by the Catholic Church to keep her from speaking.[103]

In 1922, Sanger launched the American Birth Control League as a charitable organization for education, legislation reform, medical research in contraception, and provision of services. Despite opposition from the Catholic Church—and, in some states where birth control was outlawed, the courts—birth control clinics were established around the country.[104] The entry of a new generation of more bureaucratic reformers into the movement inevitably led to a pattern of rivalries and conflict between Sanger and corporate-minded associates whose style differed from hers and who sought to replace the dedicated but less professional early recruits.[105]

Sanger left the American Birth Control League and expanded the Birth Control League of American, which she also founded, supported by backing from Noah Slee—wealthy from the invention of 3-in-One Oil—whom she married in 1922 and who, by a written contract, permitted her professional and personal independence for the duration of their marriage, which ended with Slee's death in 1943. Noah Slee's wealth enabled Sanger to live well, return the generosity shown her by friends, and educate her sons—Stuart and Grant—at good private schools and then at Yale and Princeton, respectively.[106]

In 1926, she published the third book of what she considered her trilogy; entitled *Happiness in Marriage,* it stressed the role birth control could play in marriage. Controversy surrounding the book arose from her frank discussion of lovemaking techniques that, years earlier had mesmerized Mabel Dodge. Ironically the book did not sell well, nor did her next book, *Motherhood in Bondage,* a selection from the many letters desperate women had sent her over the years. She turned from writing and made her New York birth control clinic a priority, working in the twenties to get support from the medical profession while maintaining autonomy as male medical professionals became involved with the movement. Her clinic enabled young women medical school graduates, who had been denied hospital affiliation because of gender, to get experience. She was a demanding leader whose workers were not well paid, but she was capable of rewarding faithful associates, and with intensified fund-raising from affluent supporters, the league expanded during the Depression while rival birth control organizations struggled for survival. During this period, the league distributed diaphragms and referred women for therapeutic abortions.[107]

Sanger's biographer, Ellen Chesler, has pointed out that the insistence of Sanger and the earlier feminists on sexual satisfaction as a woman's right came under attack from Betty Friedan and feminists of a later generation as a diversion from accomplishment.[108] But this assertion did not apply to Sanger, a strikingly attractive woman who drew men to her all her life. She had many affairs, often more than one at a time. She was able to love and leave or love simultaneously the many men in her life—who included Havelock Ellis and H. G. Wells—without alienating them; even her husband Noah, whom she abandoned for long periods in their marriage and who certainly knew of her infidelities, never ceased to love her. Unlike Elizabeth Gurley Flynn, Mary Heaton Vorse, or Emma Goldman, she was never left heartbroken, and she turned on its head Lord Byron's claim that love for man was a thing apart but was woman's whole existence—for, in the pattern of the modern captain of industry, she never was diverted by her sexuality from her tenacious dedication to her cause.

In the thirties, she built a national birth control movement and was honored by mainstream women's organizations, yet effort after effort to get a birth control bill through Congress failed due to the influence of the Catholic Church, even when Franklin D. Roosevelt was elected and Eleanor became involved in women's issues.[109] Eventually, because of breakthrough developments in contraception research and postwar concern about population expansion, attitudes on birth control shifted. The 1965 Supreme Court decision in *Griswold v. Connecticut* established the private use of contraception by married Americans as a constitutional right. Ill and senile in

Tucson, Arizona, Sanger lived to know of this decision, but she did not live to witness long-overdue congressional action in 1970 rewriting the Comstock laws to remove the stigma of obscenity from contraception or the Supreme Court decision two years later in *Eisenstadt v. Baird* extending the right of contraception to unmarried persons. Having achieved worldwide recognition for her work, Sanger died of arteriosclerosis in September 1966, and the *New York Times* ran a front-page obituary.[110]

Sanger's leadership of the birth control movement was a titanic achievement, accurately described in Mabel Dodge's tribute that what Sanger did was "like another attempt to release the energy in the atom."[111] But success also marked the lives of other activists. Rose Schneiderman and Pauline Newman became increasingly influential in the years after World War I, not through organizing, but through forming alliances with sympathetic women of other classes, women who respected their expertise as leaders, such as Eleanor Roosevelt, who befriended Schneiderman, and Frances Perkins, who appointed Newman to numerous federal and state labor committees. Through connections with these and other sympathetic women and with male politicians like Al Smith, Robert Wagner, and Franklin Roosevelt, they gained more benefits for working-class women than from male colleagues in their own unions.

Through their friends, Schneiderman and Newman entered a network that would enable them to function at the center of a movement that permanently changed government's relationship to American workers. Between 1919 and 1947, they worked to bring into being many of the goals they had envisioned as shop workers through passage of legislated minimum wage, maximum hours, and uniform safety standards. They wrote memos to political leaders, including the president, sat on government commissions, and testified at congressional hearings. Through the prestige their activities brought them and through the professional and personal support of their women friends, they were removed from the isolation of their status as unmarried Jewish working-class women.[112]

Elsie Clews Parsons's research in the American Southwest resulted, after twenty-five years of investigation, in two volumes of *Pueblo Indian Religions,* published in 1939. Her research in Mexico produced *Mitla, Town of Souls* in 1936. Her work as a folklorist, which involved recording dictation from African-American, Native-American, and West Indian sources, resulted in three volumes of *Folklore of the Antilles, French and English* and extensive publications on African-American folklore. She was president of the American Folklore Society from 1919 to 1920 and served as associate editor of the society's journal from 1918 until her death in 1941. In 1940, Elsie Clews Parsons was the first woman elected president of the American Anthropological Association.[113]

Mabel Dodge also made her most important achievement in the Southwest, where she went with her third husband, Maurice Sterne, whom she married in 1917 after divorcing Edwin Dodge the previous year. But in Taos, New Mexico, she found herself falling under the "magnetic drag" of the eyes of a Pueblo Indian, Tony Luhan.[114] She divorced Sterne in 1922 and married Luhan in 1923. She built an estate, Los Gallos, and helped to create an artists' colony that, in a larger way, resembled the "evenings" on lower Fifth Avenue. She brought in a stream of creative people in an effort to establish a "bridge between cultures." Her visitors included D. H. and Frieda Lawrence; Lawrence based characters on Dodge in his American fiction, notably *The Plumed Serpent*. Later visitors included Georgia O'Keeffe and Ansel Adams. Dodge died in August 1962.[115]

Susan Glaspell had gone to Greece with her husband, George Cram Cook, in 1922. After Cook's sudden death in 1923, she returned to the United States and resumed her work as a playwright. Some years later, she married the writer Norman Matson. She received the Pulitzer Prize in 1931 for *Allison's House*, a play based on the life of Emily Dickinson, but after that year, she returned to novels. In her discussion of Glaspell's work, the critic Edythe M. McGovern has described her 1931 novel, *Ambrose Holt and Family*, as a clear connection of the spirit of the twentieth- century woman and the best qualities of the pioneer. In McGovern's view, the novel that followed, *The Morning Is Near Us* (1939), did not have much relevance to the Great Depression, but in her final novels, *Norma Ashe* (1942) and *Judd Rankin's Daughter* (1945), Glaspell recognized the failures inherent in the midwestern isolationist attitudes that had been appropriate for the original pioneers. In her best writing, she consistently emphasized the need for human beings to utilize what is useful from the past and adapt it courageously to the future.

Glaspell's main significance stems from her Provincetown connection, not only as a playwright whose most lasting work probably will be the much-anthologized feminist one-acter, "Trifles," but more importantly as a participant in a movement that permanently changed the course of the American theater. Glaspell, who died in 1948, developed a broad humanistic point of view that transcended narrow midwestern regionalism and super-patriotism. [116]

Dorothy Day went to Washington to picket the White House with the suffragists after the suppression of *The Masses*. She was arrested and sentenced to a hard thirty days in prison.[117] Day got a job with *The Liberator* when she returned to New York, but found it lacked the "charm" of her old job at *The Masses,* and quit to become a nurse-in-training at King's County Hospital. After a year, she left to travel, then returned to her native Chicago, where she again worked for *The Liberator,* which had relocated there as a "Communist monthly" under Robert Minor's editorship. While caring for a sick friend who was being sheltered in a room at the IWW headquarters, Day and the woman were arrested during a Palmer "Red Raid," and she was again jailed, enduring a worse experience—including a strip search—than she had had in Washington. While in Chicago, Day wrote an autobiographical novel, *The Eleventh Virgin,* which was published in 1924 and for which she sold the film rights.[118]

She returned to New York, bought a small house on Staten Island, and entered into a common-law marriage with Forster Balling, an English anarchist. She gave birth to a daughter, Tamar Terese, in 1927, and that same year, yielding to a religiosity her radicalism and bohemianism never had quelled, became a Catholic.[119] Day had a brief stint in Hollywood as an MGM screenwriter, earning enough to support herself and her daughter for six months in Mexico.[120] However, when her daughter fell ill and Day's funds ran out, she wrote to Mary Heaton Vorse, who sent her money.[121] Day returned to New York, where she worked for *The Commonweal,* the first Catholic publication for which she had written. Her job took her to Washington to report on the demonstration there by unemployed workers. Day traveled with Mary Heaton Vorse, sharing dollar-a-night lodgings and lunch wagon meals in order to have money left over to contribute to food for the demonstrators. When Day returned to New York, she found waiting for her in her apartment Peter Maurin, the French-born religious visionary under whose guidance she established the Catholic Worker Movement, which was to be her life's work from then on until her death.[122]

The impact of this band of great-hearted women on the social, political, economic, and cultural life of the United States is almost impossible to reckon. For many, hardship, personal betrayal, political repression, even imprisonment and exile, illness, and early death followed the exuberant, confident years before the Great War. Yet the memoirs and personal correspondence of their later years reveal no bitterness; indeed, they reflect the credo expressed by Crystal Eastman in a letter to her brother: "To live greatly—that's the thing, and it means joy and sorrow both."[123]

Their lives went in different directions, yet the connections among the women of Heterodoxy remained strong. At the center of the circle is Mary Heaton Vorse, whose files at the Walter Reuther Library at Wayne State University are filled with letters from her fellow activists giving information about or inquiring after one another, recalling old times, or thanking Vorse for loans, which—despite a constant concern for money, she always seems to have been able to give.

Susan Glaspell, Vorse's neighbor in Provincetown, wrote Vorse in a typewritten letter from Greece that she often thought of her, but especially on that day because she was making jelly and

> it seems you should be here with me that together we might gently tip our glasses, and give one another a reassuring word, as so often in my kitchen or yours in Provincetown. I am sometimes homesick for our kitchens, and, oh how I longed, in making the jelly, for that glorious white preserving kettle you gave me for a going-into-our-new-house present.

Glaspell gave Vorse news from letters by mutual friends, told her she missed contact with work and home and being with friends who were writing, claimed that her husband looked well as a Greek peasant, and added a handwritten note at the end of her letter that the jelly had jelled.[124]

In November 1930, Inez Haynes Irwin wrote Vorse, describing her effort to bring old members of Heterodoxy back into the fold and asking Vorse to talk to them about *Strike!* the following January.[125] Elizabeth Gurley Flynn had written to Vorse the previous February, after Vorse had completed *Strike!*, expressing pleasure that Vorse was doing her own work again. "It always seemed a pity to me," she acknowledged, "you had to leave it so often for issues that weren't always so important and I fear that I was a party to dragging you off several times."[126] In January 1940 Flynn wrote to Vorse asking if Heterodoxy still met; if so, she must have been dropped from the list, for she never got notices.[127] Babette Deutsch, whose poems for *The Masses* and *The Liberator* had been the prelude of a long career, wrote Vorse in March 1956 that while she was working against a deadline on a book, she looked "back on the weeks we spent with you as some incredibly placid and enriching time."[128] In October 1930 Dorothy Day recalled the time she and Vorse had spent together in Mexico, where Vorse had gone after writing *Strike!*; "You remember I told you in Mexico how I felt like an exile away from my little bungalow? You remember how we both sat drawing plans of our houses, both of us trembling with love for our hearthstones?"[129]

In March 1937, after Elizabeth Gurley Flynn had returned to the Bronx and was, with great enjoyment, resuming political activities, she wrote Vorse asking what she was doing and stating that she expected "any day to hear you have either joined a group of sit-down strikers some where or gone off to Spain." Flynn was thrilled by the growth of the CIO and would have been glad to return to the Iron Range to work for the organization. She was sorry for people like her former IWW comrade Joe Ettor and her former lover, Carlo Tresca, who were living in the past and could not see what the CIO meant to American labor. "We are living in great days," she declared, "a time when dreams are coming true." Flynn concluded her letter with words that expressed the optimism of her generation of activists: "We can't go on forever on past reputations and dead organizations. Life goes on."[130]

Notes

Chapter 1

1. Joan Kelly, "Did Women Have a Renaissance?" in *Women, History, and Theory: The Essays of Joan Kelly* (Chicago: University of Chicago Press, 1984), 19.
2. Frances Trollope, *Domestic Manners of the Americans* (Barre, MA: Imprint Society), 54, 90-91.
3. Sandra Adickes, "Mind Among the Spindles," *Women's Studies* 1 (1973): 279-91.
4. Supreme Court of Wisconsin (August Term, 1875), 245.
5. Inez Haynes Irwin, "Adventures of Yesterday," ts. Inez Haynes Irwin Papers, Arthur and Elizabeth Schlesinger Library, Radcliffe College, 280.
6. Isadora Duncan, *My Life* (New York: Boni and Liveright, 1927), 217, 252; Floyd Dell, *Women as World Builders: Studies in Modern Feminism* (1913; Westport, CT: Hyperion Press, 1976), 43-44.
7. Margaret Sanger, *An Autobiography* (1938; Elmsford, NY: Maxwell Reprints, 1970), 68-70.
8. Mabel Dodge Luhan, *Intimate Memories*, vol. 3, *Movers and Shakers* (1936; New York: Kraus Reprints, 1971), 37-39, 80-83.
9. Susan Glaspell, *The Road to the Temple* (New York: Frederick A. Stokes Company, 1927), 235-36.
10. Dorothy Day, *The Long Loneliness: An Autobiography* (New York: Image Books, 1959), 66.
11. Basil Rauch, "Taggard, Genevieve," in *Notable American Women: A Biographical Dictionary, 1607-1950*, ed. Edward T. James (Cambridge: Harvard University Press, 1971), 4: 421-23.
12. Genevieve Taggard, introduction, *May Days: An Anthology of Verse from The Masses and The Liberator* (New York: Boni and Liveright, 1925), 2-3.
13. Mary Heaton Vorse, *I've Come to Stay: A Love Comedy of Bohemia* (New York: The Century Company, 1919), 6-7.
14. Dee Garrison, *Mary Heaton Vorse: The Life of an American Insurgent* (Philadelphia: Temple University Press, 1989), 3-5.

15. Sanger, *An Autobiography,* 88-89.
16. Garrison, 17.
17. Arthur E. Waterman, "Glaspell, Susan Keating," in *Notable American Women,* 2: 18.
18. Barbara Miller Solomon, *The Company of Educated Women: A History of Women and Higher Education in America* (New Haven: Yale University Press, 1985), 52, 64.
19. Zona Gale, foreword, *The Living of Charlotte Perkins Gilman: An Autobiography,* by Charlotte Perkins Gilman (1935; Madison: University of Wisconsin Press, 1990), xxxiv-xxxvi.
20. Blanche Wiesen Cook, ed., *Crystal Eastman on Women and Revolution* (New York: Oxford University Press, 1978), introduction, 6.
21. Peter Hare, *A Woman's Quest for Science: Portrait of Anthropologist Elsie Clews Parsons* (Buffalo: Prometheus Books, 1985), 19-22.
22. Elizabeth Gurley Flynn, *Rebel Girl, An Autobiography: My First Life (1906-1926)* (New York: International Publishers, 1955), 53-54.
23. Rose Pastor Stokes, "I Belong to the Working Class," ts. microfilmed at Yale University, 1971; collection of Tamiment Library, New York, 99-122.
24. Emma Goldman, *Living My Life* (New York: Dover, 1970), 1: 11, 63, 425.
25. Emma Goldman, "The Tragedy of Women's Emancipation," *Mother Earth,* March 1906: 9-18.
26. Goldman, *Living My Life,* 2: 565-71.
27. Richard Pearson Hobson, quoted. in "Hobson on Race Suicide," *New York Times,* December 17, 1907, 2.
28. Max G. Schlapp, "Race Suicide," *New York Times,* August 13, 1911, sec. 5, 6.
29. Ellen Chesler, *Woman of Valor: Margaret Sanger and the Birth Control Movement in America* (New York: Simon and Schuster, 1992), 376.
30. "Suffrage Army Out on Parade," *New York Times,* May 5 1912, sec. 2, 1.
31. Ibid.
32. Harriot Stanton Blatch, "Unpoliced Women's Parade," letter, *New York Times,* May 6, 1912, 12.
33. Winifred Harper Cooley, "How It Feels To March In a Suffragette Parade," *The World,* May 6, 1912, 18.
34. "The Uprising of the Women," editorial, *New York Times,* May 5, 1912, sec. 2, 12.
35. "Rich and Poor Marched for Suffrage," *New York Times,* May 12, 1912, sec. 5, 7.
36. Ana Cadogan Etz, letter, *New York Times,* May 12, 1912, sec. 7, 5.
37. Crystal Eastman, "Now We Can Begin," *The Liberator,* December 1920, 23-25.
38. Alice Wexler, *Emma Goldman in Exile: From the Russian Revolution to the Spanish Civil War* (Boston: Beacon Press, 1989), 9.

39. "Rose Pastor Stokes in Shirtwaist Fight," *New York Times*, January 2, 1910, sec. 6, 8.

40. "Socialism's Grip on American Colleges," *New York Times*, April 7, 1912, sec. 5, 3; "10,000 Men and Women March for Equal Suffrage," *New York Times*, May 12, 1912, sec. 7, 7.

41. Mary Heaton Vorse, *A Footnote to Folly: Reminiscences of Mary Heaton Vorse* (New York: Farrar and Rinehart, 1935), 8.

42. Irwin, "Adventures of Yesterday," Inez Haynes Irwin Papers, 416.

43. Joseph Freeman, *An American Testament* (New York: Farrar and Rinehart, 1936), 103.

44. Max Eastman, "Revolutionary Progress," editorial, *The Masses*, March 1917, 22.

Chapter 2

1. Floyd Dell, *Homecoming: An Autobiography* (1933; Port Washington, NY: Kennikat, 1960), 218, 242.

2. Max Eastman, *Love and Revolution: My Journey Through An Epoch* (New York: Random House, 1964), 20.

3. Sanger, *An Autobiography*, 68-69.

4. Quoted in Garrison, *The Life of an American Insurgent*, 69-70.

5. Luhan, *Intimate Memories*, 3: 39.

6. Dell, *Homecoming*, 218.

7. Taggard, *May Days*, 1-3.

8. "Billion Dollar Subways World's Biggest Undertaking," *New York Times*, July 7, 1912, sec. 3, 14; "Soaring Prices on Fifth Avenue," *New York Times*, June 16, 1912, sec. 7, 1.

9. Ronald H. Bayor, *Neighbors in Conflict: The Irish, Germans, Jews, and Italians of New York City, 1929-1941*, 2nd ed. (Urbana and Chicago: University of Illinois Press, 1988), 4-5.

10. "Billion Dollar Subways," *New York Times*, July 7, 1912, sec. 3, 14.

11. "Education Notes," *New York Times*, February 2, 1912, 17.

12. John Martin, "Taken From Parenthood," letter, *New York Times*, May 22, 1912, 12.

13. "Education Notes," *New York Times*, February 8, 1912, 19.

14. "Teachers in Despair Over Boy Terrors," *New York Times*, February 18, 1912, sec. 2, 5.

15. "Two Airships Soar Above the City," *New York Times*, February 14, 1912, 20.

16. "Coffyn, the Aviator, Badly Hurt in Automobile," *New York Times*, March 21, 1912, 5.

17. "Garden Show Opens in Blaze of Glory," *New York Times*, January 7, 1912, sec. 10, 1.

18. "Titanic Sinks Four Hours After Hitting Iceberg," New York Times, April 16, 1912, 1; "1595 Went to Death on Titanic," New York Times, April 19, 1912, 1.

19. "Sunken Liner Was a $7,500,000 Palace," New York Times, April 16, 1912, 3; "Titanic Could Have Been Saved," New York Times, April 24, 1912, 1.

20. "Many Needlessly Died on the Titanic," New York Times, April 20, 1912, 1.

21. "Speed Relief Work for Titanic's Survivors," New York Times, April 19, 1912, 9.

22. "Women to Care for Steerage Survivors," New York Times, April 18, 1912, 6.

23. "Women Work Hard for Rescued Folk," New York Times, April 21, 1912, 10.

24. "Statement Issued by Survivors," New York Times, April 19, 1912, 13; "Titanic Steerage Had Little Chance," New York Times, May 8, 1912, 6.

25. "High Rents Burden the Poor More Than Food Prices," New York Times, July 21, 1912, sec. 3, 8.

26. "Artist, Going Blind, Ends Life in Studio," New York Times, January 2, 1912, 22.

27. "Crippled, Fled Sons to Die by Himself," New York Times, January 3, 1912, 20.

28. "Poverty Brings End to Family of Three," New York Times, June 5, 1912, 7.

29. "Good News Too Late to Save Wife's Life," New York Times, August 20, 1912, 5.

30. "Triangle Fire Being Studied to Make Laws Recommending Changes," New York Times, March 2, 1912, 11.

31. Rheta Childe Dorr, What Eight Million Women Want (Boston: Small, Maynard, 1910), 183-86.

32. "Laundry Trust Plan Revealed By Strike," New York Times, January 2, 1912, 1.

33. Mary Jo Buhle, Women and American Socialism, 1870-1920 (Urbana, University of Illinois Press, 1983),187-89.

34. "Parade for Girl Strikers," New York Times, January 13, 1912, 7.

35. "Young Girls Tell of Laundry Hardships," New York Times, January 20, 1912, 14.

36. Buhle, 202-03.

37. Flynn, Rebel Girl, 124-26.

38. Sanger, An Autobiography, 82.

39. Mary Heaton Vorse, Letter to Arthur Bullard, February 12, 1912, Mary Heaton Vorse Collection, Box 53, Walter Ruether Library, Wayne State University.

40. Vorse, A Footnote to Folly, 13-21.

41. "Waiters Out In 17 More Places," New York Times, June 1, 1912, 1.

42. "Six Riotous Workers Land in Workhouse," *New York Times*, June 22, 1912, 24.
43. "Chambermaids Quit," *New York Times*, June 5, 1912, 3: "Urge Chambermaids to Join the Union," *New York Times*, June 9, 1912, sec. 3, 9.
44. "Won't Take Back Waiters Who Struck," *New York Times*, June 27, 1912, 9.
45. "Rioting Women Pour Kerosene on Meats," *New York Times*, June 8, 1912, 8.
46. "Pledge Housewives Not to Buy Meat," *New York Times*, June 14, 1912, 6.
47. "Gangsters Engaged in Murderous War," *New York Times*, June 6, 1912, sec. 5, 1.
48. "Gangsters Flourishing As in Old Days," *New York Times*, July 24, 1912, 3.
49. "Tong Leader Slain in Chinatown War," *New York Times*, January 6, 1912, 1; "Tong Watchers Many and Alert," *New York Times*, June 30, 1912, sec. 2, 14.
50. "Strong-Arm Squad Took 19 Gangsters," *New York Times*, June 6, 1912, sec. 2, 16.
51. "Gambler Who Defied Police Shot to Death," *New York Times*, July 16, 1912, 1.
52. "Police Admit Hired Assassins Have Fled City," *New York Times*, July 20, 1912, 1.
53. "Tells How Police Cleared Street for Murders," *New York Times*, July 29, 1912, 1.
54. "Rosenthal Murder Secrets Out; Becker Indicted, Arrested, Jailed," *New York Times*, July 30, 1912, 1.
55. "Becker Unnerved Goes to Chair," *New York Times*, July 31, 1915, 1.
56. "'Dago Frank' Confessing, Says Vallon, 'Gyp' and 'Louie' Murdered Rosenthal, Didn't Hear of Becker; Four Gunmen Die," *New York Times*, April 14, 1914, 1.
57. "Whitman Foils Efforts to Get Schepps," *New York Times*, August 20, 1912, 1; "Whitman Openly Says Police Let Gunmen Escape," *New York Times*, August 20, 1912, 1.
58. "Vice Exposure Strikes Hayes; Mayor in Charge," *New York Times*, August 17, 1912, 1; "Hayes Suspended; Vice Trusts Exposed," *New York Times*, August 17, 1912, 2.
59. "Exposes System of Newsstand Graft," *New York Times*, August 18, 1912, sec. 2, 1.
60. "People Declare War on Protected Crime," *New York Times*, August 15, 1912, 1; "The Fight Against Crime," editorial, *New York Times*, August 16, 1912, 8.
61. "Mayor Gaynor Dies in Deck Chair on Liner," *New York Times*, September 12, 1913, 1.

62. "Whitman Elected Governor by 133,000," *New York Times,* November 4, 1914, 1.

63. "Thieves Strip Home of Bank President," *New York Times,* August 14, 1912, 1.

64. "Reign of Terror Feared in China," *New York Times,* January 25, 1912, 1.

65. "May Intervene in Cuba Again," *New York Times,* January 17, 1912, 1; "Taft Means to End Boundary Fighting," *New York Times,* February 5, 1912, 6.

66. "An American Force Lands in Nicaragua," *New York Times,* August 6, 1912, 1.

67. "300,000 in Battle, Turks Routed; Constantinople in Peril; Peace Sought," *New York Times,* November 1, 1912, 1.

68. Ida Husted Harper, letter, *New York Times,* August 10, 1912, 8.

69. Ida Husted Harper, "Roosevelt Women Tricked Into It," letter, *New York Times,* August 22, 1912, 8.

70. Gertrude Atherton, "Mrs. Atherton on Bull Moosers," letter, *New York Times,* August 28, 1912, 8.

71. "Women as Party Workers," editorial, *New York Times,* August 12, 1912, 8.

72. "Women Get Seats on All Party Councils," *New York Times,* August 14, 1912, 6.

73. "Noble Husbands and Republican Wives," *New York Times,* March 11, 1877, 4.

74. "The Marriage of the President's Daughter," *New York Times,* May, 22, 1874, 1.

75. "A Costly Wedding," *New York Times,* June 1, 1871, 5.

76. Edith Wharton, *The Custom of the Country* (1913; New York: Oxford University Press, 1995), 12-13; passim.

77. Max Frankel, "'Earnest' Goals: First Times Under Ochs," *New York Times,* August 19, 1996, 1.

78. "Mayor to Girl Graduates," *New York Times,* February 1, 1912, 22.

79. "American Girls Popular in Berlin," *New York Times,* January 28 1912, sec. 3, 2.

80. "Shaftesbury Gives Millions to Bride," *New York Times,* January 19, 1912, 11.

81. "Hope Diamond Worn at McLean Dinner," *New York Times,* February 3, 1912, 11.

82. "To Be 'Big Sisters' for Little Girls," *New York Times,* June 9, 1912, sec. 2, 10.

83. "Society Women in Folk Dances," *New York Times,* February 24, 1912, 11; "Welfare Inspector at Society Dance," *New York Times,* January 4, 1912, 1.

84. "Social Workers See Real 'Turkey Trots,'" *New York Times,* June 27, 1912, 1.

85. "Making Dance Halls a Paying Proposition," *New York Times*, November 10, 1912, sec. 5, 1.
86. "Biggest Problem Not Police, but Girls," *New York Times*, August 5, 1912, sec. 5, 1.
87. "Society Women Are Oftener Bees Than Butterflies," *New York Times*, August 1912, sec. 5, 2.
88. "Multiplication of Theatres," editorial, *New York Times*, April 3, 1912, 12.
89. "Stage Affairs in General," *New York Times*, February 11, 1912, sec. 7, 8.
90. "The Women's Industrial Exhibition," *New York Times*, March 16, 1912, 5.
91. "Biggest Crowd Ever Was," *New York Times*, March 12, 1912, 2.
92. "Enlist Suffragists for a Circus Holiday," *New York Times*, April 1, 1912, 7.
93. "Stage Riot for Suffrage," *New York Times*, April 13, 1912, 2.
94. "Suffragists Start Week in Vaudeville," *New York Times*, September 10, 1912, 3.
95. Mary Heaton Vorse, Notes, 1923, Mary Heaton Vorse Collection, Box 78.
96. Judith Schwarz, *Radical Feminists of Heterodoxy: Greenwich Village, 1912-1940* (Lebanon, NH: New victoria Publishers, 1982), 29.
97. Floyd Dell, *Homecoming*, 249; Schwarz, 30.
98. Ibid., 247; Garrison, 72.
99. Constance M. Chen, *The Sex Side of Life: Mary Ware Dennett's Pioneering Battle for Birth Control and Sex Education* (New York: New Press, 1996), 152.
100. Vorse, *A Footnote to Folly*, 42; Garrison, 74.
101. Alice Beach Winter, "Discrimination," *The Masses*, February 1913: 8.
102. Cornelia Barns, "Patriotism for Women," *The Masses*, November 1914: 7.
103. Irwin, "Adventures of Yesterday," Inez Haynes Irwin Papers, 416-23; Schwarz, 26-30.
104. Mary Heaton Vorse, Letter to "Lucy," January 23, 1913, Mary Heaton Vorse Collection, Box 54.
105. Quoted in Nancy Cott, *The Grounding of Modern Feminism* (New Haven: Yale University Press, 1987), 36.
106. Quoted in Garrison, 70.
107. Glaspell, *The Road to the Temple*, 247, 250.
108. "Women's Narrow Skirts Play Hob with Textile Industry," *New York Times*, April 28, 1912, sec. 5, 5.
109. "Declining Birth Rate Spells Disaster Says Dr. Guilfoy," *New York Times*, April 28, 1912, sec. 5, 5.

Chapter 3

1. Charlotte Perkins Gilman, *The Living of Charlotte Perkins Gilman: An Autobiography* (1935; Madison: University of Wisconsin Press, 1991), 3-203.
2. Gilman, *Women and Economics* (1898; New York: Harper Torchbooks, 1966), 3, 71, 120, 231-33, 242-45, 277-80.
3. Zona Gale, foreword, *The Living of Charlotte Perkins Gilman*, xxiv-xxvi.
4. Gale, 9.
5. Irwin, "Adventures of Yesterday," Inez Haynes Irwin Papers, 413-14.
6. Luhan, *Intimate Memories*, 3: 143.
7. Gilman, *Living*, 281.
8. Luhan, *Intimate Memories*, 3: 143.
9. Louis Filler, "Dorr, Rheta Childe," in *Notable American Women*, 1: 503-5.
10. Schwarz, 32.
11. Irwin, "Adventures of Yesterday," Inez Haynes Irwin Papers, 413-14.
12. Ibid., 414.
13. Schwarz, 15.
14. Quoted in Cott, 38-39.
15. Irwin, "Adventures of Yesterday," Inez Haynes Irwin Papers, 262-70.
16. Louis Untermeyer, *From Another World: The Autobiography of Louis Untermeyer* (New York: Harcourt, Brace, 1939), 37.
17. Irving Howe, introduction, *Echoes of Revolt: The Masses, 1911-1917*, ed. William L. O'Neill (Chicago: Quadrangle Books, 1966), 5.
18. Ethel Lloyd Patterson, "Things for Dolls," *The Masses*, January 1912: 13.
19. Inez Haynes Irwin, Letter to Mary Heaton Vorse, January 19, 1912, Mary Heaton Vorse Collection, Box 53.
20. Mary Heaton Vorse, "The Day of a Man," *The Masses*, May 1912: 8.
21. Vorse, *A Footnote to Folly*, 15-19.
22. Mary Heaton Vorse, *Rebel Pen: Mary Heaton Vorse: The Life of an American Insurgent*, ed. Dee Garrison (Philadelphia: Temple University Press, 1989), 15-18.
23. Mary Heaton Vorse, Journal, 1923, Mary Heaton Vorse Collection, Box 78.
24. Garrison, 48.
25. Vorse, *A Footnote to Folly*, 1-21.
26. Ibid., 41.
27. Art Young, *On My Way: Being the Book of Art Young in Text and Picture* (New York: Liveright, 1928), 286.
28. Goldman, *Living My Life*, 1: 7-9.
29. Ibid., 1: 29.
30. Ibid., 1: 86-89.

31. Ibid., 1: 90-95.

32. Ibid., 1: 96-102, 122-32.

33. Ibid., 1: 136-45, 157, 174.

34. Ibid., 1: 296.

35. Ibid., 1: 372-84.

36. Ibid., 1: 341.

37. Ibid., 1: 418, 439-41.

38. Luhan, *Intimate Memories*, 3: 89.

39. Christopher Lasch, "Belmont, Alvine Erskine Smith Vanderbilt," in *Notable American Women*, 1: 126-27.

40. Eleanor Flexner, "Blatch, Harriot Stanton," in *Notable American Women*, 1: 172-74.

41. Buhle, 126; Francoise Basch, "The Shirtwaist Strike in History and Myth," introduction, *The Diary of a Shirtwaist Maker* by Theresa Serber Malkiel (1910; Ithaca, NY: International Labor Review Press, Cornell University, 1990), 3-72.

42. Malkiel, *The Diary of a Shirtwaist Maker*, 122.

43. Ibid., 106-03.

44. Buhle, 233, 312, 319, 326, n 2.

45. Sara Josephine Baker, *Fighting for Life* (New York: Macmillan, 1939), 4-25.

46. Ibid., 26-40.

47. Leona Baumgartner, "Sara Josephine Baker," in *Notable American Women*, 1: 86.

48. Baker, *Fighting for Life*, 56-60, 80-87.

49. Ibid., 113-15, 130-35.

50. Ibid., 116-18.

51. Ibid., 162; Baumgartner, 1: 86.

52. Sol Cohen, "Marot, Helen," *Notable American Women*, 2: 499-501.

53. Helen Marot, *American Labor Unions* (New York: Henry Holt, 1914), 68.

Chapter 4

1. Quoted in Schwarz, 6.

2. Ibid., 6-7.

3. Luhan, *Intimate Memories*, 3: 143; Garrison, 68-69.

4. Baker, 182-83.

5. Hutchins Hapgood, *A Victorian in the Modern World* (New York: Harcourt Brace, 1939), 333.

6. Schwarz, 47.

7. Ibid., 28, 80.

8. Rose Pastor Stokes, "I Belong to the Working Class: An Autobiography." Collection of Tamiment Library, New York, ts. microfilmed at Yale University Library in April 1971; 1-99.
9. Ibid., 111-25.
10. Sanger, *An Autobiography*, 74.
11. Stanley Ray Tamarkian, "Rose Pastor Stokes: The Portrait of a Radical Woman, 1905-1919," Dissertation, Yale University, 1983, 221-24.
12. "Mrs. Stokes Berates Hotel Proprietors," *New York Times*, June 1, 1912, 6.
13. "Rose Pastor Stokes in Shirtwaist Strike," *New York Times*, January 2, 1910, 6.
14. Stokes, "Working Class," 138, 178-89.
15. Hare, *A Woman's Quest for Science*, 22-78.
16. Ibid., 19-21.
17. Elsie Clews Parsons, *Fear and Conventionality* (New York: Putnam, 1914), 210-11.
18. Elsie Clews Parsons, "Facing Race Suicide," *The Masses*, June 1915: 15.
19. Hare, 20-21.
20. Luhan, *Intimate Memories*, vol. 1, *Background*, 13, 104, 113.
21. Ibid., vol. 2, *European Experiences*, 33, 48, 55.
22. Ibid., 82, 138-39.
23. Ibid., 303.
24. Ibid., 321-23.
25. Ibid., 446.
26. Ibid., 3: 3-37, 57-74.
27. Ibid., 83.
28. Ibid., 83-84.
29. Flynn, *Rebel Girl*, 127-43; Luhan, *Intimate Memories*, 3: 209-15.
30. Luhan, *Intimate Memories*, 3: 143-44.
31. Ibid., 199.
32. Ibid., 215.
33. Ibid., 303.
34. Sanger, *An Autobiography*, 11-13.
35. Ibid., 68-71.
36. Luhan, *Intimate Memories*, 3: 69.
37. Sanger, *An Autobiography*, 73.
38. Ibid., 72.
39. Ibid., 79-80.
40. Ibid., 78-79.
41. Ibid., 81-83.
42. Ibid., 84-85.
43. Chesler, *Woman of Valor*, 63.
44. Max Eastman, *Heroes I Have Known* (New York: Simon and Schuster, 1942), 9.
45. Cook, 6-13.

46. Ibid., 15.

47. Eastman, *Love and Revolution*, 69-72; Cook, 19-22

48. Paul S. Boyer, "Boissevain, Inez Milholland," in *Notable American Women*, 1: 188-200.

49. "Let Something Good Be Said," *Socialist Woman*, November, 1909: 16.

50. "Socialism's Growing Grip on American Colleges," *New York Times*, April 7, 1912, sec. 5, 3.

51. Boyer, "Boissevain, Inez Milholland," in *Notable American Women*, 1:188-200.

52. Martha Banta, *Imaging American Women: Ideas and Ideals in Cultural History* (New York: Columbia University Press, 1987), n.709; "Inez Boissevain To Be Buried Here," *New York Times*, January 7, 1916, 1.

53. Max Eastman, *Enjoyment of Living* (New York: Harper, 1948),319- 22.

54. "More Strike Waifs To Be Sent Here," *New York Times*, February 13, 1912, 8.

55. Banta, 68.

56. Undated speech, Inez Milholland Papers, Schlesinger Library, Radcliffe College, Folder 29.

57. Inez Milholland, Letter to Eugen Boissevain, November 11, 1911, Inez Milholland Papers, Folder 2.

58. "Inez Boissevain To Be Buried Here," *New York Times*, January 27, 1916, 1.

59. Banta, 709, n.; Boyer, "Boissevain, Inez Milholland," in *Notable American Women*, 1:188-200.

60. Inez Haynes Irwin, *The Story of Alice Paul and the National Woman's Party* (Fairfax, VA: Denlinger's Publishers, 1977), 187-88.

61. Irwin, *Woman's Party*, 189.

62. Cook, 18.

63. "Henrietta Rodman," *Woman's Who's Who of America: A Biographical Dictionary of Women of the United States and Canada, 1914*, John William Leonard, editor-in-chief (New York: The Commonwealth Company,1914), 697; "Henrietta A. Rodman, School Leader, Dies," *New York Times*, March 22, 1923, 19.

64. "Feminists Design a New Type Home," *New York Times*, April 5, 1914, 7.

65. "Teacher Mothers Look to Mitchel," *New York Times*, November, 17, 1914, 9.

66. Floyd Dell, *Homecoming*, 247.

67. Flynn, *Rebel Girl*, 23-64.

68. Ibid., 63, 77.

69. Ibid., 84-85.

70. Ibid., 102, 112-14.

71. Ibid., 50.

72. Ibid., 115.

73. Ibid., 117.

74. Ibid., 137.

75. Elizabeth Gurley Flynn, "The Truth About The Paterson Strike," in Rosalyn Fraad Baxandall, *Words on Fire: the Life and Writing of Elizabeth Gurley Flynn* (New Brunswick: Rutgers University Press, 1987), 119.

76. Flynn, *Rebel Girl*, 152, 334.

77. Baxandall, 20-21.

78. Flynn, *Rebel Girl*, 191.

79. Ibid., 191, 249-57.

80. Ibid., 21.

81. Baxandall, 31-35.

82. Day, *Loneliness*, 17-24.

83. Ibid., 38-47.

84. Ibid., 48-51.

85. Ibid., 65.

86. Eastman, *Love and Revolution*, 39.

87. Robert A. Rosenstone, *Romantic Revolutionary: A Biography of John Reed* (New York: Knopf, 1982), 269.

88. Day, *Loneliness*, 65-66.

89. Dorothy Day, *From Union Square to Rome* (Silver Spring, Maryland: Preservation of the Faith Press, 1940), 10.

90. Eastman, *Love and Revolution*, 22.

Chapter 5

1. Elizabeth Frost and Kathryn Cullen-DuPont, *Women's Suffrage in the United States: An Eyewitness History* (New York: Facts-on-File, 1992), 55-58, 66; Eleanor Flexner, *Century of Struggle: The Woman's Rights Movement in the United States* (New York: Atheneum,1971), 71-72.

2. Flexner, 2; Frost and DuPont, 79.

3. Frost and DuPont, 80; Flexner, 74-77.

4. Aileen Kraditor, *The Ideas of the Woman Suffrage Movement, 1890-1920* (New York: Anchor-Doubleday, 1971), 2; Anne F. Scott and Andrew M. Scott, *One Half the People: The Fight for Woman Suffrage* (Philadelphia: Lippincott, 1975), 16-17.

5. Kraditor, 2-3; Scott and Scott, 17.

6. Scott and Scott, 14, 20.

7. Flexner, 122-25.

8. Ibid., 179-80; Cott, 23.

9. Scott and Scott, 28; Cott, 22.

10. Kraditor, 39; Flexner, 138.

11. Flexner, 38; 44.

12. Ibid., 219.

13. Ibid., 221-22.

14. Ibid., 250.

15. Ibid., 252.

16. Cott, 24-25.

17. Flexner, 252-53; Cott, 25.

18. Flexner, 235-39; Cott, 270-74.

19. "10,000 Marchers in Suffrage Line," *New York Times*, May 4, 1913, sec. 2, 1; "Women in a Rage at Mayor Gaynor," *New York Times*, May 7, 1913, 11. The editors of the *Times*, while praising the success of the parade and expressing admiration for the superiority of the organizers' methods over those of the English suffragists, nevertheless took the position that achieving suffrage would not increase "either the happiness or prosperity of women in America," but would deprive women of privileges they presently enjoyed and would cost them the respect of men. "The Women's Parade," editorial, *New York Times*, May 1913, sec. 3, 6.

20. "Cabaret-Burlesque for Suffrage," *New York Times*, May 26, 1913, 4; "Suffrage Week at Circle," *New York Times*, May 29. 1913, 10; "Gen. Rosalie Jones Flies for Suffrage,"*New York Times*, May, 31, 1913, 6.

21. Schwarz, 22-23.

22. Flexner, 252-53; Cott, 28-31.

23. "To Invade Wall Street," *New York Times*, April 11, 1914, 10; "Suffrage Shop Open Today," *New York Times*, November 2, 1914, 14.

24. Cott, 38; "Talk on Feminism Stirs Crowd," *New York Times*, February 18, 1914, 2; "Adam the Real Rib, Mrs. Gilman Insists," *New York Times*, February 19, 1914, 9.

25. Cott, 35.

26. Ibid., 42.

27. Ibid, 37.

28. Ibid, 38.

29. Ibid., 36-39.

30. Hapgood, 332-34.

31. Quoted in Schwarz, 7.

32. Mary Heaton Vorse, Letter to "Family," March 10, 1915, Mary Heaton Vorse Collection, Box 55. The capable Vira (Mrs. Nelson) Whitehouse, who organized the suffrage shop in addition to many other suffrage events, succeeded Carrie Catt as chair of the New York State Woman Suffrage Party in December 1915.

33. "25,340 March In Suffrage Parade to the Applause of 250,000 Admirers; Spectacle Runs on in the Moonlight," *New York Times*, October 24, 1915 1; "Governor and Mayor Voted For Suffrage," *New York Times*, November 3, 1915, 4; "100,000 Pledged As Suffrage Fund," *New York Times*, November 5, 1915, 1; "Suffrage Vote In Detail," *New York Times*, December 25, 1915, 5.

34. Flexner, 296; "10,000 Marchers In Suffrage Line," *New York Times*, May 4, 1913, sec. 2, 1. "Suffrage and Women's Ideals," editorial, *New York Times*, April 3, 1913, 10.

35. Mrs. John Martin, "Feminism Makes Man the Drone in a Beehive," *New York Times*, April 12, 1914, sec. 6, 4.

36. "Women and the Franchise," *New York Call*, March 12, 1912, 6; "Suffragists Invade National Capital; Plead Their Cause," *New York Call*, March 14, 1912, 1; "30,000 Suffragettes In Mighty Parade up Fifth Avenue," *New York Call*, May 4, 1913, 1.

37. See, for example, typical short stories as "When the Stars Came Close" by Mollie Frank Ellis on page 13 of the *Ladies Home Journal* of July 1911 and "Her Day: The Story of a Mother And Her Man Boy" by Eleanor Hoyt Brainerd on page 9 of the same issue. Kate Wiggin's novel, *Mother Carey's Chickens*, was serialized in the 1911 issues, beginning with the February "Romance and Social Number." "The Minister's Social Helper" can be found on page 46 of the *Ladies Home Journal* issue of April 1911, as well as other issues; Dr. Emily Lincoln's "The Young Mother's Guide" can be found on page 39 of the *Ladies Home Journal* issue of February 1911, as well as other issues.

38. Kate Douglas Wiggin, Ida M. Tarbell, et al., "Do You, As a Woman, Want to Vote?" *Ladies Home Journal*, January 1911: 17.

39. "A Man's Letter to a Man," *Ladies Home Journal*, July 1912: 49.

40. Christopher Lasch, *The New Radicalism in America, 1889-1963: The Intellectual as a Social Type* (New York: Knopf, 1965), 48-51.

41. "Report of Meeting of New York Socialist Women," *Progressive Woman*, April 1909: 15.

42. Flexner, 296-302.

43. "Mrs. Belmont Stops Graft," *New York Times*, August 25, 1912, 11; Cott, 56; "Attack on Aliens Stirs Suffragists," *New York Times*, February 25, 1916, 6; Flexner, 132, 158.

44. "To Force Suffrage on Women's Clubs," *New York Times*, July 3, 1912, 12; "Mrs. Carpenter Defeated," *New York Times*, July 5, 1912, 15.

45. "Women at the Plaza Hotel Knit for Belgians and Hear Readings," *New York Herald*, November 7, 1914, 4; "Women of Society Open Shop in Fifth Avenue to Help Belgians," *New York Herald*, November 28, 1914, 7.

46. "Women to March For Peace," *New York Times*, August 8, 1914, 4; "Split On Peace Parade," *New York Times*, August 13, 1914, 4; "Protesting Women March In Mourning," *New York Times*, August 30, 1914, sec. 2, 11.

47. Cook, 11-13.

48. Baker, 182.

49. Dodge, *Intimate Memories*, 3: 144.

50. Mary Heaton Vorse, quoted in Garrison, 88.

51. Vorse, "The Women's Peace Congress," in *Rebel Pen*, 302-10.

52. Garrison, 89-90.

53. Cook, 17.

54. Cott, 57; Scott and Scott, 38-39; Inez Milholland, 1916 speech, Inez Milholland Papers, Folder 29.

55. Kraditor, 192-95; Irwin, *Woman's Party*, 334; Cott, 58-59; Scott and Scott, 39.

56. Kraditor, 200; Scott and Scott, 39-42.

57. Cott, 59.

58. Day, *Loneliness*, 70-80; Irwin, *Woman's Party*, 289.

59. "Women to Map War Work," *New York Times*, February 22, 1917, 20; "Suffragists to Pledge Aid to Nation," *New York Times*, February 26, 1917, 9; Cott, 60-61; Irwin, *Woman's Party*, 369.

60. "Women Carry City," *New York Times*, November 7, 1917, 1; "New Suffrage Drive Planned By Women," *New York Times*, November 7, 1917, 3.

61. Cott, 52; Flexner, 63.

Chapter 6

1. Charlotte Perkins Gilman, review of *Women and Labour*, by Olive Schreiner, *The Forerunner*, July 1911: 197.

2. Olive Schreiner, *Women and Labour* (London: T. Fisher Unwin, 1911), 114-15.

3. Ibid., 122-23.

4. Ibid., 191-92.

5. Ellen Key, *Century of the Child* (New York: G. P. Putnam's Sons, 1909), 50-95.

6. Ellen Key, *Love and Ethics* (New York: B. W. Huebsch, 1911), 47-50.

7. Ellen Key, *The Woman Movement* (1912; Westport, CT: Hyperion Press, 1976), 132-36.

8. Charlotte Perkins Gilman, "On Ellen Key and the Woman Movement," *The Forerunner*, February 1913: 35.

9. Buhle, 33-34, 40.

10. Ibid., 125-27.

11. Ibid., 131-38.

12. Josephine Conger-Kaneko, "The National Movement," *Socialist Woman*, May 1908: 5.

13. Buhle, 147-50.

14. Ibid., 184-89.

15. Nancy Schrom Dye, *As Equals and As Sisters: Feminism, the Labor Movement, and the Woman's Trade Union League of New York* (Columbia, MO: University of Missouri Press, 1980), 13-17.

16. Ibid., 34-45.

17. Ibid., 18-27.

18. Ibid., 45-47, 59.

19. Ibid., 48; Buhle, 187-88.
20. Ibid., 49-50, 120.
21. Ibid., 63-69, 82-86.
22. Meredith Tax, *The Rising of the Women: Feminist Solidarity and Class Conflict, 1880-1917* (New York: Monthly Review Press, 1980), 218-22.
23. Dye, 92-94.
24. Annaliese Orleck, *Common Sense and a Little Fire: Women and Working Class Politics in the United States, 1900-1965* (Chapel Hill: University of North Carolina Press, 1995), 17, 25.
25. Ibid., 40.
26. Ibid., 44-46, 302.
27. Dye, 88-97; Stein, *The Triangle Fire*, 177-203.
28. Dye, 97-98.
29. Ibid., 99.
30. Ibid., 100; Orleck, 75-76.
31. Ibid.,101-02; Tax, 232.
32. Elizabeth Gurley Flynn, "Women in Industry Should Organize," in Baxandall, *Words on Fire*, 91-96.
33. Dye, 105, 111-13.
34. Ibid., 113-19.
35. Ibid., 120-28.
36. Ibid., 136.
37. Ibid., 137-39.
38. Inez Milholland, article for *Harper's Weekly*, May 30, 1914, 12-14; Inez Milholland Papers, Folder 38.
39. Unidentified newspaper photo, Inez Milholland Papers, Folder 45; "Women to Sell Automobiles, Showing Own Sex How to Drive," *New York Herald*, November 23, 1914, 18.
40. Ruth Markowitz, *My Daughter, the Teacher: Jewish Teachers in New York City* (New Brunswick: Rutgers University Press, 1993), 133.
41. Charlotte Perkins Gilman, "Women Teachers, Married and Unmarried," *Forerunner*, November 1910: 8-10.
42. Ibid., 134.
43. "Mother-to-Be Begins War by Going back to Teach," *The World*, October 16, 1914, 16; "Teacher-Mother Goes High in Her Appeal," *The World*, October 19, 1914, 6; "Teacher-Mother Is Suspended for Trial on Charges," *The World*, November 12, 1914, 1; "Teacher-Mother Appeals to Finley," *The World*, November 20, 1914, 5; "Wants a Teacher's Union," *New York Times*, January 31, 1916, 1; "Says Mother Teacher Surpasses the Soldier," *The World*, October 16, 1914, 4; "Women Teachers Hiss Miss Strachan," *New York Times*, November 14, 1914, 8; "A Mother," letter, *The World*, November 17, 1914, 10; "Mayor Reassures Mother-Teachers Under Board's Ban," *The World*, November 18, 1914, 6.
44. Markowitz, 133-34.

45. Ibid., 135-39.
46. Ibid., 141.
47. Conversation with Lucille Swaim, Director of Negotiations, United Federation of Teachers of New York City, June 7, 1996.
48. "Miss Rodman Arraigned," *New York Times*, November 18, 1914, 7; "Teacher Mothers Look to Mitchel," *New York Times*, November 17, 1914, 9; "Try Miss Rodman for School Satire," *New York Times*, December 23, 1914, 12; Floyd Dell, "The Village School Board," *The Masses*, March 1915: 11; George McAdam, "Feminist Apartment House to Solve Baby Problem," *New York Times*, January 24, 1915, sec. 7, 9; "To Reimburse Miss Rodman," *New York Times*, January 23, 1915, 8.

Chapter 7

1. Chesler, 66-68.
2. Ibid., 69.
3. "Hobson on Race Supremacy," *New York Times*, December 7, 1907, 2.
4. "Decrease in Births Alarms Physicians," *New York Times*, April 7, 1912, 9; Max G. Schlapp, "Race Suicide," *New York Times*, August 13, 1911, sec. 5, 6.
5. Goldman, *Living My Life*, 2: 552-53. The conference was named for the English clergyman and economist Thomas Robert Malthus (1766-1834) who advocated maintaining population in proportion to the means of subsistence.
6. Ibid., 554; 569-70.
7. Sanger, *An Autobiography*, 68-70; Chesler, 56.
8. Sanger, 72; Chesler, 82-83.
9. Sanger, 77; Chesler, 67.
10. Chesler, 61-63; Sanger, 89-92.
11. Chesler, 97-98.
12. Max Eastman, "The Woman Rebel," editorial, *The Masses*, May 1914: 5; "Margaret Sanger," editorial, *The Masses*, November 1914: 20; "Birth Control and Emma Goldman," editorial, *The Masses*, May 1916: 15.
13. Chesler, 97, 130.
14. Goldman, *Living My Life*, 1: 36, 120.
15. Luhan, *Intimate Memories* 3: 70-71.
16. Chesler, 290-91.
17. Goldman, *Living My Life*, 2: 556-57.
18. Goldman, Letter to Sanger, April 9, 1914, Margaret Sanger Papers, Library of Congress.
19. Emma Goldman, Letter to Sanger June 22, 1914, Margaret Sanger Papers, Library of Congress.
20. Chesler, 99, 103-04.

21. Chesler, 109, 126-27.
22. Emma Goldman, Letter to Margaret Sanger, December 7, 1915, Margaret Sanger Papers, Library of Congress.
23. Emma Goldman, Letter to Margaret Sanger, December 8, 1915, Sanger Papers, Library of Congress.
24. Margaret Sanger, *Motherhood in Bondage* (1928; Elmsford, NY: Maxwell Reprint Company, 1956), xii, xvi, 47, 126, 183, 378.
25. Chesler, 130-31.
26. Ibid., 140-41.
27. Ibid., 142-43.
28. Ibid., 154-55.
29. Ibid., 159.
30. Sanger, *An Autobiography*, 249-50.
31. "Welcome For Mrs. Sanger," *New York Times*, March 16, 1917, 12.
32. Chesler, 161.
33. "Punished Teachers Supported By Union," *New York Times*, November 17, 1917, 3; "Enemy Aliens Face Closer Supervision," *New York Times*, November 17, 1917, 3.
34. Chesler, 161-63.
35. Quoted in Chesler, 163.
36. Hapgood, 170.
37. Chesler, 156-57, 162.

Chapter 8

1. Candace Serena Falk, *Love, Anarchy, and Emma Goldman: A Biography* (New Brunswick: Rutgers University Press, 1984), xii, 2-3.
2. Ibid., 4.
3. Ibid., 57.
4. Ibid., 75.
5. Ibid., 72.
6. Ibid., 140, 150-52.
7. Emma Goldman, "Marriage and Love," *The Traffic in Women and Other Essays on Feminism* (1911; New York: Times Change, 1970), 37-46.
8. Luhan, *Intimate Memories*, 2: 446 (Dodge was Mabel's second husband; her first husband, Karl Evans, had been killed in a shooting accident during the early years of their marriage); *Intimate Memories*, 3: 33.
9. Luhan, *Intimate Memories*, 3: 216.
10. Ibid., 310.
11. Ibid., 234.
12. Max Eastman, *Venture* (New York: Albert and Charles Boni, 1927), 200.
13. Luhan, *Intimate Memories*, 3: 260.

14. Floyd Dell, *Intellectual Vagabondage: An Apology for the Intelligentsia* (New York: Doran, 1926), 139.
15. Ibid., 216.
16. Luhan, *Intimate Memories*, 3: 187; Hapgood, 350.
17. Vorse, *A Footnote to Folly*, 57; Sanger, *An Autobiography*, 71; Chesler, 58.
18. Quoted in Chen, *Sex Side*, 138.
19. Flynn, *Rebel Girl*, 152-53.
20. Helen C. Camp, *Iron in Her Soul: Elizabeth Gurley Flynn and the American Left* (Pullman, WA: Washington State University Press, 1995), 113.
21. Luhan, *Intimate Memories*, 3: 303.
22. Virginia Gardner, *Friend and Lover: The Life of Louise Bryant* (New York: Horizon, 1982), 34-38.
23. Dell, *Intellectual Vagabondage*, 139; Mary V. Dearborn, *Queen of Bohemia: The Life of Louise Bryant* (Boston and New York: Houghton Mifflin, 1996), 111.
24. William Carlos Williams, *Autobiography of William Carlos Williams* (New York: Random House, 1951), 142.
25. Cott, 44.
26. Dearborn, *Queen of Bohemia*, 66.
27. Hapgood, 320.
28. Dell, *Homecoming*, 288.
29. Cott, 43; Schwarz, 59.
30. Quoted in Garrison, 71.
31. Orleck, 122, 127, 134-35.
32. Ibid., 136-39, 145.
33. Irwin, "Adventures of Yesterday," Inez Irwin Papers, 416; Elizabeth Irwin, "New Methods In Education," address to Public Education Association panel, May 1936, in Elizabeth Irwin Papers, Little Red Schoolhouse; "Says 'Little School' Lags in Its Results," *New York Times*, May 7, 1932; "Parents Cease Efforts to Save Special School," *New York Herald Tribune*, May 7, 1932 in Elizabeth Irwin Papers; "Progressive Training Vs. Pupil Cost," *New York Times*, September 25, 1932 in Elizabeth Irwin Papers; Schwarz, 68.
34. "Anthony, Katherine Susan," in *Twentieth Century Authors: A Biographical Dictionary of Modern Literature*, Stanley J. Kunitz and Howard Haycroft, eds. (New York: H. W. Wilson, 1942), 32-33.
35. M. Patricia Carlton, "Caroline Pratt: A Biography," Dissertation, Teachers College, Columbia University, 1986, 8.
36. Caroline Pratt, *I Learn from Children* (1948; New York: Perennial Library-Harper, 1990), 7-9, 12-15.
37. Ibid., 26, 38-43; Carlton, 15.
38. Hapgood, 333-34.
39. Luhan, *Intimate Memories*, 3: 143-44.
40. Hare, 39-41, 60-61.

41. Gilman, *Living,* 281; Ann J. Lane, *To Herland and Beyond* (New York: Pantheon, 1990), 330; Mary A. Hill, *A Journey from Within: The Love Letters of Charlotte Perkins Gilman, 1897-1900* (Perkins, PA: University of Pennsylvania Press,1995), 19-25.

42. Irwin, "Adventures of Yesterday," Inez Haynes Irwin Papers, 341,404-8, 514, 550-51, 573, 589.

43. Inez Milholland, Letter to Eugen Boissevain, November 11, 1913, Inez Milholland Papers, Folder 2.

44. Inez Milholland, Letter to Eugen Boissevain, November 1913, Inez Milholland Papers, Folder 2.

45. Boyer, "Boissevain, Inez Milholland," in *Notable American Women,* 1: 188-90.

46. Inez Milholland, Letter to Eugen Boissevain, Inez Milholland Papers, Spring 1915, Folder 2.

47. Dell, *Homecoming,* 304, 309.

48. Eugen Boissevain, Letters to Inez Milholland, Inez Milholland Papers, Spring 1915, Folder 6.

49. Eugen Boissevain, Letter to Inez Milholland, June 17, 1915, Inez Milholland Papers, Folder 7.

50. Eugen Boissevain, Letters to Inez Milholland, May-June 1915, Inez Milholland Papers, Folders 6 and 7.

51. Inez Milholland, Letters to Eugen Boissevain, August 1915–January 1916, Inez Milholland Papers, Folder 3.

52. Sharon M. Vardamis, introduction, Inez Milholland Collection, Schlesinger Library; Inez Milholland, Letters to Eugen Boissevain, June 1915–January 1916, Folder 3.

53. Inez Milholland, Letters to Eugen Boissevain, March 30–April 28, 1915, Inez Milholland Papers, Folder 4.

54. Eugen Boissevain, Letters to Inez Milholland, April 3-30, 1916, Inez Milholland Papers, Folder 8.

55. Mrs. John Milholland, Letter to Eugen Boissevain, March 30–April 28, 1916, Inez Milholland Papers, Folder 4.

56. Eugen Boissevain, Letter to Inez Milholland, April 8, 1916, Inez Milholland Papers, Folder 8

57. Inez Milholland, Letters to Eugen Boissevain, March 30–April 28, 1916, Inez Milholland Papers, Folder 4.

58. Eugen Boissevain, Letter to Inez Milholland, April 12, 1916, Inez Milholland Papers, Folder 8.

59. Inez Milholland, Letters to Eugen Boissevain, October 8-20, 1916, Inez Milholland Papers, Folder 5.

60. William M. Sealy, Letter to Inez Milholland, Inez Milholland Papers, Folder 23.

61. Tribute from the NAACP, Inez Milholland Papers, Folder 17.

62. Various documents, Inez Milholland Papers, Folder 24.

63. Eastman, *Enjoyment of Living*, 322, 324; Crystal Eastman, Letters to Eugen Boissevain, Inez Milholland Papers, Folder 18.

Chapter 9

1. Garrison, 99-100.
2. Hapgood, 391-92.
3. Garrison, 107; Dearborn, 51.
4. Hapgood, 394.
5. Glaspell, 256.
6. Dearborn, 58-59.
7. Glaspell, 290, 303, 315-19.
8. Quoted in Cook, 20.
9. Emma Goldman, *Living My Life*, 1: 379, 474, 2: 610.
10. Emma Goldman, "The Traffic in Women," in *Traffic in Women*, 19-32.
11. Emma Goldman, "Love and Marriage," in *Traffic in Women*, 37-46.
12. Emma Goldman, "Woman Suffrage," in *Traffic in Women*, 51-63
13. Gilman, *Living*, 304-5.
14. Irwin, "Adventures of Yesterday," Inez Haynes Irwin Papers, 420.
15. Charlotte Perkins Gilman, "Our Androcentric Culture, or the Man-Made World," *Forerunner*, March 1910: 20-22.
16. Charlotte Perkins Gilman, "Suffrage," *Forerunner*, May 1910: 30.
17. Charlotte Perkins Gilman, "The Woman of Fifty," *Forerunner*, April 1911: 96-98.
18. Art Young, *Art Young: His Life and Times* (New York: Harper, 1948), 271-75.
19. Eastman, *Enjoyment of Living*, 394; Eastman, *Love and Revolution*, 16.
20. "Announcement," *The Masses*, December 1912: 2.
21. Freda Kirchwey, "To a Soapbox Orator," *The Masses*, February 1915: 8. For a major study of the women contributors to *The Masses*, see Margaret C. Jones, *Heretics and Hellraisers: Women Contributors to The Masses, 1911-1917* (Austin: University of Texas Press, 1993).
22. Susan Glaspell, "Joe," *The Masses*, January 1916: 9.
23. Babette Deutsch, "Ironic," *The Masses*, June 1917: 48.
24. Babette Deutsch, "Extra," *The Masses*, November-December 1917: 37.
25. Amy Lowell, "The Poem," *The Masses*, April 1915: 21.
26. Amy Lowell, "The Grocery," *The Masses*, June 1916: 8.
27. Typical advertisements include those for *The Sexual Life of Woman* by E. Heinrich Kisch, M.D., of the University of Prague in *The Masses*, February 1917: 39; *Woman: Her Sex and Love Life* and *Sexual Problems of Today* by Dr. William Robinson, M.D. ("American Authority on Sexology"), in *The Masses*, March 1917: 39; *The Sexual Crisis* ("Magna Carta of

the *new* woman's movement") by Grete Meisel-Hess, in *The Masses*, April 1917: 37.

28. Helen Hoyt, "Gratitude," *The Masses*, August 1916: 18.
29. Helen Hoyt, "Return," *The Masses*, September 1915: 16.
30. Helen Hoyt, "Menaia," *The Masses*, September 1915: 16.
31. Margaret Hunt Hetzel, "Aprille's Love Song," *The Masses*, July 1917: 45.
32. Nann Clark Barr, "You," *The Masses*, November-December 1917: 39.
33. Alice May Richards, "The Lips of My Lover," *The Masses*, November-December 1917: 39.
34. Flora Shufelt Rivola, "The Mothers Meeting," *The Masses*, July 1917: 13.
35. Nan Apotheker, "In the Hallway," *The Masses*, September 1917: 43.
36. Nan Apotheker, "Bohemia—From Another Angle," *The Masses*, February 1917: 39.
37. Helen Hoyt, "To Love on Feeling Its Approach," *The Masses*, September 1915: 16.
38. Lydia Gibson, "Not Years," *The Masses*, August 1917: 23.
39. Nan Apotheker, "Morning after Thought," *The Masses*, January 1917: 20.
40. Louise Bryant, "Dark Eyes," *The Masses*, July 1917: 28.
41. Louise Bryant, "Lost Music," *The Masses*, June 1917: 43.
42. Williams, *Autobiography*, 142.
43. Hortense Flexner, "The Fire Watcher," *The Masses*, September 1913: 16.
44. Jean Starr Untermeyer, "Deliverance," *The Masses*, October-November 1915: 16.
45. Jean Starr Untermeyer, *Private Collections* (New York: Knopf, 1965), 34-38.
46. Margaret Haughawout, "Wyrd," *The Masses*, March 1917: 41.
47. Flora Shufelt Rivola, "Mother," *The Masses*, May 1917: 41.
48. Claire Bu Zard, "Comfortable," *The Masses*, September 1917: 41.
49. Claire Bu Zard, "A Question," *The Masses*, June 1917: 47.
50. Mary Carolyn Davies, "College," *The Masses*, July 1916: 26.
51. Virginia Brastow, "A House with Green Blinds," *The Masses*, January 1917: 6.
52. Jeanette Eaton, "Rebellion," *The Masses*, August 1917: 3.
53. Lydia Gibson, "Lies," *The Masses*, October 1913: 15.
54. Ruza Wenclaw, "The 'New Freedom' for Women," *The Masses*, March 1917: 42.
55. Sarah N. Cleghorn, "The Mother Follows," *The Masses*, December 1913: 7.
56. Elizabeth Waddell, "Them and Their Wives," *The Masses*, November 1914: 20.
57. Sarah N. Cleghorn, "And Thou, Too, America," *The Masses*, June 1916: 8.
58. Mary Carolyn Davies, "To the Women of England," *The Masses*, April 1916: 7.

59. Babette Deutsch, "Extra," *The Masses*, November-December 1917: 37.
60. Elizabeth Waddell, "The Job," *The Masses*, February 1916: 18.
61. Florence Ripley Martin, "The Dream," *The Masses*, June 1916: 17.
62. Elizabeth Waddell, "For Lyric Labor," *The Masses*, September 1917: 39.
63. Margaret E. Sangster, "Proportionately," *The Masses*, November-December 1917: 3.
64. Hortense Flexner, "The Winds of Spring," *The Masses*, May 1915: 18.
65. Margaret French Patton, "The Sound of the Needles," *The Masses*, June 1916: 4.
66. Marguerite Wilkinson, "The Food Riots," *The Masses*, May 1917: 33.
67. Vorse, *A Footnote to Folly*, 38.
68. Garrison, 68.
69. Mary Field, "Names," *The Masses*, January 1913: 7.
70. Sarah N. Cleghorn, "Comrade Jesus," *The Masses*, April 1914: 14.
71. Rose Pastor Stokes, "A Waiter," *The Masses*, June 1914: 18.
72. Rose Pastor Stokes, "Paterson," *The Masses*, November 1913: 11.
73. Elizabeth Waddell, "Chivalry," *The Masses*, May 1916: 11.
74. The account of Leo Frank's arrest, conviction, defense, murder, and exoneration was composed from the following articles in the *New York Times*: "Frank Convicted of Girl's Murder," August 26, 1913, 18; "Frank Sentenced to Die," August 27, 1913, 3; "W. J. Burns to Sift the Frank Mystery," February 19, 1914, 1; "Evidence for Frank Hidden, Say Counsel," February 21, 1914, 1; "Frank Plea Opposed at Atlanta Meeting," June 6, 1915, 4; "Frank's Fate Now in Slaton's Hands," June 17, 1915, 10; "Outsiders Corroborated by Georgians," editorial, June 17, 1915, 10; "Slaton Commutes Frank's Sentence," June 22, 1915, 1; "Governor Slaton's Courageous Act," editorial, June 24, 1915, 14; "Threaten Boycott of Georgia Jews," June 24, 1915, 5; "They Knew Support Was Lacking," editorial, June 24, 1915, 10; Troops to Guard Slaton," June 25, 1915, 5; "Leo M. Frank Kidnapped at Night from Georgia State Prison Farm by Armed Men in an Automobile," August 17, 1915, 1; "Frank Lynched After 100-Mile Ride," August 18, 1915, 1; "Mob Had Plotted Crime for Weeks," August 18, 1915, 1; "Marietta Citizens Laud Mob's Work," August 18, 1915, 2; "Save Body from Mob," August 18, 1915, 2; "Prison Head, in Irons, Saw Mob Seize Frank," August 18, 1915, 2.
75. Martha Greening, "Prepared," *The Masses*, March 1916: 3.
76. Emma Goldman, *Living My Life*, 2: 653-60.
77. Josephine Bell, "A Tribute," *The Masses*, August 1917: 28.
78. Young, *On My Way*, 293-94; Dell, *Homecoming*, 313-14.
79. Eastman, *Enjoyment of Living*, 406-07.
80. Alice Carpenter, et al., letter, *The Masses*, February 1916: 2.
81. Max Eastman, "Knowledge and Revolution," editorial, *The Masses*, January 1913: 5.
82. Eastman, *Heroes I Have Known*, 1-9.

83. Eastman, *Love and Revolution*, 4-14.

84. Max Eastman, "Knowledge and Revolution," editorial, *The Masses*, July 1913: 5.

85. Eastman, *Love and Revolution*, 21.

86. Max Eastman, editorial, *The Masses*, April 1913: 6.

87. Max Eastman, "Starting Right," editorial, *The Masses*, September 1913: 5.

88. Max Eastman, "Confessions of a Suffrage Orator," *The Masses*, October-November 1915: 7-9.

89. Max Eastman, "Knowledge and Revolution," editorial, *The Masses*, January 1913: 5.

90. Eastman, *Enjoyment of Living*, 384.

91. Ibid., 385.

92. Vorse, *A Footnote to Folly*, 119-31.

93. Dell, *Homecoming*, 236.

94. Dell, *Women as World Builders*, 20.

95. Floyd Dell, "The Nature of Woman," *The Masses*, January 1916: 16.

96. Floyd Dell, "Feminism for Men," *The Masses*, July 1914: 19.

97. Rosenstone, 109.

98. John Reed, "Where the Heart Is," *The Masses*, January 1913: 8.

99. Eastman, *Enjoyment of Living*, 406-07.

100. Marie Louise Van Saanen, "The Game," *The Masses*, May 1916: 9.

101. Eileen Kent, "Moon Madness," *The Masses*, May 1917, 20.

102. Adriana Spadoni, "A Rift of Silence," *The Masses*, February 1913: 12.

103. Phyllis Wyatt, "The Checked Trousers," *The Masses*, June 1917: 18.

104. Helen Forbes, "The Hunky Woman," *The Masses*, May 1916: 12.

105. Helen Hull, "Mothers Still," *The Masses*, October 1914: 14.

106. Helen Hull, "Unclaimed," *The Masses*, May 1916: 20.

107. Helen Hull, "Usury," *The Masses*, September 1916: 7.

108. Dorothy Weil, "A New Woman," *The Masses*, January 1916: 17.

109. Mary Heaton Vorse, "Time and the Town," ts. draft in the Mary Heaton Vorse Collection, Box 12, 9-10.

110. Mary Heaton Vorse, "The Two-Faced Goddess," *The Masses*, December 1913: 12.

111. Mary Heaton Vorse, Ms. notes for 1923 (undated), Mary Heaton Vorse Collection, Box 78.

112. Mary Heaton Vorse, "Tolerance," *The Masses*, February 1914: 12.

113. Mary Heaton Vorse, "The Story of Michael O'Shea, *The Masses*, November 1913: 16.

114. Mary Heaton Vorse, "The Happy Woman," *The Masses*, April 1915: 18.

115. Mary White Ovington, *The Walls Came Tumbling Down* (New York: Harcourt Brace, 1947), 11, 107.

116. Mary White Ovington, "The White Brute," *The Masses*, October-November 1915: 17.

117. Mary White Ovington, Letter to readers, *The Masses*, January 1916: 2.

118. Elizabeth Hines Hanley, "Chivalry," *The Masses*, June 1916: 2.

119. Helen Hull, "Till Death," *The Masses*, January 1917: 5.

120. Carolyn Wedin Sylvander, "Helen Rose Hull," in *American Women Writers: A Critical Reference Guide from Colonial Times to the Present in Four Volumes*, Lina Mainieiro, ed. (New York: Frederick Ungar, 1980), 2: 347-49.

121. Helen Hull, *Islanders* (New York: Macmillan, 1927). {passim}

122. Jones, *Heretics and Hellraisers*, 177.

123. Mabel Dodge Luhan, "The Eye of the Beholder," *The Masses*, October 1917: 10.

124. Lois Palken Rudnick, *Mabel Dodge Luhan: New Woman, New World* Albuquerque: University of New Mexico Press, 1984), 135-36.

125. Mabel Dodge Luhan, "A Quarrel," *The Masses*, September 1916: 17.

126. Mabel Dodge Luhan, "The Parting," *The Masses*, October 1916: 8.

127. Mabel Dodge Luhan, *Intimate Memories*, 3: 435.

128. Ibid., 505.

129. Ibid., 199; Rudnick, 115.

130. Isabel R. Meyers, "Culture and Crochet," *The Masses*, February 1917: 22.

131. Kate Richards O'Hare, "Booze and Revolution," *The Masses*, April 1915: 21.

132. Kate Richards O'Hare, *Kate Richards O'Hare: Selected Writings and Speeches*, Eds. Phillip S. Foner and Sally McMillan (Baton Rouge: Louisiana State University Press, 1982), 2-30.

133. Luhan, "The Secret of War," *The Masses*, November 1916: 8; *Intimate Memories*, 3: 16.

134. Louise Bryant, "Two Judges," *The Masses*, April 1916: 18.

135. Louise Bryant and John Reed, "News From France," *The Masses*, October 1917: 5.

136. Mary Heaton Vorse, *A Footnote to Folly*, 133-34.

137. Mary Heaton Vorse, "Accessories Before the Fact," *The Masses*, November 1916: 6.

138. Elsie Clews Parsons, "Marriage: A New Life," *The Masses*, September 1916: 27.

139. Elsie Clews Parsons, "Engagements," *The Masses*, November 1916: 14.

140. Irwin, "Stray Thoughts on Chivalry," *The Masses*, October-November 1915: 2.

141. Inez Irwin, "Adventures of Yesterday," Inez Haynes Irwin Papers, 293-323.

142. Irwin, "At the Industrial Hearings," *The Masses*, March 1915: 8.

143. Inez Irwin, "Shadows of Revolt," *The Masses*, June 1915: 7.

144. Inez Irwin, "At the A. F. of L. Convention," *The Masses*, February, 1916: 8.

145. Irwin, "Adventures of Yesterday," Inez Haynes Irwin Papers, 341.

146. Irwin, *Angel Island* (New York: Henry Holt and Company, 1914), {passim}.
147. Helen Marot, "Revolutionary Spirit at Seattle," *The Masses*, January 1914: 16
148. Eastman, *Love and Revolution*, 453.
149. Helen Marot, "Actors and Teachers," *The Masses*, June 1916: 16.
150. Helen Marot, "Revolution and the Garment Trade," *The Masses*, August 1916: 29.
151. Helen Marot, "Educating the Teachers," *The Masses*, September 1916: 31. Julia A. Deane of Taunton, Massachusetts protested Marot's characterization of teachers as occupiers of pedestals, for women who "drudge in schools" never feel their positions are secure. Letter to Editor, *The Masses*, November 1916: 31.
152. Helen Marot, "Railroads and Revolution," *The Masses*, November 1916: 5.
153. Helen Marot, "The Railroad Question," *The Masses*, April 1917: 10.
154. Theresa Malkiel, "Hedda Gabbler," *Progressive Woman*, February, 1910: 3-4.
155. Josephine Conger-Kaneko, "Publisher's Preface," *Coming Nation*, July 1914: 5.
156. Buhle, 307.
157. Day, *From Union Square to Rome*, 74-80.

Chapter 10

1. Cook, 13.
2. Rebecca Zurrier, *Art for the Masses: A Radical Magazine and Its Graphics, 1911-1917* (Philadelphia: Temple University Press, 1988), 61.
3. Eastman, *Love and Revolution*, 118-23; Dell, *Homecoming*, 326-27.
4. Eastman, *Love and Revolution*, 63.
5. Ibid., 72-74.
6. Max Eastman, "The Chicago Conventions," *The Liberator*, September 1919: 5.
7. Rosenstone, 285; announcement of John Reed's death in *The Liberator*, November 1920: 11.
8. Eastman, *Love and Revolution*, 265.
9. Joseph Freeman, *An American Testament* (New York: Farrar and Rinehart, 1936), 245.
10. Cook, 28.
11. Eastman, *Love and Revolution*, 221.
12. Ibid., 269-72.
13. "Announcement," *The Liberator*, October 1924: 1.
14. Freeman, 249.

15. Floyd Dell, "Explanations and Apologies," *The Liberator*, June 1922: 25.
16. Max Eastman, "A Militant Suffrage Victory," editorial, *The Liberator*, March 1918: 7.
17. Vorse, *A Footnote to Folly*, 162-212.
18. Mary Heaton Vorse, "The Steel Strike," *The Liberator*, January 1920: 16.
19. Mary Heaton Vorse, "The Hopper," *The Liberator*, April 1920: 34.
20. Mary Heaton Vorse, "Courage," *The Liberator*, March 1923: 11.
21. Mary White Ovington, "Bogalusa," *The Liberator*, January 1920: 31.
22. Inez Haynes Irwin, "Just Before the Drive," *The Liberator*, May 1918: 10.
23. Crystal Eastman, "In Communist Hungary," *The Liberator*, August 1919: 5; Crystal Eastman, "An Interview with Bela Kun," *The Liberator*, March 1920: 16.
24. Gardner, 188-91; Louise Bryant, "Last Days of John Reed," *The Liberator*, February 1921: 11.
25. Gardner, 210-11.
26. Ibid., 222-33.
27. "Women Voters of New York City," *New York Times*, November 8, 1917, 8.
28. Suffragists at Cooper Union," *New York Times*, November 9, 1917, 12.
29. "Antis Report Rush to New League," *New York Times*, November 17, 1917, 4.
30. "Suffragists Deny Pro-German Help," *New York Times*, November 20, 1917, 17.
31. Cott, 61.
32. "Public Schools of Disloyalty," editorial, *New York Times*, November 16, 1917, 10.
33. Ibid., "Resolution Blocked by Woman Teacher," *New York Times*, November 22, 1917, 13.
34. Goldman, *Living My Life*, 2: 610, 615-22, 671-73.
35. Flynn, *Rebel Girl*, 246, 280-81.
36. Cott, 96, 150-52.
37. Gilman, *Living*, 318-19.
38. Cott, 62-63, 86.
39. Gilman, *Living*, 313, 316, 320.
40. Cott, 74.
41. Ibid., 74, 88.
42. Ibid., 86-87.
43. Ibid., 154.
44. Ibid., 155.
45. Ibid., 45.
46. Alice Wexler, *Emma Goldman in Exile: From the Russian Revolution to the Spanish Civil War* (Boston: Beacon Press, 1989), 9, 12, 15, 25-26.
47. Goldman, *Living My Life*, 2: 739-40.
48. Emma Goldman, *My Disillusionment in Russia* (1925; New York: Thomas Crowell, 1970), 193-200.

49. Goldman, *Living My Life*, 2: 796-806.
50. William D. Haywood, *Bill Haywood's Book: The Autobiography of Big Bill Haywood* (1929; New York: International Publishers, 1983), 310, 324, 361-62.
51. Goldman, *Living My Life*, 2: 904-06.
52. Wexler, 69, 92-95, 120-21.
53. Ibid., 154-61.
54. Ibid., 193-209, 230-41.
55. Ibid., 173-78.
56. Dorothy Day, *Loneliness*, 57.
57. Wexler, 112.
58. Ibid., 186.
59. Garrison, 135-38.
60. Ibid., 157-58.
61. Ibid., 167-68, 172-73, 175-76.
62. Ibid., 180.
63. Goldman, *Living My Life*, 2: 906.
64. Garrison, 180.
65. Ibid., 184-88.
66. Mary Heaton Vorse, Undated notes for January, February, March, 1923, Mary Heaton Vorse Collection, Box 78.
67. Mary Heaton Vorse, Undated notes for January, February, March, 1925, Mary Heaton Vorse Collection, Box 80.
68. Day, *Loneliness*; Numerous notebook entries in Mary Heaton Vorse collection.
69. Mary Heaton Vorse, Undated notes for August, September, 1928, Mary Heaton Vorse Collection, .Box 81.
70. Mary Heaton Vorse, Undated notes for January, February, March, 1925, Mary Heaton Vorse Collection, Box 80.
71. Garrison, xiii.
72. Mary Heaton Vorse, Undated notes, circa 1946, Box 87, Mary Heaton Vorse Collection.
73. Garrison, xiv.
74. Mary Heaton Vorse, Undated notes, January 1930, Box 81, Mary Heaton Vorse Collection.
75. Mary Heaton Vorse, Undated notes, April 1940, Box 84, Mary Heaton Vorse Collection.
76. Gilman, *Living*, 324, 332-35.
77. Stokes, "Working Class," {passim}.
78. Rose Pastor Stokes, *The Woman Who Wouldn't* (New York: Putnam, 1916), {passim}.
79. Cook, 24-25.
80. Ibid., 23-29.
81. Ibid., 31-32.
82. Ibid., 33-36.

83. Gardner, 210-11, 222-33.
84. Louise Bryant, *Mirrors of Moscow* (New York: Thomas Seltzer, 1923), 114-16.
85. Gardner, 236-69; Dearborn, 248-49.
86. Louise Bryant, *Mirrors of Moscow*, 113.
87. Gardner, 270-94; Dearborn, 300.
88. "Wants to Rush the Case of 'Insubordinate' Teacher," *The World*, November 18, 1914, 16; "Harriet Rodman, School Leader, Dies," *New York Times*, March 22, 1923, 19.
89. Helen C. Camp, *Iron in Her Soul: Elizabeth Gurley Flynn and the American Left* (Pullman, WA: Washington State University. 1995) 89; Baxandall, 23, 30-36.
90. Ibid., 189.
91. Baxandall, 46-52.
92. Ibid., 56-58.
93. Ibid., 61.
94. Ibid., 68-69.
95. Baxandall, 69-71; James S. Allen, introduction, *Rebel Girl*, 9-11.
96. Inez Haynes Irwin, "Adventures of Yesterday," Inez Haynes Irwin Papers, 548-50.
97. Inez Haynes Irwin, Letter to Mary Heaton Vorse, January 18, 1920, Mary Heaton Vorse Collection, Box 57.
98. Lynn Masel-Walters and Helen Loeb, "Irwin, Inez Haynes," in *American Women Writers*, 2: 370-72.
99. Chesler, 172
100. Ibid., 201; Chen, 223.
101. Ibid., 203-04.
102. Ibid., 196.
103. Ibid., 218-19.
104. Ibid., 223, 231-33.
105. Ibid., 238, 239.
106. Ibid., 243-52.
107. Ibid., 265, 268, 273-77, 289-301.
108. Ibid., 308.
109. Ibid., 341.
110. Ibid., 376, 467.
111. Luhan, *Intimate Memories*, 3: 70.
112. Orleck, 124, 126.
113. Hare, 20-21.
114. Luhan, *Intimate Memories*, vol. 4, *Edge of Taos Desert*, 16-17, 321; Rudnick, 134, 141.
115. Rudnick, 157, 169, 195-224, 315.
116. Edythe M. McGovern, "Glaspell, Susan," *American Women Writers*, 2: 144-46.
117. Day, *Loneliness*, 70-80.

118. Ibid., 94-106.
119. William D. Miller, *Dorothy Day: A Biography* (New York: Harper, 1982), 165-67.
120. Day, *Loneliness,* 158-61.
121. Dorothy Day, Undated letters to Mary Heaton Vorse, 1929-1931, Mary Heaton Vorse Collection, Box 60.
122. Day, *Loneliness,* 158-162.
123. Eastman, *Love and Revolution,* 504.
124. Susan Glaspell, Undated letter to Mary Heaton Vorse, Mary Heaton Vorse Collection, Box 68.
125. Inez Haynes Irwin, Letter to Mary Heaton Vorse, November 18, 1930, Mary Heaton Vorse Collection, Box 60.
126. Elizabeth Gurley Flynn, Letter to Mary Heaton Vorse, February 5, 1930, Mary Heaton Vorse Collection, Box 60.
127. Elizabeth Gurley Flynn, Letter to Mary Heaton Vorse, January 7, 1940, Mary Heaton Vorse Collection, Box 66.
128. Babette Deutsch, Letter to Mary Heaton Vorse, March 30, 1956, Mary Heaton Vorse Collection, Box 67.
129. Dorothy Day, Letter to Mary Heaton Vorse, October 30, 1930, Mary Heaton Vorse Collection Box, 60.
130. Elizabeth Gurley Flynn, Letter to Mary Heaton Vorse, March 22, 1937, Mary Heaton Vorse Collection, Box 63.

BIBLIOGRAPHY

Archival Collections

Library of Congress, Washington, D.C.
  Margaret Sanger Papers
Walter Reuther Library, Wayne State University, Detroit.
  Mary Heaton Vorse Collection
Arthur and Elizabeth Schlesinger Library, Radcliffe College, Cambridge.
  Inez Haynes Irwin Papers
  Inez Milholland Papers
Elizabeth Irwin High School, New York City.
  Elizabeth Irwin Papers
Tamiment Library, New York.
  Rose Pastor Stokes, ts. "I Belong to the Working Class."

Major Newspapers and Periodicals

Examined for articles by and about major activists (in chronological order). For citations to individuals in these publications and others, please see endnotes.

New York Times, 1870s, 1908-1923, 1932
Socialist Women/Progressive Woman, 1908-1911
Mother Earth, 1908
The Forerunner, 1910-1911
The Masses, 1911-1917
The Liberator, 1918-1922.
Ladies Home Journal, 1911-1912
New York Call, 1912-1913
The World, 1912-1914
New York Herald, 1914
New York Herald Tribune, 1932

Unpublished Sources

Carlton, M. Patricia. "Caroline Pratt: A Biography." Dissertation. Teachers College, Columbia, 1986.

Tamarkian, Stanley Ray. "Rose Pastor Stokes: The Portrait of a Radical Woman 1905-1919." Dissertation. Yale University, 1983.

Vardamis, Sharon. Introduction. Inez Milholland Collection, Schlesinger Library.

Primary and Secondary Sources

Adickes, Sandra. "Mind Among the Spindles." *Women's Studies* 1: (1973): 279-91.

Baker, Sara Josephine. *Fighting for Life*. New York: Macmillan, 1939.

Banta, Martha. *Imaging American Women: Ideas and Ideals in Cultural History*. New York: Columbia University Press, 1987.

Baxandall, Rosalyn Fraad. *Words on Fire: The Life and Writing of Elizabeth Gurley Flynn*. New Brunswick: Rutgers University Press, 1987.

Bayor, Ronald H. *Neighbors in Conflict: the Irish, Germans, Jews, and Italians of New York City, 1929-1941*, 2nd ed. Urbana: University of Illinois, 1988.

Bryant, Louise. *Mirrors of Moscow*. New York: Thomas Seltzer, 1923.

Buhle, Mari Jo. *Women and American Socialism, 1870-1920*. Urbana: University of Illinois Press, 1983.

Camp, Helen C. *Iron in Her Soul: Elizabeth Gurley Flynn and the American Left*. Pullman, WA.: Washington State University Press, 1995.

Chen, Constance M. *The Sex Side of Life: Mary Ware Dennett's Pioneering Struggle for Birth Control and Sex Education*. New York: New Press, 1996.

Chesler, Ellen. *Woman of Valor: Margaret Sanger and the Birth Control Movement in America*. New York: Simon and Schuster, 1992.

Cook, Blanche Wiesen. ed. *Crystal Eastman on Women and Revolution*. New York: Oxford University Press, 1978.

Cott, Nancy. *The Grounding of Modern Feminism*. New Haven: Yale University Press, 1987.

Day, Dorothy. *From Union Square to Rome*. Silver Spring, MD.: Preservation of the Faith Press, 1940.

———. *The Long Loneliness: An Autobiography*. New York: Image Books, 1959.

Dearborn, Mary V. *Queen of Bohemia: The Life of Louise Bryant*. Boston: Houghton, 1996.

Dell, Floyd. *Homecoming: An Autobiography*. 1933. Port Washington, NY: Kennikat, 1960.

———. *Intellectual Vagabondage: An Apology for the Intelligentsia*. New York: Doran, 1926.

———. *Women as World Builders: Studies in Modern Feminism.* 1913. Westport, CT: Hyperion Press, 1976.

Dorr, Rheta Childe. *What Eight Million Women Want.* Boston: Small, Maynard, 1910.

Duncan, Isadora. *My Life.* New York: Albert and Charles Boni, 1927.

Dye, Nancy Schrom. *As Equals and As Sisters: Feminism, the Labor Movement, and the Women's Trade Union League of New York.* Columbia, MO: University of Missouri Press, 1980.

Eastman, Max. *Enjoyment of Living.* New York: Harper, 1948.

———. *Heroes I Have Known.* New York: Simon and Schuster, 1942.

———. *Love and Revolution: My Journey Through an Epoch.* New York: Random House, 1964.

———. *Venture.* New York: Albert and Charles Boni, 1927.

Falk, Candace Serena. *Love, Anarchy, and Emma Goldman: A Biography.* New Brunswick: Rutgers University Press, 1984.

Flexner, Eleanor. *Century of Struggle: The Woman's Rights Movement in the United States.* New York: Atheneum, 1971.

Flynn, Elizabeth Gurley. *Rebel Girl, An Autobiography: My First Life (1906-1926).* New York: International Publishers, 1955.

Freeman, Joseph. *An American Testament.* New York: Farrar and Rinehart, 1936.

Frost, Elizabeth and Kathryn Cullen-DuPont. *Women's Suffrage in the United States: An Eyewitness History.* New York: Facts-on-File, 1992.

Gardner, Virginia. *Friend and Lover: The Life of Louise Bryant.* New York: Horizon, 1982.

Garrison, Dee. *Mary Heaton Vorse: The Life of an American Insurgent.* Philadelphia: Temple University Press, 1989.

Gilman, Charlotte Perkins. *The Living of Charlotte Perkins Gilman: An Autobiography.* 1935. Madison: University of Wisconsin Press, 1991.

———. *Women and Economics.* 1898. New York: Harper Torchbooks, 1966.

Glaspell, Susan. *The Road to the Temple.* New York: Frederick Stokes, 1927.

Goldman, Emma. *Living My Life.* 2 vols. New York: Dover. 1970.

———. *My Disillusionment in Russia.* 1925. New York: Thomas Crowell, 1970.

———. *The Traffic in Women and Other Essays on Feminism.* 1911. New York: Times Change, 1970.

Hapgood, Hutchins. *A Victorian in the Modern World.* New York: Harcourt Brace, 1939.

Hare, Peter. *A Woman's Quest for Science: Portrait of Anthropologist Elsie Clews Parsons.* Buffalo: Prometheus Books, 1985.

Haywood, William. *Bill Haywood's Book: The Autobiography of Big Bill Haywood.* 1929. New York: International Publishers, 1983.

Hill, Mary A. *A Journey from Within: The Love Letters of Charlotte Perkins Gilman, 1897-1900.* Perkins: University of Pennsylvania Press, 1995.

Howe, Irving. Introduction. In *Echoes of Revolt: The Masses, 1911-1917.* William L. O'Neill, ed. Chicago: Quadrangle Books, 1966. 17-24.

Hull, Helen. *Islanders.* New York: Macmillan, 1927.

Irwin, Inez Haynes. *The Story of Alice Paul and the National Woman's Party.* 1921. Fairfax, VA: Denlinger's Publishers, 1977.

———. *Angel Island.* New York: Henry Holt and Company, 1914.

James, Edward, ed. *Notable American Women: A Biographical Dictionary, 1607-1950.* 4 vols. Cambridge: Harvard University Press, 1971.

Jones, Margaret C. *Heretics and Hellraisers: Women Contributors to* The Masses, *1911-1917.* Austin: University of Texas Press, 1993.

Kelly, Joan. "Did Women Have a Renaissance?" in *Women, History, and Theory: The Essays of Joan Kelly.* Chicago: University of Chicago Press, 1984.

Key, Ellen. *Century of the Child.* New York: Putnam, 1909.

———. *Love and Ethics.* New York: B. W. Huebsch, 1911.

———. *The Woman Movement.* 1912. Westport, CT: Hyperion Press, 1976.

Kraditor, Aileen. *The Ideas of the Woman Suffrage Movement, 1890-1920.* New York: Anchor-Doubleday, 1971.

Kunitz, Stanley J. and Howard Haycroft, eds. *Twentieth Century Authors: A Biographical Dictionary of Modern Literature.* New York: H. W. Wilson, 1942.

Lane, Ann J. *To Herland and Beyond.* New York: Pantheon, 1990.

Lasch, Christopher. *The New Radicalism in America, 1889-1963: The Intellectual as a Social Type.* New York: Knopf, 1965.

Luhan, Mabel Dodge. *Intimate Memories.* 4 vols. 1936. New York: Kraus Reprints. 1971.

Malkiel, Theresa Serber. *The Diary of a Shirtwaist Maker.* 1910. Ithaca: International Labor Review Press, Cornell University Press, 1990.

Maniero, Lisa, ed. *American Women Writers: A Critical Reference Guide from Colonial Times to the Present in Four Volumes.* 4 vols. New York: Frederick Ungar, 1980.

Marot, Helen. *American Labor Unions.* New York: Henry Holt, 1914.

Markowitz, Ruth. *My Daughter, the Teacher: Jewish Teachers in New York City.* New Brunswick: Rutgers University Press, 1993.

Miller, William D. *Dorothy Day: A Biography.* New York: Harper, 1982.

O'Hare, Kate Richards. *Kate Richards O'Hare: Selected Writings and Speeches.* Edited by Phillip S. Foner and Sally McMillan. Baton Rouge: Louisiana State University Press, 1982.

O'Neill, William. ed. *Echoes of Revolt.* Chicago: Quadrangle Books, 1966.

Orleck, Annaliese. *Common Sense and a Little Fire: Women and Working Class Politics in the United States, 1900-1965.* Chapel Hill: University of North Carolina Press, 1995.

Ovington, Mary White. *The Walls Came Tumbling Down.* New York: Harcourt, Brace, 1947.

Parsons, Elsie Clews. *Fear and Conventionality.* New York: Putnam, 1914.

Pratt, Carolyn. *I Learn from Children.* 1948. New York: HarperCollins, 1990.

Rosenstone, Robert A. *Romantic Revolutionary: A Biography of John Reed.* New York: Knopf, 1982.

Rudnick, Lois Palken. *Mabel Dodge Luhan: New Woman, New World.* Alburquerque: University of New Mexico Press, 1984.

Sanger, Margaret. *An Autobiography.* 1938. Elmsford, New York: Maxwell Reprint Company, 1971.

———. *Motherhood in Bondage.* 1928. Elmsford, New York: Maxwell Reprint Company, 1956.

Schreiner, Olive. *Women and Labour.* London: T. Fisher Unwin, 1911.

Schwarz, Judith. *Radical Feminists of Heterodoxy: Greenwich Village, 1912-1940.* Lebanon, NH: New Victorian Publishers, 1982.

Scott, Anne F. and Andrew M. Scott. *One Half the People: The Fight for Woman Suffrage.* Philadelphia: Lippincott, 1975.

Solomon, Barbara Miller. *The Company of Educated Women: A History of Women and Higher Education in America.* New Haven: Yale University Press, 1985.

Stein, Leo. *The Triangle Fire.* 1962. New York: Carol and Graf, 1983.

Stokes, Rose Pastor. *The Woman Who Wouldn't.* New York: Putnam, 1916.

Taggard, Genevieve. ed. *May Days: An Anthology of Verse from The Masses and The Liberator.* New York: Albert and Charles Boni, 1925.

Tax, Meredith. *The Rising of the Women: Feminist Solidarity and Class Conflict, 1880-1917.* New York: Monthly Review Press, 1980.

Trollope, Frances. *Domestic Manners of the Americans.* 1832. Barre, MA: Imprint Society, 1969.

Untermeyer, Jean Storr. *Private Collections.* New York, Knopf, 1965.

Untermeyer, Louis. *From Another World: The Autobiography of Louis Untermeyer.* New York: Harcourt, Brace, 1939.

Vorse, Mary Heaton. *A Footnote to Folly: Reminiscences of Mary Heaton Vorse.* New York: Farrar and Rinehart, 1935.

———. *I've Come to Stay: A Love Comedy of Bohemia.* New York: Century, 1919.

———. *Rebel Pen: The Writing of Mary Heaton Vorse.* Dee Garrison, Ed. Philadelphia: Temple University Press, 1989.

Wexler, Alice. *Emma Goldman in Exile: From Russian to Spanish Civil War.* Boston: Beacon, 1989.

Wharton, Edith, *The Custom of the Country.* 1913. New York: Oxford University Press, 1995.

Williams, William Carlos. *Autobiography of William Carlos Williams.* New York: Random House, 1951.

Woman's Who's Who of America: A Biographical Dictionary of Women of the United States and Canada, 1914. John William Leonard, Editor-in-Chief. New York: The Commonwealth Company, 1914.

Young, Art. *On My Way: Being the Book of Art Young in Text and Picture.* New York: Liveright, 1928.

Zurrier, Rebecca. *Art for the Masses: A Radical Magazine and Its Graphics, 1911-1917.* Philadelphia, Temple University Press, 1988.

INDEX

Printed in the United States
879200001BA